Scattered and Gathered

†

STUDIES IN WORLD CATHOLICISM

Other Titles in This Series

Beyond the Borders of Baptism: Catholicity, Allegiances, and Lived Identities. Edited by Michael L. Budde. Vol. 1, 2016. ISBN 9781498204736

New World Pope: Pope Francis and the Future of the Church. Edited by Michael L. Budde. Vol. 2, 2017. ISBN 9781498283717

Forthcoming Titles in This Series

Fragile World: Ecology and the Church. Edited by William T. Cavanaugh

A Living Tradition: The Holy See, Catholic Social Doctrine, and Global Politics 1965–2000. A. Alexander Stummvoll

A Church with the Indigenous Peoples: The Intercultural Theology and Ecclesiology of JTatik Samuel Ruiz García. Michel Elias Andraos

Scattered and Gathered

Catholics in Diaspora

EDITED BY
Michael L. Budde

CONTRIBUTORS

Michel Elias Andraos
Gioacchino Campese, CS
Ondina Cortés, RMI
Daniel G. Groody, CSC
Linh Hoang, OFM
Jaisy Joseph
Simon C. Kim

Dorian Llywelyn, SJ
Daniel McNeil
Cecile L. Motus
Mark R. Mullins
Dominic Pasura
Robert Schreiter, CPPS
Matthew John Paul Tan

CASCADE *Books* • Eugene, Oregon

SCATTERED AND GATHERED
Catholics in Diaspora

Studies in World Catholicism 3

Copyright © 2017 Wipf and Stock Publishers. All rights reserved. Except for brief quotations in critical publications or reviews, no part of this book may be reproduced in any manner without prior written permission from the publisher. Write: Permissions, Wipf and Stock Publishers, 199 W. 8th Ave., Suite 3, Eugene, OR 97401.

Cascade Books
An Imprint of Wipf and Stock Publishers
199 W. 8th Ave., Suite 3
Eugene, OR 97401

www.wipfandstock.com

PAPERBACK ISBN: 978-1-5326-0709-7
HARDCOVER ISBN: 978-1-5326-0711-0
EBOOK ISBN: 978-1-5326-0710-3

Cataloguing-in-Publication data:

Names: Budde, Michael L., editor.

Title: Scattered and gathered : Catholics in diaspora / edited by Michael L. Budde.

Description: Eugene, OR: Cascade Books, 2017 | Studies in World Catholicism 3 | Includes bibliographical references and index.

Identifiers: ISBN 978-1-5326-0709-7 (paperback) | ISBN 978-1-5326-0711-0 (hardcover) | ISBN 978-1-5326-0710-3 (ebook).

Subjects: LCSH: Immigrants—Religious life | Emigration and immigration—Religious aspects | Emigration and immigration—Social aspects.

Classification: BV4466 S35 2017 (print) | BV4466 (ebook).

Manufactured in the U.S.A.   09/13/17

Scripture quotations marked (NRSV) come from the New Revised Standard Version Bible: Catholic Edition, copyright © 1989, 1993 National Council of the Churches of Christ in the United States of America. Used by permission. All rights reserved worldwide.

Scripture quotations marked (NIV) come from the Holy Bible, NEW INTERNATIONAL VERSION®, NIV® Copyright © 1973, 1978, 1984, 2011 by Biblica, Inc.® Used by permission. All rights reserved worldwide.

Scripture quotations marked (NAB) come from the New American Bible, revised edition © 2010, 1991, 1986, 1970 Confraternity of Christian Doctrine, Washington, D.C. and are used by permission of the copyright owner. All Rights Reserved. No part of the New American Bible may be reproduced in any form without permission in writing from the copyright owner.

Contents

Contributors | vii
Acknowledgments | ix

Introduction by Michael L. Budde | 1

1: Religion Displaced and Replaced:
What We Have to Learn from Diaspora Communities | 11
ROBERT SCHREITER, CPPS

2: Levantine Catholic Communities in the Diaspora
at the Intersection of Many Identities and Worlds | 23
MICHEL ELIAS ANDRAOS

3: A New Creation: The Catholic Faith in Diaspora | 40
SIMON C. KIM

4: Harmony in Faith:
Asian and Pacific Catholics in the United States | 52
CECILE L. MOTUS

5: Passing Over:
A Theological Vision of Migration | 62
DANIEL G. GROODY, CSC

6: "One Does Not Live By Bread Alone. . . ." (Matt 4:4):
The Relational Turn of Theologies of Migration
in the Twenty-First Century | 76
GIOACCHINO CAMPESE, CS

7: The Love of Many Lands:
Theology, Multiplicity, and Migrant Identity | 96
MATTHEW JOHN PAUL TAN

8: Becoming a Multicultural Church in the Context of Neo-Nationalism:
The New Challenges Facing Catholics in Japan | 112
MARK R. MULLINS

9: Diaspora as Mission?
Toward a Theological Interpretation of the Experience of the Cuban
Catholic Community in South Florida | 131
ONDINA CORTÉS, RMI

10: Diasporic Devotions | 142
DORIAN LLYWELYN, SJ

11: Negotiations In-Between:
Indian Catholics in Diaspora | 167
JAISY JOSEPH

12: Vietnamese Catholics and Diaspora:
Re-imaging Mary as Vietnamese | 179
LINH HOANG, OFM

13: From America, with Hate:
Bond and the "Black Shirley Temple" | 190
DANIEL MCNEIL

14: Rootedness and Openness:
Experiences, Practices, and Theologies of Zimbabwean Catholics
in Britain | 202
DOMINIC PASURA

Bibliography | 221
Scripture Index | 241
Subject Index | 243

Contributors

Michel Elias Andraos: Associate Professor of Intercultural Studies and Ministry at the Catholic Theological Union, Chicago

Michael L. Budde: Professor of Catholic Studies and Political Science and Senior Research Professor at the Center for World Catholicism and Intercultural Theology at DePaul University, Chicago

Gioacchino Campese, CS: Resident Professor at the Scalabrinian International Migration Institute in the Pontifical Urbaniana University, Rome

Ondina Cortés, RMI: Assistant Professor of Practical Theology at St. Thomas University, Miami

Daniel G. Groody, CSC: Associate Professor of Theology and Director of the Center for Latino Spirituality and Culture at the University of Notre Dame, South Bend

Linh Hoang, OFM: Associate Professor of Religious Studies at Siena College, Loudonville

Jaisy Joseph: Doctoral Candidate in Systematic Theology at Boston College

Simon C. Kim: Assistant Professor of Theology at the University of Holy Cross, New Orleans

Dorian Llywelyn, SJ: Director of the Ignatian Center for Jesuit Education at the University of Santa Clara

Daniel McNeil: Associate Professor of History at Carleton University, Ottawa

Cecile L. Motus: Former Assistant Director at the Secretariat for Cultural Diversity of the US Conference of Catholic Bishops

Mark R. Mullins: Professor of Japanese Studies at the University of Auckland

Dominic Pasura: Lecturer in Sociology at the University of Glasgow

Robert Schreiter, CPPS: Professor of Systematic Theology and Vatican Council II Chair of Theology at the Catholic Theological Union, Chicago

Matthew John Paul Tan: Adjunct Senior Lecturer at the University of Notre Dame Australia and Member of the Archdiocese of Sydney's Ecumenical and Interfaith Commission

Acknowledgments

NOTHING OF IMPORTANCE GETS done through the Center for World Catholicism and Intercultural Theology without the work of many people. The present volume owes much to William Cavanaugh, director of the Center; Stan Chu Ilo, CWCIT research professor; Francis Salinel, the Center's administrative director; and Anna Kreutz Beck, CWCIT student assistant; and to the administration of DePaul University, for its ongoing support of the Center and its mission.

Absolutely nothing involving the Center's publishing work gets done without the exemplary work of Karen Kraft, the Center's communications and publications project manager. From manuscript preparation and copyediting to untold other tasks, Karen enables the Center to have an outsized impact relative to its size and resources. I am grateful for her diligence, competence, and unflagging spirit of collegiality.

Introduction

MICHAEL L. BUDDE

Christianity is the story of people on the move. From its forebears in the Hebrew Bible (Abram, Moses, Jacob, and more) to the dramatis personae of the New Testament (the Holy Family in flight to Egypt, the mobile ministry of Jesus, the globetrotting missions of Paul), Christianity witnesses the movement of people across God's map of creation. One name given the early followers of Jesus—people of "the Way"—speaks to activity, outreach, and sojourning through this world.

At the same time, Christian history speaks to the rootedness of God's people, of the goodness that flows from their being told to "build houses and live in them; and plant gardens and eat their produce . . . Seek the welfare of the city where I have sent you into exile, and pray to the Lord on its behalf" (Jer 29:5, 7; NAS). Monastic communities often take vows of stability, promising to stay in one place and find God there; the deep connections between Christianity and various human cultures are themselves the products of marinades centuries in the making.

The message of Jesus has left a global footprint, thanks in part to Jesus' directive to his followers to go to "the ends of the earth" (Acts 1:8). Carried by slaves and slave traders, conquerors and refugees, adventurers and plodders, the Way of Jesus has found its way into nearly all corners of the world. Today's Christians—and those who find them to be of interest—find themselves engaging a far-flung phenomenon, one that seeks to be the most local and most transnational at the same time; distinct and unique in its particularities, the church nonetheless affirms a unity that joins near and far, familiar and unfamiliar, those on the move and those in place.

For most people, past and present, becoming part of a diaspora is often part of a violent process. While some people move for adventure and excitement, most are pushed—by starvation, state-building, war, ecological collapse, political machinations, or similarly deadly processes. What often gets lost in the postmodern celebration of interculturality and hybridity is that such processes have simultaneously been the products of choice and coercion, bricolage and brigandage. It is important not to lose sight of the fact that for most people in most of history, moving has been hard—physically, emotionally, financially, spiritually, and politically. That it has often led to good and worthwhile outcomes should not shield us from the suffering and sacrifices undergirding all of it.

When Christians have been moved, or received new people, sharing their habitations and cultures, the Church has moved with them. The interplay, and sometimes tensions, between being rooted and being people of pilgrimage through this world has shaped the faith life and practices of Christians on the move and those momentarily in place. The ecclesial commitment both to Christian universality (catholicity) and particularity (distinctive ways of being Church in a given culture and context) shapes the interactions of Christians in evermore surprising ways around the world. Being a people of the Way doesn't always mean one can dictate or predict the contours of the road ahead—only the destination.

Moving the Conversation Forward

From April 7–9, 2014, DePaul University's Center for World Catholicism and Intercultural Theology (CWCIT) hosted an international conference on matters of movement, displacement, cultural rootedness, and more as concerns for Christians worldwide. This gathering, under the title "Scattered and Gathered: Catholics in Diaspora," brought together scholars from a variety of fields and theological perspectives to engage a range of challenging and often difficult matters. While focusing primarily on Catholic experiences, the insights and challenges identified by participants will be of value to Christians in other traditions as well as to Catholic leaders and scholars. Drawn from around the world, contributors to this volume bring historical and geographical breadth of vision to matters that predate the contemporary world even as they have helped shape that world.

Setting the Stage

No one has contributed more to the understanding of Christianity and the worldwide interaction of cultures than Robert Schreiter, professor of theology at Catholic Theological Union. In "Religion Displaced and Replaced: What We Have to Learn from Diaspora Communities," Schreiter offers a significant-yet-succinct framing of important sociological and cultural theories and dynamics relevant to understanding Catholic communities in dispersion around the world.

Schreiter offers a useful distinction between the study of *transnationalism*—which studies the relations of cultural groups to one another and to the state, in which cultural groups become something of a putative supra-nation claiming identity and loyalty—and *diaspora*, which looks at the networks and relations between members of a national group outside their country of origin. In looking at Catholic faith in relation to diaspora, he offers a review of the concept of diaspora and diaspora studies over time, from attention to biblical Judaism to a more generalized sense of peoples dispersed and connected across borders and boundaries. In particular, he explores how immigrants transform physical space into a sense of place, demonstrating the affective processes that create a sense of belonging and comfort in the new spaces they inhabit. In this sense, human movement not only dis-places people and their religion, it also re-places it somewhere new—a dynamic that can be both challenging and beneficial. Displacement and replacement can be a source of creativity, theologically and otherwise, for newcomers and locals alike.

Such is apparent in the contribution of Michel Andraos, associate professor of intercultural studies and ministry at Catholic Theological Union. In "Levantine Catholic Communities in the Diaspora at the Intersection of Many Identities and Worlds," he offers a timely exploration of Christians in the Levant (the Eastern shores of the Mediterranean, which includes Syria, Lebanon, Jordan, Palestine, Iraq, and Israel); for millennia, this region has been a cultural crossroads for Christians of all kinds. The Levant has also been an area of long interaction with Islam, and Christians here have extensive experience both in dispersion and in living as minorities—within the Ottoman Empire, later as clients of the West, and now in states with varied religious and cultural dispositions. Centuries of fluctuating fortunes and tumult impelled significant emigration of Christians from the region, to the extent that more Levantine Christians live in diaspora than in the region—a situation that occurred before the mass exodus of people fleeing the recent bloody war in Syria. Andraos provides a cultural and pastoral overview of Levantine Christians in North America, looking at their experiences to date and highlighting some possible future trajectories. He identifies several key pastoral challenges, ranging from declining church participation rates and "spiritually homeless" people to clericalism and problems in clergy formation—problems known to many diasporic Christian communities, as he notes, even as they take a particular configuration among Middle Eastern Christians in North America.

Catholic Mission and Identity

Before Korean Catholics spread around the world, the faith found its way to the Korean peninsula in a distinctive fashion, according to Simon Kim in "A New Creation: The Catholic Faith in Diaspora." A priest in the Diocese of Orange in California, Kim is a theologian and leader in the Korean diaspora. He notes that Catholicism came to Korea via Koreans who encountered it in China—creating a situation in which, as he says, the Koreans "evangelized themselves" rather than having Catholicism "planted by foreigners." He says, "Nowhere else did Christianity spread in this manner, as missioners were invited into Korea only after the neophytes understood for themselves the need for ordained clergy in the celebration of the sacraments." [45]

A similar lay-centered and lay-sustained quality typified Korean Catholicism as people migrated from the peninsula to places like the United States: "[t]he laity carried the faith across national borders and laid the foundations for ecclesial communities in the United States before the arrival of native-speaking clergy." [46]

When Korean clergy did arrive, they often saw themselves as an extension of the church in Korea, and thereby left it to lay people to bring stability and the requisite adjustments to the new situation. As a result, Korean Catholicism in diaspora created a tradition of effective lay leadership that continues to the present.

In "Harmony in Faith: Asian and Pacific Catholics in the United States," Cecile Motus offers a short set of reflections on the experiences of this third-largest segment of the Catholic community in the United States. Having previously served as the assistant director in the Secretariat for Cultural Diversity of the US Conference of Catholic Bishops, Motus provides an overview of the rich cultural backgrounds that Asian/Pacific Catholics have brought to the United States, and how these have begun to interact with the other cultures of US Catholicism.

As Motus notes, across the different ways that Catholicism has been lived across Asia and the Pacific, one sees some commonalities against the backdrop of US Catholicism. She describes these communities as Asian in spirit, whose Catholicism provides a source of identity and a sense of home, all of which anchored in a deep sense of popular religiosity. Her overview describes the ways in which other parts of the Catholic community in the United States have responded to these newcomers—a story with good and bad experiences, and a variety of pastoral strategies and initiatives.

Cross-Cultural Communities in a Postmodern World

University of Notre Dame theologian Daniel Groody describes migration as "one of the most defining issues of our time" [62] in "Passing Over: A Theological Vision of Migration." The numbers are staggering, as he suggests: 740 million internal migrants worldwide in 2013, and another 232 million from one country to another. [62] He offers a theological starting point for rethinking migration as he builds around the Passover narratives as "a way of understanding the challenges of passing over from the dehumanized dimensions of migration to those that lead to life, justice, and solidarity." [63] This involves four senses of "passing over": from being a migrant to being a person; from injustice to justice; from otherness to neighborliness; and from nationalism to the Reign of God.

Groody provides a clear and nuanced introduction to the basis for Christian thinking on human dignity and persons, the variegated origins and differential claims of rights, and a more adequate vision of justice than that on offer in conventional political discourse and advocacy. The fourfold passings-over he sees as necessary for Christians constitute "a challenge to reimagine the world in a different way and to live out of a different narrative. . . . These scriptural narratives help us reevaluate the prepackaged values fed to us by society and popular media, including dehumanizing narratives about migration." [74]

Christian theology and social ethics needs to integrate migration and movement more fully with all aspects of theology, rather than simply ignoring it or considering it as just one more subspecialty in an already overcrowded theological menu. That is the assertion of Gioacchino Campese, a professor at the Scalabrinian International Migration Institute at the Pontifical Urbaniana University in Rome. In "One Does Not Live by Bread Alone: The Relational Turn of Theologies of Migration in the Twenty-First Century," he offers a wide-ranging pastoral, political, and theological comparison of two contested ports of entry for migrants approaching the prosperous North—the Italian island of Lampedusa, where Pope Francis lamented the "globalization of indifference," and the US-Mexico border towns of Nogales (Arizona and Sonora).

In both places, Campese finds an ecology of fear surrounding citizens, churches, and government actors—and a range of inadequate or incomplete responses that put off the hard but essential work necessary to move beyond a short-term crisis mentality to one of long-term cooperation, incorporation, and new creation. He also explores the tradeoffs involved in ethnonational churches as responses to social and ecclesial marginalization.

Multiplicity of Identities

Theologian Matthew John Paul Tan, who teaches philosophy and theology at Campion College in Australia, brings contemporary social theory into conversation with core Catholic convictions in "The Love of Many Lands: Theology, Multiplicity, and Migrant Identity." As he notes, "The migrant has now become one of a class of outsiders that has become demonized, excluded, or even *in*cluded in exploitative ways." [96] He suggests that migrant identity needs to become an important theological concern, with multiple identities being accepted as a legitimate way of being in the world. As he suggests, rather than seeing migrants and multiplicity as "problems to be overcome," he believes one should see "the migrant as an icon of the church which images a divine reality, rather than looking at them as a distortion of that reality." [97]

Drawing on the thought of Saints Augustine and Bonaventure, Tan finds theology able to contribute to such discussions by reflecting more deeply on unity, division, and sin. He suggests that the Word is what unifies the distinct persons of the Trinity, and that the Eucharist reconciles the divisions of humanity in and through the Body of Christ—two areas of classical Christian theology with much to contribute to a reconfigured appreciation for migrants and plural communities of affiliation in the contemporary world.

The challenges of multiple identities and national homogeneity are highlighted in "Becoming a Multicultural Church in the Context of Neo-Nationalism: The New Challenges Facing Catholics in Japan." A professor of Japanese studies at the University of Auckland, Mark Mullins examines the ups and downs of the Catholic community in Japan—a small section of the population which has had to prove its Japan-ness since the sixteenth century, but which found itself hosting rising numbers of Catholic immigrants. A country that has long prided itself on cultural homogeneity as a key to national identity, Japan began allowing guest workers to take low-end jobs beginning in the 1980s; many of these immigrants were Filipinos who brought varieties of Catholic thought and practice quite different from that practiced by Japanese Catholics.

As Mullins notes, the challenges to Japanese Catholics have been significant—having focused on making Catholicism an inculturated, Japanese way of life, they now find themselves having to consider being multicultural and welcoming to all Catholics, not merely Japanese ones. All of this has been made more difficult by a rising tide of nationalism in the Japanese political mainstream, with a vigorous affirmation of ethno-national "Japan-ness" in the public realm. This nationalism has led to a revitalized Japanese civil religion—focused on the national anthem, the flag, World War II memorials and cemeteries, and more—which leaves no room for foreigners or multicultural hospitality. Mullins notes that many Japanese bishops have leveled prophetic critiques against such chauvinism and have generated an admirable range of pastoral initiatives aimed at welcoming newly arrived Catholics in Japan; however, he also suggests that a deeply divided Japanese Catholic laity may be ignoring the bishops on such matters.

The Latin American Catholic Diaspora

An entirely different experience provides the backdrop to "Diaspora as Mission? Toward a Theological Interpretation of the Experience of the Cuban Catholic Community in South Florida." Ondina Cortés, assistant professor of practical theology at St. Thomas University, charts the experiences and theological implications of the massive influx of Cuban Catholics—one-tenth of the island's population left after the Revolution of 1959, most ending up in southern Florida—for newcomers and host communities alike. Later waves of immigrants provided different challenges for all concerned, be it for material assistance or the preservation of communal identity.

Significantly, however, Cortés notes that the host Catholic communities also benefited in important ways from the infusion of new Catholics from Cuba. Some Cuban Catholics looked upon their exile as a call to evangelize, to lives dedicated to mission and service to the Gospel in a new land. Such resulted not in a loss, but in new opportunities to spread the Good News across borders and cultures. All of this is well illustrated, she suggests, in the role of Our Lady of Charity, a Cuban devotion that has become important not only to the Cuban diaspora in Florida but to the Church more generally.

Devotions in diaspora also draw the attention of Dorian Llywelyn, a Jesuit theologian who provides anthropological insights as well in "Diasporic Devotions." From the far reaches of the world—a remote Chilean island named Chiloe, where poverty has forced migrants to a small city 1,500 miles away in search of work—Llywelyn (director of the Ignatian Center for Jesuit Education at Santa Clara University) offers the story of popular religiosity, images, and sacramentality that have survived various church and social reforms aimed at eliminating popular religion and its devotions elsewhere in Latin America. The islanders' special devotion to Our Father Jesus of Nazareth, a product of Jesuit and Franciscan missions, originated as a peacemaking initiative among rival island peoples that generated civic celebrations enduring across time and many changes.

While the statue of Our Father Jesus of Nazareth anchors celebrations and religious activities on the island, a copy of the statue among Chilotes in diaspora has helped them create a new identity that keeps alive their culture of origin as they adapt to life on the mainland. In this ethnography informed by theological sensitivity, Llywelyn provides a tour de force of popular religion, sacramentality, and the power of indigenous/mestizo cultures in the face of powerful economic, cultural, and political currents that would submerge the Chilotes into a homogenizing mass.

Asian Catholic Diaspora

Jaisy Joseph is a theologian specializing in non-Roman Christianities (including the Syriac, Greek, and Coptic traditions) and a leader in the Syro-Malabar Catholic Church (an Eastern Catholic church in India, in communion with the Church of Rome). She brings her scholarly and pastoral experience to bear in "Negotiations In-Between: Indian Catholics in Diaspora."

Joseph draws attention to "Christians of the in-between," those who experience "the reality of living in-between the culture of their ancestors and the culture of their residence." [168] People of the in-between struggle with religious practices from India that they have judged to be inappropriate in the US ecclesial and cultural context, and with past liturgical conflicts originating in India that have raised questions of enforced uniformity versus legitimate diversity. Syro-Malabar Christians in diaspora are multi-perspectival in their approach to knowledge, says Joseph—which allows for creativity and fluidity in theological work, the capacity to create community in new circumstances, and hopes for prophetic witness of many sorts. She suggests that although migration has been an underexplored topic in theological circles, experiences like those of Asian Catholics in diaspora may be useful in enriching Christian consciousness and reflection moving forward.

Diaspora is a hot topic in Asian American studies, according to Linh Hoang, professor of religious studies at Siena College. In "Vietnamese Catholics and Diaspora: Re-Imaging Mary as Vietnamese," he notes the need to include explicit discussions of race in diaspora studies, something he sees as an underexplored area in Asian American scholarship. The fragmentation of identities caused in large measure by processes of globalization have a profound effect on collective identities, in his view, making it especially difficult to parse the meanings of race and ethnicity for many Asian and Asian American communities.

In his exploration of the Vietnamese Catholic diaspora—a case study of race, ethnicity, and diaspora—Hoang contrasts the divergent pictures and receptions of Mary in the lives of Catholics in Vietnam and elsewhere. He contrasts a major Marian apparition in La Vang in Vietnam—a visitation which offered protection and well-being—with the hierarchically sanctioned later apparitions at Lourdes and Fatima, which spoke of apocalyptic judgment. These appearances, with their very different messages, were well received by the faithful even as they presented challenges to the Catholic hierarchy and pastoral leaders. Matters of race and identity figure prominently among Vietnamese Catholics in sometimes surprising ways; Hoang notes the curious reality of popular white European images of Mary and the Church among Catholics in Vietnam, while many Vietnamese Catholics in the United States are drawn toward representations of Mary with distinctly Vietnamese features.

African Catholic Diaspora

Paradoxes, contradictions, and tragedy abound in viewing another case study, this one offered by Daniel McNeil in "From America with Hate: Bond and the 'Black Shirley Temple.'" McNeil relates the story of Philippa Schuyler, the daughter of a blonde Texas woman and a black journalist and author from New York City. Schuyler had so many talents of such a high level that early in her life she became known as the "black Shirley Temple," a child prodigy whose life unfolded as a series of twists, contradictions, and surprises. Schuyler rejected the racist America that rejected her heritage, even as she attacked black culture as retrograde; she was a writer of Catholic literature whose complex mix of racial, political, and religious attitudes made her life "a special blend of irony, tragedy, and farce," as McNeil says.

McNeil, an associate professor of history at Carlton University in Canada, asks why a mixed-race woman with considerable gifts came to locate herself as a defender of white supremacy and the John Birch Society, and why would she position herself as a female Ian Fleming—the creator of James Bond, the colonial white spy at play in the world of marginalized peoples and lands—by writing novels of sex and race and hierarchy? And why should we care? McNeil asks and answers such questions with attention both to the factors of Schuyler's life and the larger forces of her time; in particular, he offers a provocative comparison with another author concerned with racial identity, power, and domination—the influential Afro-Caribbean scholar and Marxist theoretician, Frantz Fanon.

Another sort of case study—this of a group rather than an individual—comes courtesy of Dominic Pasura, a sociologist specializing in transnationalism and migration at the University of Glasgow. He offers the results of a study he conducted in 2009–2010 among Zimbabwean Catholics in the United Kingdom, presented here as "Rootedness and Openness: Experiences, Practices, and Theologies of Zimbabwean Catholics in Britain." Among African nations sending its citizens abroad, Zimbabwe is notable in seeing perhaps two to three million of its people leave (out of a population of 13 million) in the years after independence, including many members of its middle and professional classes. Approximately 200,000 Zimbabweans moved to the United Kingdom, where they comprise a community that mixes asylum seekers, refugees, laborers, students, and professionals.

Pasura suggests that the particular/local and transnational aspects of Catholicism are not opposed to one another, but in fact presuppose and require one another. He explores the ways in which Zimbabwean Catholics have become a force for Catholic revitalization in the heart of secular Europe, as well as a conduit for ideas and practices in Zimbabwe. In addition, he explores whether and to what extent the notion of "diaspora" usefully applies to transnational religious communities, and why it is controversial in some quarters as people attempt to understand an era of massive human movements, hybrid identities, and wide-ranging cultural interactions.

I

Religion Displaced and Replaced: What We Have to Learn from Diaspora Communities

ROBERT SCHREITER, CPPS

Introduction: Religion and Diaspora Studies

The vast flow of migrating peoples that now encircles the planet has set off a whole new era in transnational and diaspora studies. What happens to people as they leave their home territories and settle in new places? How does this affect their views and their relationships to the places they call home? How do the circumstances under which they left—be they economic "push" and "pull" factors, the trauma of armed conflict or persecution, or now escaping environmental meltdown and catastrophes—shape their understandings of themselves, where they came from, and where they land after their journeys? And what of those places that become their new "homes," so to speak? What are the historical horizons out of which a nation views its newcomers? How is a nation changed by those who arrive at their borders? In the midst of globalization's flows of capital, goods, and ideas, where does the more problematic flow of peoples find its place?

These, and a host of other questions, fuel current discussions in migration, and the overarching fields of transnational and diaspora studies. Indeed, the paired fields of study—transnational and diaspora studies—are not entirely discrete areas of inquiry. They often address the same populations, and certainly address the same contexts, albeit viewed from different perspectives. It might be helpful here to provide a rough definition of each, especially in light of their relation to each other. Transnational studies follow the flow of human populations across national boundaries, and have indeed those boundaries of the nation-state always in the forefront of their concerns. How migrating populations see themselves, and are seen by others, is measured against conceptions of the nation-state. It should be recalled here that the Western notion of the nation-state, as it emerged in the seventeenth and eighteenth centuries, saw itself as a collection of *nations* in the sense of distinct cultures. Indeed, the meaning of the Latin word *natio* is equivalent to what we now call "culture," in the modern sense of that term.[1] The nation-state was then a collection of "nations" that are bound together via contract in the abstract conception of the *state*, which was to be understood as a kind of *ersatz* nation or supra-culture embracing the various nations as though it were a nation itself. Peoples migrating into a nation-state, then, are perceived either as losing their own nation-affiliation and merging into the supra-culture of the nation-state, or resisting that amalgamation and maintaining some measure of cultural identity. Current discussions of multicultural policy in so-called multicultural nation-states are usually designed along those lines of relative allegiance to one or other "nation" within the "nation-state." Thus, "assimilation," "integration," "autonomy," and the like are all calibrated according to the metrics of the nation-state, which is seen as needing to be preserved at all costs. Not only is this framework at play in terms of immigration, but also in discussions and policy-formation regarding culturally autonomous regions within nation-states as different as Spain (the issues of Catalonia and the Basque Territory) and the Philippines (in the Bangsamoro Peace Agreement for Mindanao in that country).

Diaspora studies, on the other hand, look less to the relation of the new, arriving populations to the nation-state, and more to their formation of communities within the new country. Diaspora is not equivalent to dispersal. An immigrant population may enter a country, and may or may not congregate into distinct enclaves. Sometimes national policy is such as to discourage or even obfuscate such community formation. Such was the case, for example, with the first wave of settlement of Vietnamese refugees in the United States in 1975. They were deliberately located at dispersed locations so as to avoid the kind of concentration of people that occurred with the exodus from Cuba in the 1960s—with all the political consequences that such a concentration of Cuban exiles in Miami has created down to the present time. Diaspora, in the current understanding of the concept, means that immigrating populations form an enclave that sets up new networks of relationships both among the immigrants themselves, and with both the host country and with the homeland. These networks, both those that help

---

1. The older concept "natio" is maintained, for example, at the University of Uppsala in Sweden, where the student body was housed in colleges representing the thirteen different "nations" of Sweden (Gotland, Göteborg, etc.).

constitute the diaspora community itself and those that define its relationships to other communities, are the horizons or frameworks by which the diaspora communities are understood and interacted with.

I wish to focus here upon diaspora communities rather than their transnational relationships. As already noted, diaspora and transnational relationships cannot be completely separated, yet concentrating on diaspora and diasporic relationships yield particular insights not only into the movement of peoples today, but also upon their impact on how we see more "settled" populations and—perhaps more importantly—how we view the whole.

In order to do this, I will begin with a closer investigation of some of the dynamics of diaspora communities as they are being discussed in the current literature. Then the focus will move to the role of religion within those dynamics. More specifically, the experience of Catholic faith within the diaspora will be examined further under the two experiences of "place" within the diaspora experience: of being "dis-placed" from one's homeland, and of being "re-placed" in the setting of a new (diasporic) community within a new context. Some of the meanings of this, both for the diaspora communities themselves but also for the larger religious social configurations in which they find themselves, will be the object of our investigation. What I am trying to do then—although admittedly only in a bare outline— is to bring together some of what we are learning about the dynamics of religion in migrant communities as diaspora communities within the larger discussion about diaspora communities going on today.

The Dynamics of Diaspora

The term "diaspora" in its original Greek setting, meant "spread throughout." It referred to peoples who were (usually) forcibly relocated to another place. It gained greater currency in the Septuagint translation of the Hebrew Bible to refer to the relocation of the Jews from the Northern and Southern Kingdoms into the Babylonian exile; later, the expulsion of the Jews from Judea in the first century CE came to be included as well. "Diaspora" has continued to have special reference to the Jewish experience of such dispersion, although it has come to denote the forced relocation of other peoples as well, most notably that of Africans in the Atlantic slave trade,[2] and the imperial relocations of peoples such as populations from India throughout the British Empire. It can refer as well to dispersions that have come about

---

2. See here especially Gilroy, *Black Atlantic*.

through the pursuit of commerce, such as that of the Chinese diaspora communities throughout the world.

As a discrete field of inquiry, "diaspora studies" is relatively recent.[3] It builds upon studies of specific communities (especially Jewish communities) but has broadened out in attempts to take a more comprehensive view of the phenomenon. As already noted, it distinguishes itself from the broader field of transnational studies in taking the diaspora community as its point of departure.

The literature being collected on diaspora studies is configured methodologically by a sense of dialectic, a back-and-forth between two foci. There are two distinctive sets of dialectics that come most into play. The first of these is "continuity-discontinuity," referring to the temporal experience of populations in relation to their homeland. There is a strong sense of "then" (at home) and "now" (an experience of alienation). The second is "space and place," a more spatially constructed experience about the location one inhabits in relation to the homeland.

"Continuity-discontinuity" captures especially the experience of rupture or alienation from one's previous experience as one is propelled into a new, different, and sometimes hostile environment. Many of the features of one's life that heretofore anchored one's identity are swept away. In the new environment, others are not aware of one's status or position in the previous society, one's achievements, or one's view of oneself. In the midst of the experience of profound disruption, which is part of the migrant experience (and even more so for the refugee), the past that is encountered is one served up by memory. That remembered past often takes on a more uniform, uninterrupted, and smooth patina than was likely the case in the unfolding of the actual events. The past—and the homeland—become romanticized as an almost unfallen state of nature compared to the travails of the present.

Indeed, the discontinuities of the present, where one is not recognized, where one might even be rendered invisible, can overwhelm and indeed drive this dialectic between present and past. The stress under which first-generation migrants and refugees live, even when they freely embrace their new setting, can be considerable. It is marked especially by this disjunction between present and past.

As one probes more below the surface of the tumultuous present and the serene past, one may find that the symmetry of continuity-discontinuity might be better expressed by what Daniel Barber has called a dialectic of

---

3. It has gained sufficient status to merit at least a partial "handbook" status. See Quayson and Daswani, *Companion to Diaspora*.

"integrity-discontinuity."[4] In other words, the experience of the past is not so much one of an objective, disinterested flow of events, as it is a moral configuration that sheds a harsh light on the brokenness and alienation of the present. The past coheres in a moral, even aesthetic, unity that is contrasted with the disheveled, disordered experience of the present. It implies that any progress toward a more coherent experience of self and community in the present will be patterned upon, and be judged against, the remembered experience of the past. The emphasis here on the "remembered" experience of the past is of crucial importance, since the past was rarely as ordered as it may now be remembered. Nor is that past so stable that it continues to be replicated in what is now the present of that homeland. This latter dynamic is played out, often tragically, in the experience of first-generation migrants who are able to return to their homelands after an extended absence, only to discover how much their homeland has "changed" from the one that they carry in their memories.

The dialectic of continuity-discontinuity, then, is a powerful force in shaping the experience of diaspora communities. It provides a representation of the homeland in memory—that ever-changing relationship between the past and the present. It continues to shape the defining boundaries between the diaspora community and other communities in their new setting. And it shapes, both subtly and not-so-subtly, relations within the diaspora community itself. That diaspora communities are so often fissiparous and riven with disputes that to outsiders seem to be over trivial matters is indicative of how this dialectic continues to be at work. The moral dimension that Barber's proposal of integrity versus continuity suggests helps clarify the emotional intensity that often marks the adversarial relationships that emerge in these communities.

The second set of dialectics that give methodological shape to diaspora studies is between "space" and "place." "Space" refers to the coordinates into which diaspora groups are thrust. It is to be understood as encompassing both physical and social space. The physical space may not be such to foster human relationships and flourishing. One thinks here of the refugee camp or the slum-like dwellings into which refugees and migrants are often deposited. The physical space itself bespeaks marginalization or even invisibility. The physical space carries with it all kinds of social indicators as well. It may involve a marginalization that forms a ghetto or segregation from "proper" members of the settled community. The social space in which diaspora groups find themselves speaks of their relative social status vis-à-vis other communities in the same physical space as well.

4. Barber, *On Diaspora*.

Students of human geography have come to regard as important how "space" is turned into "place," that is, how a physical space comes to be inhabited and remade by human groups.[5] On this view, space may represent the physical coordinates of a location, whereas place encompasses the social relationships that fill that space. Those relationships are not only physical ones, but cultural, ideational, and spiritual ones as well. Thus, the social relations that make "space" a "place" may not be entirely in the spatial order. They encompass sounds (especially language and song), smells (especially the aromas of food), and feelings (such as euphoria or unity). Indeed, as one author has put it, they provide a "sensorium" out of which place is produced.[6] Place, then, becomes as much an act of the imagination as it is the result of any social engineering or social analysis. In other words, to assess the "place" that a diaspora community creates requires an assessment of what Pnina Werbner has called the "affective economy" that is woven out of the spaces, sounds, smells, and the social imaginary of that community.[7] That social imaginary is best captured in the polyvalent term, "home." At what point does a diaspora community become home to its inhabitants? Or does it live perpetually within the thrall of one's native land?

Discontinuity versus continuity (or integrity), space versus place: these dialectics lay out coordinates from which diasporas can be mapped and followed in their ongoing development within host countries and vis-à-vis their homelands. We need to turn next to the study of religion within diaspora communities.

Religion in Diasporas and Diaspora Communities

To this point in time, religion has been a relatively under-researched area in diaspora studies.[8] Most commonly, it appears when extremist religious views are held by the diaspora community, and such views are seen as causal factors in antisocial behavior. One thinks of second-generation migrant youths in Europe who come to subscribe to a violent interpretation of Islam, or controversies around women wearing a veil in some of those same countries. Such a relative lack of attention can be ascribed to biases

---

5. See especially Tuan, *Space and Place*. An earlier writer on this topic that has also been influential in the English-speaking world was Lefebvre, *Production of Space* (French original, *La production de l'espace*). It should be noted that there is not a consistent usage of the terms "space" and "place" in the literature. This is partially due to the fact that "social space" overlaps considerably with notions of "place."

6. The phrase comes from Shenar, "Bollywood in Israel," 226–54.

7. Werbner, "Migration and Transnational Studies," 106–24.

8. One good overview may be found in McLoughlin, "Religion, Religions," 125–38.

about religion often held in the secularist academy—that religion is a private affair on the verge of disappearance altogether, or that it is consistently a negative factor in human relations. The resurgence of religion in the 1990s and the questioning of Max Weber's secularization hypothesis as applicable to human societies in general have caused some rethinking of the role of religion in international studies in general. And this awareness is causing some reconsideration of religion in transnational and diaspora studies. To be sure, religion has always been a kind of subtext in studying transnational phenomena, but it has often not been allowed to surface.[9]

The study of migrant communities, on the other hand, has provided a good deal of focus upon religion in those communities. This has been the case especially in the United States, but also in parts of Europe, notably in Great Britain. In the United States, the work of R. Stephen Warner and of Helen Rose Ebaugh come immediately to mind, both for their own work and the mentoring they have provided to younger scholars. In addition, a group of newer scholars has added significantly to this literature.[10] While these studies have generally not focused specifically on the diaspora phenomenon as such, they can contribute much to our understanding of it.

A place to begin is a summary of research findings on immigrant religion published by Stephen Warner.[11] I will not review all six points he makes there, but concentrate on two of them that are most significant for our purposes here. The first is that religion provides a source of continuity in the migration experience, between the homeland and the new location. As a source of continuity, it can be a stabilizing factor amid the challenges to identity that inevitably arise out of the migration experience. This is a significant feature for diaspora studies, in that it provides an anchor in the stormy seas of the migration experience. At the same time, of course (and this is another of Warner's points), those new challenges also change the experience of religion of the migrant. An example of the latter is how immigrant religious practice will take on American congregational patterns. The religions of India, for example, whose practice entails episodic visits to a temple or shrine, may take on the Sunday communal worship patterns in the United States—not so much out of any doctrinal change but rather from the fact that congregating around religious practice creates a place where one's own language may be spoken and understood, where one can enjoy the social status that is denied during the rest of the week, and where

9. Paul Gilroy speaks of a "politics of transfiguration" in *The Black Atlantic*, for example.

10. Warner and Wittner, *Gatherings in Diaspora*; Ebaugh and Chafetz, *Religion across Borders*.

11. Warner, "Religion and New (Post-1965) Immigrants," 232–52.

children may be socialized into homeland patterns and find endogamous marriage partners.

Religion in diaspora provides both a transnational and a local focus for the immigrant. The transnational dimension is enhanced if the religious tradition is itself avowedly transnational as are the so-called "world religions." Here Roman Catholicism—by incorporating "catholicity" in its very name—lays clear claim to transnationality. It is intended to be and to be experienced as always extending beyond the local or even national "community." The transnational character gives the diaspora community a kind of compass by which to orient itself, mapping its own moral and spiritual geography onto the political maps of nation-states. By providing such an orientation, it can lessen the sharp feelings of discontinuity with the immediate environment in which it finds itself.

At the same time, it can provide a unique perspective on the local. The local is more than the opposite of the global or the global manqué. It can reveal hidden dimensions of the global as well as critique its totalizing dimensions. The "foreignness" of the diaspora community can call into question how other local social configurations view or relate to global phenomena. What might be taken for granted as inevitable or self-evident is contested by a diaspora community. An example would be the supervision of teenagers. Many migrant communities are surprised how unsupervised and un-chaperoned teenagers are allowed to be in the dominant culture of the United States. With that dominant culture, this unsupervised character is taken for granted or even lauded for respecting their freedom.

Religion Displaced

It is time to turn more directly to religion in diaspora communities. Following the direction of diaspora studies, I would like to concentrate on the dialectics of continuity-discontinuity, and space and place by looking more closely at dis-placement, or the rupture of place, and re-placement in its double sense of resituating and substituting.

The experience of rupture and displacement is a defining characteristic of a diaspora community. It operates with a bifocal perspective: one eye, as it were, on its current location, and the other eye on its homeland. This perspective is acute in the first generation, and either fades or can be maintained in subsequent generations, depending upon the relative size of the community and its relation to the dominant culture of its host country. In the fading process, usually language is the first thing to go: the generation born in the host country is likely to be more fluent in that country's language than in the language of their parents. Mores or patterns of behavior specific to the home country are the next to fade. Usually the one thing that may endure is food. What may have been peasant food or food of the poor in the home country often becomes special food for festive occasions in the diaspora community.

Religious practices may follow the same trajectory as other artifacts of culture. Hymns in the home language may fade from use as fewer people understand the words. Practices that may have anchored faith in the home country (such as attendance at a 4:00 or 5:00 a.m. Mass in rural villages in Vietnam) may not be replicated in the diaspora setting. The practices that survive may be attached to festive moments in the calendar: liturgical festivals such as Christmas or Easter, or key transitions in life such as weddings. In such instances, being displaced from the home setting means that the context for some practices has been lost; it renders those practices more abstract to the experience of younger members of the diaspora community.

The loss of home can beget nostalgia in a diaspora community, a yearning for an imagined past. Holding on to practices—or even onto place—can keep the nostalgia alive. In Chicago, for example, Our Lady of Pompeii parish, the "home" parish for Italian immigrants to that city's "Little Italy," was slated to be closed and consolidated with a neighboring parish some years ago. There was strong public protest against this proposal, coming especially from the children and grandchildren of immigrants who no longer lived in that neighborhood. The archbishop eventually bowed to this pressure, and Our Lady of Pompeii was "reopened" as a shrine. While it continues to attract the descendants of Italian immigrants, it also attracts a considerable number of other Catholics who are attracted by its programming and the dynamic "rector" of the shrine. What started as an act of nostalgia has taken on other dimensions. Our Lady of Pompeii has thus been a sign both of dis-placement (a site of nostalgia) and re-placement (a site for the New Evangelization) of religion.

Religion can be a site for nostalgia in a dis-placed community, but it can also have other functions. It can also foster attempts to forge new bonds with the home community. Benedict Anderson identified this already thirty years ago in his now classic study, *Imagined Communities*.[12] There he spoke of "long-distance nationalism without responsibility." There he was talking of how diaspora communities would engage in the politics of their home country without having to live with the consequences. The involvement of Irish immigrants and descendants of Irish immigrants in Boston who provided financial support for the Irish Republican Army is an example of

---

12. Anderson, *Imagined Communities*.

this. There are religious examples as well. Last year I was contacted by a Sri Lankan diaspora community, asking my evaluation of a proposed program on forgiveness that they had developed for use in Sri Lanka, to deal with the lingering effects of the civil war that had taken place there. They were looking for an evaluation of the program. A few months later, I was in Sri Lanka myself, invited to work with the Religious Conference of that country on issues of reconciliation between Tamils and Sinhalese. One of the things that I discovered rather quickly was how far away those two groups were from talking about forgiveness. So much had to happen there before talk about forgiveness could even begin. I am not calling the diaspora community that produced this program on forgiveness irresponsible; they created the program out of a deep sense of solidarity with those in their homeland. But even with the best of intentions, they were out of touch with where most Sri Lankans found themselves at that moment in time.

Religion displaced can seem to lead to a whole range of negative outcomes. But are there some positive ones as well? Diaspora religion in a largely secular and pluralist setting, such as North America or Europe or Australia, can help cultivate a sacramental vision. That is to say that the meaning of signs or signifiers may also be more complex than is first imagined. That complexity reaches beyond what Charles Taylor called the "buffered self," a self that believes that there is this world and nothing more beyond it.[13] A number of writers have pointed to this sacramental quality as constitutive of the Catholic imagination. They have spoken of the "Catholic imagination" (Andrew Greeley) or the "analogical imagination" (David Tracy).[14] The experience of displaced religion may open up such an imagination, not only around things religious, but also for other cultural values as well. The significant role that migration plays in the biblical story of both Testaments would suggest that this "sacramental" imagination is not solely the property of Catholic or high liturgical traditions within Christianity. Being "par-oikoi," "beyond the household" as the etymology of the word "parish" suggests, might be something endemic to a faith that finds here on earth "no lasting city." Being diasporic may be central to our Christian religious identity.

Religion Re-placed

To speak of religion re-placed is to speak both of religion being resituated and being substituted. Let me speak of diaspora religion in both situations.

13. Taylor, *Secular Age*.
14. Greeley, *Catholic Imagination*; Tracy, *Analogical Imagination*.

Religion may be part of the luggage a migrant brings to a new country. That religion might be seen as a replication of what religion was in the homeland. But it inevitably will undergo change in the new context. Some of those changes are brought about by outside pressures. Some temples of Reform Judaism in the United States resituated the Sabbath observance to Sunday mornings in order to be attuned to the predominantly Christian culture of the United States. Others reflect changes that have gone on in the immigrants themselves.

A striking example of the latter case are two remarkable Catholic Church buildings of Vietnamese communities in suburban Washington, DC (Vietnamese Martyrs) and in Orange County, California (Our Lady of La Vang). What is striking about both of these is that the architecture is that of a Buddhist pagoda or temple such as one might see in Vietnam. The Catholic churches in Vietnam, however, until recently, were typically built in the neo-Gothic or neo-Romanesque style of nineteenth-century French churches. In Vietnam, this style marked the "foreign" character of Catholic faith in a non-Christian country. In the United States, these two churches reflect the "Vietnamese-ness" of the Catholics who worship there. These worship spaces have become "home," "places" for those who gather there. These designs were not suggested by outsiders, but rather developed by the parishioners themselves. They "re-placed" their faith and their identities in a remarkable way.

The replacement can also be substitutional. A classic case in this country is recounted in Robert Orsi's book, *The Madonna of 115th Street*, a study of what happened when different diaspora communities inhabited the same space.[15] Our Lady of Mount Carmel Church in New York City's Harlem area was, as the choice of the name might suggest, originally a church for Italian immigrants. One of the religious practices they brought with them from their home country was a large outdoor procession held on the feast of Our Lady of Mount Carmel. When the population of the neighborhood changed from Italian to Puerto Rican, the Hispanic community took over this celebration and made Our Lady of Mount Carmel their own.

But there has been a further development since Orsi published his book in 1988. Today, Our Lady of Mount Carmel has a substantial Haitian population. They have brought with them a practice of *vodou*, and the church basement even provides a meeting place for vodou.[16]

Replacement of diaspora religion can take on other forms of substitution as well. It was noted that Our Lady of Pompeii in Chicago now attracts

---

15. Orsi, *Madonna of 115th Street*.
16. McAlister, "Madonna of 115th Street Revisited," 123–60.

more than Italian-Americans. It is significant to know that today the majority of practitioners of *candomblé*, an African-Catholic diaspora religion in Brazil, are not of African descent.

Conclusion

The experience of religion in diaspora communities is marked by dialectics of continuity (or integrity) and discontinuity, and turning spaces into places. One can speak of religion being displaced (experiencing rupture and trauma) and of being replaced (in both means of being resituated and being substituted). For Catholics, the transnational network which is the Roman Catholic Church adds an additional feature. It is possible to bring in personnel from different parts of the world to serve local congregations. The world was used to this in the missionary movement, but today the movement comes more from the so-called "newer" churches of Africa and Asia into the longer established churches in Europe and the United States. Other forms of aid can be sought within this transnational network as well. It has also been suggested that diaspora communities may reveal something of the very heart of Christian identity: its sacramental vision. Others have looked to diaspora communities as "creative minorities" to revitalize a seeming moribund church in a secularized culture. Whatever the reading, the emerging field of diaspora studies, drawing upon the work that has been done in the study of migration, may well become a rich resource for living out the catholicity of Christian faith as we truly become a world church—not just in terms of demographics, but in terms of relationships as well.

2

Levantine Catholic Communities in the Diaspora at the Intersection of Many Identities and Worlds

MICHEL ELIAS ANDRAOS

"Like my grandmother, I understood questions of identity, how being torn in two often leaves something less than one." (Anthony Shadid, House of Stone)

Introduction

Like other immigrant communities from traditional, sociocentric cultures and societies, the Levantine Catholic communities in the diaspora face the challenge of critically reflecting on their religious and cultural identities and traditions, reinterpreting them in new cultural contexts, and passing them on to the next generation. In order for the religious and cultural reinterpretations in the new context to survive, they would have to be meaningful to the second generation of these communities who find themselves simultaneously belonging to two or more cultural worlds, religious practices, and language, and constantly negotiating these worlds as they forge their new in-between identities. The cultural and religious challenges Levantine Catholic communities face in this complex process, their relation to their churches, and the role their churches play in this complex process are the main topic of this chapter. Adding new layers to this complexity are the tragic situation in the Middle East today, the ongoing suffering in the homelands of origin of Levantine Christians, and the continuing influx of new waves of immigrants escaping these situations.

The word "Levantine" in the title is used on purpose instead of the "Middle East" or "Near East."[1] "Levant," or *al-mashreq* in Arabic, refers to the eastern part of the Mediterranean. The region includes the countries of Syria, Iraq, Jordan, Palestine, Israel, and Lebanon. Before and after France and Great Britain (the European colonial powers of the time) partitioned the region into small countries in the aftermath of World War I, the peoples of that region experienced a shared history and culture as a result of long interaction. Migration movements have been part of the region's life throughout history and continue to be the case today. Ecclesially, most of the Levant, especially the coastal areas, has been part of the ancient church of Antioch since the early Christian period. Ancient Antioch, not unlike the region today, was a meeting place of many cultural traditions, Christian theological trends, and religions. During the early Islamic period, it became the birthplace of an Islamo-Christian civilization, which deeply impacted both Christianity and Islam to the present day.[2] To paraphrase the late Anthony Shadid in *House of Stone*, his recent novel, there is part of Islam in every Middle Eastern Christian—and, I would add, the same is true for Levantine Muslims.[3] Today, most heads of Eastern churches of the Levant are titular patriarchs of Antioch and the East. They preside over the churches of the different rites of the church of Antioch such as Syriac, Melkite, Maronite, etc., and they reside in the main metropoles of the region, mainly Damascus and Beirut.

Definitions of diaspora are problematic, depending on the field of research and the particular cultural group in discussion. William Safran defines diasporas as "'expatriate minority communities' that are dispersed from a 'center' to two or more locations; sustain a 'memory, vision, or myth about their original homeland'; believe that full acceptance in the host country is impossible; view the ancestral home as a place of return; are committed to the homeland's restoration; and have their identities constituted in large part by their relationships with their homelands."[4] The author notes that,

---

1. Like the terms "Middle East" and "Near East," "Levant" is also a loosely defined European designation. It refers to the lands from where the sun rises toward Europe. I use "Levantine" more than the two other designations, because this is the term being used more often nowadays by Christian communities in the Middle East to describe their shared identity as *al-maseeheyoun al-mashriqeyoun*, Levantine Christians. The other two terms are also used in this essay, and they all refer to the same region. The Catholic affiliation of these churches will be explained below.

2. See Bulliet, *Case for Islamo-Christian Civilization*. Bulliet's focus is not the early Islamic period, but his arguments are equally valid for describing what happened during the first centuries of Islam in the Levant.

3. Shadid, *House of Stone*, 61.

4. Safran, "Diasporas in Modern Societies," 83–84, quoted by Weaver, *Mapping*

although this definition might seem paradigmatic of the Jewish experience, it equally applies to Palestinian, Armenian, Greek, and other communities. I would also say that it applies to most of the Levantine Christian communities I will be discussing in this essay.[5] While this essay is not a scientific study of the Levantine Christian communities in the North American diaspora, I am using the term "diaspora" in the title in its broad meaning to describe the experience of immigration in North America of these communities and their present relation to their homelands and mother churches.

The first part of this essay provides a general overview with a particular focus on the historical developments during the late Ottoman and European colonial intervention in the region that continues to have an impact on the identity and self-understanding of Levantine Catholic communities to the present day. The second part examines some selective aspects of the complex collective identity of the Levantine Catholic communities, focusing primarily on their multiple religious and ethnic belonging, education, and experience of war and violence. The essay concludes with a reflection on the role of the churches and includes some final theological reflections on healing, reconciliation, and peace.

A General Historical Overview

The Levantine communities in discussion are the Maronite, Melkite (Byzantine Catholic or Greek Catholic), Syriac Catholic, Armenian Catholic, Chaldean, and Latin (or Roman Catholic).[6] To this group one could add the Coptic Catholic community, which makes the seven Catholic families of the Middle East. The Coptic churches do not, strictly speaking, consider themselves as part of the Levantine churches and culture. With a distinct history, culture, liturgy, and spirituality, they have more in common with the East African churches than with the Levant. Their historical ecclesial point of reference is Alexandria rather than Antioch. However, there has historically been much interaction between these two cultural worlds, including in the

---

Exile and Return, 14.

5. Safran's definition of diaspora quoted above is contested because of its lack of fluidity. Nevertheless, it is helpful in my experience for understanding certain aspects of the Levantine Christian diaspora.

6 For a brief description of the Christian communities in the Middle East, which also includes demographic information, see Bailey and Bailey, *Who Are the Christians in the Middle East?* Given the volatile situation of migration in the region, especially because of the recent and ongoing wars in Syria and Iraq, numbers about Christian communities in almost all the countries of the region are in flux. For other helpful statistical background information, see also "Guide: Christians in the Middle East."

modern period, and many Coptic churches are part of the different councils of bishops and churches of the Middle East, whether Catholic, Orthodox, or Protestant. The total number of native members[7] of the Christian communities in the entire Middle East today—Catholic, Orthodox, and Evangelical—is less than 10 million.[8] Without the Copts of Egypt, who form the largest group, the number is less than half of that. The members of the churches in communion with Rome in the whole region would be roughly in the range of two million. Exact numbers are almost impossible to obtain.

The word "Catholic" in the name of each of the ecclesial communities mentioned above refers to their affiliation or communion with the Roman Catholic Church. Except for the Maronite church, which claims older ties with Roman Catholicism that date back to the early Middle Ages, the Roman Catholic association of all the other Eastern churches is a relatively modern development. Conversion to Catholicism, as Robert Haddad notes, happened in a particular political and economic context around the eighteenth century as the Ottoman Empire began to decline and the power of Western European states and their intervention in the region were on the rise.[9] Haddad argues that the conversion of Eastern Christians to Catholicism during that period was influenced by similar historical reasons as the earlier conversion of some Christians to Islam under the Muslim empire, namely better access to economic and political power. Haddad notes that this shift of power began around the middle of the seventeenth century. He argues,

> The oft-cited shift in the balance of power from the Ottoman Empire, the most powerful Muslim state, to Europe, principally to the lands of Latin Christendom, produced at last an alternative to conversion to the faith of the Prophet. This would prove to be conversion to the Unia whose very establishment and growth were intimately related to that shift in the balance of

---

7. Pew Research Center, "Global Christianity." Here, see the interactive map, "Catholics in Middle East-North Africa," at http://www.pewforum.org/interactives/global-christianity/#/middleeast. According to these 2010 Pew Research statistics, there are about 2 million Catholics in Saudi Arabia and the surrounding Gulf countries, almost all migrant workers mostly from Southeast Asia and other countries in the Middle East. Most of these Christians would be Roman Catholic and do not originally belong to the traditional, native churches of the Middle East.

8. For a variety of political and historical reasons, reliable sources for statistics of Christian communities in the Middle East are difficult to find. For what appears to be the most recent reliable estimates, see the interactive map, "Christians in Middle East-North Africa," at http://www.pewforum.org/interactives/global-christianity/#/middleeast. All in Pew Research Center, "Global Christianity."

9. Haddad, "Conversion and Continuity," 449–59.

power which, by the early twentieth century, had brought most of the globe, including the Muslim portions of it, under this or that variety of European hegemony.[10]

Over time, these commercial and political benefits became a relationship of patronage between Eastern Christians who converted to Catholicism and the West, France in particular, argues Joseph Maïla. "In the middle of the eighteenth century," notes Maïla, "France was recognized by the Holy See and by the European powers as the protector of Christians [of the Levant] affiliated to Rome."[11] Within a century or so, the Eastern Christian communities that united with Rome changed from minorities within the Ottoman Empire to children of the West.[12]

The new relationship with the West, particularly since the seventeenth century, I would argue, has shaped the identity of the Levantine Christian Catholic communities in ways that continue to the present time. These communities also began to associate themselves culturally with the West, which complicated their relationship with both the West and the East, especially with Islam, and put them at the intersection of these two cultural worlds to the present day. This complex aspect of the Levantine Catholic Christian identity also extends to the diaspora communities, which I will discuss below.

Many Levantine Catholics today would prefer to attribute their union with Rome to other reasons such as orthodoxy, continuity of apostolic tradition, and so on. Getting into the details of this debate, however, is outside the scope of this essay. Haddad's thesis and analysis, in my opinion, are historically plausible and helpful for a postcolonial understanding of both the history and the future of the relations between Western European Christianity and Levantine Christian communities.[13]

Another aspect that shaped the Levantine churches and their relation to their communities during the late Ottoman period, and which also continues to have an impact to the present day, is the making of the Middle Eastern Christian communities, among other religious groups, into *millets*, or nations, that is autonomous groups with distinct political status and identity. Within the millet system, the church hierarchy was given political power to play the intermediary role between the empire and the community. This role allowed the church hierarchy, in collaborations with the

10. Ibid., 453.
11. Maïla, "Arab Christians," 35.
12. Ibid., 40.
13. For a summary of the perspective of the Middle Eastern Catholic church leaders on this point, see Andraos, "Christian Communities," 1–4.

elite, to manage the internal affairs of the community and to also represent the community to the Ottoman rulers. Originally designed for managing religious diversity in the empire, the millet system shaped, in a profound way, the power relations between the church hierarchy, the elite, and the common members of their communities. This period became formative for the identity of the Levantine churches. Churches were at the same time a political community and an ethnic group with some autonomy. The millet system survived the Ottoman period and was reinforced by Western European colonial powers after the end of World War I and the defeat of the empire. It became commonly known as sectarianism and continued to serve the same purpose of managing and manipulating power relations between the different ethnic/religious communities, new states, and colonial powers.[14] Understanding the origin and function of the millet system during the formative period of the power structure within the Christian churches is very important as a background for understanding Middle Eastern church-community relations and the role churches and church hierarchy continue to play today within, as well as between, the different communities, including in the diaspora. These power relations within the Levantine church communities have been contested in a variety of ways, but they have proven, over time, to be resistant to change. As far as I know, there is no pastoral process in any of the Levantine dioceses in the diaspora that has succeeded in moving beyond this legacy of hierarchical, clerical power structure that dates at least to the late Ottoman period. I will come back to this topic below.

The North American Diaspora

There are more members who belong to the Levantine Christian communities in the diaspora (including North America, Latin America, Europe, and Australia) than there are in the Middle East. In North America, there are roughly about one million people affiliated with the seven above-mentioned Eastern Catholic churches. Exact numbers in the diaspora are difficult to find, since there is no official census that gives such information. The main sources of information are the communities' diocesan offices and their websites, which are not very reliable and often vary from one source to another. Like other immigrant groups, members of these communities in North America mostly live in large metropolitan areas such as Boston, New York, Detroit, Chicago, St. Louis, Los Angeles, Toronto, Montreal, Halifax,

---

14. On the topic of sectarianism among the Middle East's Christian communities, see Masters, *Christians and Jews in the Ottoman Arab World*; Makdisi, *Culture of Sectarianism*; and Robson, *Colonialism and Christianity in Mandate Palestine*.

Edmonton, etc. The diocesan sees of the Eastern Catholic churches are located in some of these big cities, and their bishops participate in the local conferences of Roman Catholic bishops, since they are considered to be in full communion with Rome.

Early waves of immigration from the Levant to North America started in the late nineteenth century.[15] Already in the 1880s, there were Levantine communities and churches in cities such as Montreal and New York. The Melkite church—St. John the Baptist in the Chicago area, for example—dates to the early 1900s. Newer waves arrived during the period between the two world wars, especially in the years following World War II as the need for labor increased in North America's industrial cities. Other more recent waves arrived in the 1970s as a result of new wars and conflicts in the Middle East, some of which are still ongoing. Palestinian Christian immigration increased after the 1967 war and Israel's occupation of new areas of Palestine. Many people left Lebanon between 1975 and 1990, during the years of the so-called civil war, but immigration is still ongoing because of the constant political and economic instability throughout the whole region. The wars in Iraq and, more recently, in Syria are having a devastating impact on all of the region's communities and countries and causing another wave of massive displacement, internal migration, and immigration. For the most part, immigration from the region has been involuntary and forced because of a sequence of wars and other human security factors, yet, on the other hand, it has been desirable because of the opportunities it offers for a better life. First-generation working class immigrants rarely have an easy life in their newly adopted countries; however, they are often considered lucky by those left behind because they were able to escape the wars, violence, economic hardships, and political instability.

While there are some recent scholarly studies on today's Middle East Christian communities,[16] there are very few scholarly works on the Levantine Christian communities in diaspora, even in North America. My intention in the remainder of this essay is not to offer an analysis regarding the degree of integration or assimilation of these communities in their new

15. For a good source of information on the early Middle Eastern immigration to North America, see Abu-Laban, *Olive Branch on the Family Tree*. The book focuses on immigration to Canada, but it also contains a good deal of information about the United States, as immigration from the Middle East to both countries happened around the same time, and the churches in both countries were, and continue to be, connected. See in particular 128–44, the section on immigration and the role of religious institutions in chapter 6.

16. Surprisingly, there are only few publications in the English language that provide scholarly analyses of the situation of the Christian communities in the Levant. For a general overview, see Pacini, *Christian Communities in the Arab Middle East*.

societies; rather, what I intend to do is to give a cultural and pastoral overview based on my own experience, observations, and research. I will identify some of the pastoral challenges these communities are facing, focusing mainly on their life experience. I conclude by sharing some theological and pastoral insights reflecting on my hope for the future of these communities in North America.

Cultural and Religious Identity at the Intersection of Many Worlds

For immigrant groups, cultural adaptation is a lifelong challenge, and the Levantine Christian communities in North America are no exception. Identity, both social and individual, is the product of complex social and cultural processes. It is common knowledge in the social sciences that cultural identities are socially constructed, dynamic, hybrid, and fluid. Cultural identities are normally constructed within particular contexts and webs of social relations in a place, community, and ecology. In order to survive, the systems of cultural and religious values that newcomers bring with them to a new place or social ecology must be reinterpreted in a way that is meaningful in the new context, unless these newcomers live in their own ghetto. When the new context is very different from the one in which they grew up, which is the case of Levantine communities in North America, the task is even more challenging. Communities of Western European origin, for example, would have less difficulty reinterpreting their cultural and religious values in North America, where the dominant culture, for the most part, is still Euro-American. This is not the case for communities of Middle Eastern origin. In addition, reconstructing both individual and collective cultural identities in a new context becomes even more challenging when the immigrant group's culture or religion is considered inferior by the majority or by other dominant cultures. In such a situation, the new groups often experience cultural racism and rejection. The experience of many communities from Middle Eastern origin in post-September 11 North America is a good example.

Given the complexity and broad spectrum of the discussion about cultural and religious identities, I limit my comments below to some snapshots of identity tensions that Levantine Catholic communities experience at the intersection of the cultural and religious worlds to which they belong or from which they come. These snapshots are by no means exhaustive and are not intended to represent the complex experience of these communities. They only offer some examples to illustrate my argument.

"Catholic" but Not Fully Roman Catholic

One of the intersections at which Levantine Catholic communities in diaspora find themselves is their eastern and Catholic identities. Belonging simultaneously to the Roman Catholic Church as people of Middle Eastern origin, mostly Arabic speaking, and to their more ancient and particular eastern churches, has never been easy to reconcile.

Overemphasizing their Catholic identity and association with the Roman Catholic Church in the diaspora is always a temptation, given the unequal cultural power relations and the Levantine immigrant communities' need for cultural acceptance. Another reason for this identification, I believe, might be their insecurity about their Catholic identity, for the historical reasons mentioned above. While the face of the Roman Catholic Church in North America is changing due to Catholic immigration from Latin American and South Asian countries, among other places, and is becoming increasingly diverse, Levantine Catholic churches do not seek full integration in that diverse church. They want to be Catholic while at the same time maintaining an independent and autonomous presence as particular Eastern rite churches.

The hesitation to belong to the larger Roman Catholic community is not only on the part of the Levantine churches. It is mutual. It took the Roman Catholic Church in North America a long time to recognize the immigrant Levantine Catholic churches as being in communion with them. Quoting scholar Yvonne Haddad, Robert Younes notes that "despite being Christians with a history going back to the earliest foundations of the Christian faith, many Middle Eastern Christians had difficulty being accepted by their American co-religionists."[17] The author uses the example of the Maronite church, which was only recognized by the Roman Catholic Church in the United States in the 1960s. And the Greek Catholic Melkite Church in the United States, he notes, was not recognized by Rome as a separate entity distinguished from the Melkite Church in the Middle East until 1966.[18] Even though the juridical question has been resolved, at the cultural level, being or not being part of the Roman Catholic Church in the North American diaspora continues to be a shadow area where these two identities intersect but do not fully mix.

---

17. Younes, "Yvonne Haddad on Issues," 61.
18. Ibid.

Middle Eastern but Not Fully "Arab"

People of Middle Eastern origin have been racialized as "Arab Americans" and "Muslims" in post-September 11 North America. In order to avoid this racialization, many Levantine Christians try to distance themselves from their Middle Eastern and Arab identity by emphasizing their Christian and Catholic sense of belonging. The identification of being Arab and Middle Eastern with being Muslim is not new, and it is not only a diaspora question. It existed in both the Middle East as well as in the West, long before September 11, 2001. Being Arab or not has also been an internal debate within the Middle Eastern Christian communities, both in their old countries as well as in the diaspora. In the early 1960s, just to give one example, Mary Sengstock did a study on the Chaldean community in Detroit. She recounts the following: "In one family, two immigrant cousins were described as 'Christian Arabs.' 'I'm not an Arab!' exclaimed one. 'Well I am!' his cousin retorted. In another family, a Chaldean immigrant described himself as an Arab, at which point his fiancée, also an immigrant, burst into tears."[19] Because Chaldeans, as well as other Middle Eastern Christians from different ethnic groups, are considered marginal in the Arab world, some choose not to identify as Arabs. When they immigrate, this debate does not disappear and continues to be part of negotiating their new identity in the diaspora. Generally, when Levantine Catholic Christians immigrate to North America, they identify themselves mostly with white Euro-Americans for reasons of religion and the other cultural aspects related to their "western Christian education" at home, which is part of the colonial legacy discussed above. Many adopt racist attitudes toward other peoples of color, which are normally part of the Euro-American, white cultural experience. What contributes to this fact is that the official US census considers immigrants of Middle Eastern origin as white. Their recent new racialization as "Arab Americans," however, puts an end to their association with the white, Euro-American culture.

When I meet new people in North America who learn that I am a Christian originally from Lebanon, I am often asked: when did you or your family convert to Christianity? At first, the question used to puzzle me. But now that I have a rehearsed my answer, I normally reply: "I am a convert. My ancestors converted to Christianity about 2000 years ago," which is, of course, not true. Even though Christian communities have been continuously present in the region since the beginning of Christianity, the historical continuity of these communities since that time is a myth, which many of us

---

19. Sengstock, "Traditional and Nationalist Identity," 201.

Middle Eastern Christians believe and like to brag about. But I have come to realize, like Anthony Shadid, that there is a Muslim in every Middle Eastern Christian.

Forging an identity at the intersection of being Middle Eastern Christian, Arab, Muslim, and, at the same time, part of the Roman Catholic Church in the diaspora is very confusing at times, to say the least, and it is very unlikely that this confusion will be clarified in the near future.

"Western" Educated, but Not Really Western

Levantine Christians, especially Catholics, are normally proud of their Western, Christian education and the ability to speak one or more European languages fluently. This education is certainly an advantage that helps them in their cultural integration when they immigrate to Western countries. However, being educated by Western institutions also has its downside in terms of creating a false cultural identity and self-image.

Western educational institutions have existed in the Levant for several centuries. Many were already established before the time of some Levantine Christian communities' conversion to union with Rome, in the early part of the eighteenth century. European Roman Catholic missionaries normally ran them. With the expansion of the Western missionary movements in the early nineteenth century, missionaries from the United States joined the Europeans in the Levant, which led to multiplying the number of these institutions.[20] Western missionary schools and universities had a significant impact on Levantine Christians and contributed in important ways to raising their social and economic status, which eventually tilted the balance of power and the status quo that was established with the Muslim communities for centuries under the Ottoman rule.[21] Western education also influenced the Middle Eastern Christian communities' formation of a worldview and their self-understanding, particularly in relation to believing in the superiority of Western Christian beliefs and practices and having negative views of both Eastern Christianity and Islam, attitudes that many Middle Eastern Catholic Christians continue to harbor to the present. Ussama Makdisi, a pioneer historian of the Western missionary movement in the Middle East, argues that essentializing the difference with Islam and the Muslim communities, as we know it today, is a product of nineteenth- and

---

20. See the recent and important study on this topic by Tejirian and Simon, *Conflict, Conquest, and Conversion*.

21. On the topic of the shifting power relations in the nineteenth-century Levant, see Masters, *Christians and Jews in the Ottoman Arab World*.

early twentieth-century French and British colonial politics in the region, which was to a great extent communicated through the educational systems.[22] In addition, Makdisi notes that European powers "singled out the Christian communities of the Ottoman Empire for special protection from the Muslim population."[23] On this point, Joseph Maïla rightly argues that

> the constant concern shown by the European consuls for the Christian minorities, attested in numerous diplomatic documents, as well as the number of times they intervened on their behalf at the Sublime Porte, turned them into political patrons of Europe, and made them extremely dependent psychologically on the West. From minorities within the [Ottoman] Empire, Christians became children of the West.[24]

Levantine Christians, who were among the first to immigrate to North America, carried with them this colonial legacy. They tend to be proud of their European educational identity while at the same time having negative views of, and dissociating themselves from, the Arabic and Islamic Middle Eastern culture. This creates an internal tension of identity association and, to a certain extent, a false self-image, a typical product of a colonized mind. In post-September 11 North America, however, there has been no distinction in the new racialization process between Levantine Christians and other peoples from the Middle East. They have all been racialized together as Arab Americans.

The role of religion and education in the process of colonizing peoples' cultures and minds is vast and complex. Levantine Catholic Christians have been at this intersection in their homelands for centuries before immigrating to North America, and like the debate about Arab and Middle Eastern identity, this too is a complex debate. The Catholic churches and their institutions have been implicated as major actors in the global process of colonization, and the Middle East was no exception. To what extent the Levantine churches in the diaspora can be part of reversing this process of colonization in the life of their communities is a debatable question, and it requires more discussion than I can include in this essay.

---

22. Makdisi, *Artillery of Heaven*. See also Khalaf, *Protestant Missionaries in the Levant*.

23. Makdisi, "Reconstructing the Nation-State," 24.

24. Maïla, "Arab Christians," 40.

Traumatized Communities

Another important aspect of the Levantine communities' identity in the diaspora that is rarely addressed is their experience of collective trauma as a result of the war and violence many of their members experienced firsthand before coming to North America. They are communities in need of deep personal and social healing and reconciliation. The entire Middle East has been in turmoil for most of the nineteenth and twentieth centuries. The memory of collective trauma of war and violence is a shared experience by these communities, without exception. Many people in these communities lost members of their families and close friends who were killed in violent ways in the various wars. Others lost their homes and possessions and were displaced more than once before they were able to immigrate. Many continue to be part of divided families; part of the family is here, and part is still over there, sometimes living in danger and poverty. Families here often experience fear and worry out of concern for those they left behind. This concern causes permanent stress and anxiety. The Middle East is constantly in the news and always seems to be on the brink of a new war, in addition to its continuing conflicts and violence. Old traumas are relived with every new episode of war and violence, and there have been many of those. Over the past few decades, hardly a year has passed without a major new act of violence or war. Continuing conflicts such as the occupation of the Palestine and the suffering and oppression of the Palestinians affect all the peoples of the region. In many ways, the region's peoples are interconnected; they are one people in different states. Whatever happens in one area affects the rest and also has an impact on the communities in the diaspora.

In addition to the trauma of wars, there is also the pain of uprootedness from land, culture, ecology, extended family, and more. This also is an experience of violence that deeply affects members of the Levantine communities. In their pastoral ministry, church communities and parishes, unfortunately, rarely take seriously the need of their people for healing from these traumas, and their need for reconciliation. I have yet to see one parish or diocese in the diaspora that has developed a ministerial program to attend to these areas of pastoral care. Going to church sometimes has the opposite effect. Wounds are reopened in church gatherings because they bring alive old memories. Old experiences of the conflicts are often carried over without creating the spaces and ministry for healing and reconciliation.

An added dimension to these traumas of war and violence is the foreign policy of countries such as the United States and Canada which support war and invasions that cause the killing of many innocent people in the region. In the name of promoting democracy and freedom, such countries continue to exercise colonial politics in the Middle East, unconditionally supporting aggressive states that oppress their and other people and occupy their land. The colonization of the Middle East never came to an end. The political and military support for unjust countries and regimes adds to the pain and trauma of the people from the region who live here. This is a real daily life experience for Levantine communities in the North American diaspora. Instead of experiencing healing, their pain and trauma are often deepened. This is another identity contradiction resulting from being simultaneously part of two worlds, where one is exercising power unjustly over the other. Like the other identity tensions mentioned above, this, too, is unlikely to disappear in the near future.

The Role of the Churches

For the particular historical formation of church-community relations mentioned above, churches play a primary role in the life of the Levantine communities and in the process of their identity construction. This role, however, is not always positive or helpful, as I will discuss below. Churches make significant social and cultural contributions, yet at the same time, have important pastoral shortcomings. I begin with the positive contribution.

In a study on the Orthodox Eastern Churches in the United States, Alexei Krindatch[25] notes that the parishes of these churches "have become the centers not only of religious but also of social life. First, they served to attract and consolidate newly arriving immigrants in certain geographic areas. Second, their functions transcend religious needs and include, for instance, financial aid for the needy paid by the richer members of the ethnic community, help in finding a first job and place to live, legal assistance, free English language lessons, etc. At the beginning of a new millennium, these 'immigrational services' are still an essential part of the social work of many OCs [Orthodox churches] in the United States."[26] What Krindatch has said about the social role of the OCs I believe is also true for the most of the Levantine Catholic churches with which I am familiar.

One of the most common challenges of Levantine churches and parishes in diaspora is the fact that many of their members, after a period of a decade or two, stop going to church and practicing their religion. They begin to find the religious practices of their churches irrelevant to their new cultural experience. The churches' strong emphasis on maintaining

---

25. Krindatch, "Orthodox (Eastern Christian) Churches in the United States at the Beginning of a New Millennium," 533–63.

26. Ibid., 551.

old religious traditions comes to have little meaning to average community members because of the minimal impact these traditions have on sustaining them in their present daily life struggles. In parishes I observed in cities like Montreal, Toronto, and Chicago, there is hardly any substantial pastoral effort made toward reinterpreting tradition in meaningful ways for the new cultural experience of the communities. In many parishes, the excessive emphasis on maintaining vague traditional practices and values, keeping the community's original ethno-religious identity, and sustaining the churches' institutional structures, drives many people away from the church. This seems to be a chronic problem that parishes face across the board.

Given the complexities of interpreting traditions in new contexts, and the churches' general failure in doing so adequately, many Levantine Christians find themselves spiritually homeless. Certain levels of cultural integration in society are easier to achieve, but sustaining traditional spiritualties that are important for people's daily life is not easy. People need to find other sources in the new culture for nurturing their spirituality. The churches' contribution in this regard is crucial, but in my experience, it has unfortunately been very limited and inadequate. In the churches, people paradoxically live in spiritual poverty while hearing their pastors constantly boast in Sunday homilies about the spiritual richness of their ancient religious traditions. Many of these affirmations during the various liturgies and on churches' websites are rhetorical and carry no real meaning for the people.

Other limitations and pastoral failures concern the formation of the clergy. New clergy often come from the old homelands and are not familiar enough with the reality of immigration and the new culture. The ideas they preach about religious tradition and culture are often not helpful for the community. For example, not long ago, I attended a liturgical celebration that was designed for the young people from all the parishes in the diocese of a major Canadian city. The message communicated to the young people throughout the service, including the homily by the bishop, focused primarily on nurturing an ethno-religious ideology from the old country and warning these young people of the negative secular values of the society in which they live. This kind of religious teaching and orientation puts these young people in a place of confrontation with their new cultural and social values in the name of faithfulness to God and to their "authentic" Eastern Christian spiritual and religious tradition. I am not sure to what extent this kind of religious orientation is helpful for the young generation of Levantine communities in the diaspora. In my opinion, this is contrary to interpreting religious traditions in the new context in a way that helps the members of the community, especially the young generation, to live a healthy, integrated Christian and spiritual life.

Clericalism is another perennial pastoral problem in the Levantine churches. The clerical mentality and attitudes carried over from the old countries, which evolved in the particular historical context discussed above, are not relevant in the new context. The style of exercising of clerical power would need to change. Immigrants from traditional societies experience social transformation in the new egalitarian society and no longer accept traditional, authoritarian ways of exercising clerical power. Common problems of abuse of authority are a lack of consultation in the decision-making processes in the parishes and dioceses, pyramidal ecclesial power structures, and dealing with financial matters without transparency. Unresolved, these problems create mistrust between the clergy and the community. Situations and stories of corruption are fairly common. Educated parishioners find it difficult to serve their communities effectively in such circumstances. They stop going to church, which adds to their feelings of uprootedness and loss of community.

A Concluding Reflection

Many of the points discussed above are not unique to the Levantine Catholic communities in diaspora; they equally apply to other immigrant groups and their churches. The particular historical context of the Levantine Catholic churches, and the challenges of forging new communal and individual identities at the intersection of the many identities and worlds discussed above, are complex processes. Of all the pastoral shortcomings in this regard, I would identify as a high pastoral priority initiatives focusing on the ministries of healing and reconciliation in Levantine Catholic churches' parishes and dioceses, given the magnitude and complexity of the trauma and continuing violence in the Middle East. This pastoral project could not happen without active participation from the churches and their leadership. But such participation would require a shift in ecclesial thinking and the presence of prophetic voices at the level of church leadership, neither of which are the case at the moment. In addition, I believe that building bridges of collaboration across the Levantine Christian communities, as well as across interreligious lines with the other Levantine Muslim communities who coexist in the same cities and share the same struggles, would make a significant contribution to healing and reconciliation, not only among the diaspora communities, but also to peace in the hosting countries as well as in the Middle East. At a time of high tension between Western societies and

Muslim communities, such a witness could become an important sign of hope and peace.

3

A New Creation: The Catholic Faith in Diaspora

SIMON C. KIM

Introduction

The struggle for identity arises through the departure from one's previous realities into the environs of another. While Jesus was alive, the question of identity for his followers was never in doubt since Jesus considered himself a faithful Jew. Through a physical departure from the past and an embrace of the unknown does the question of identity arise. This concept was certainly evident among the disciples after Jesus's death especially when their mission moved them to other locales. In his overview of the early church, Joseph Kelly begins,

> In the Acts of the Apostles, the evangelist Luke reports how Jesus's disciples, both men and women, including Jesus's mother, got together and determined that Jesus's work on earth must be continued by the community, guided, as Luke says, by the Holy Spirit. But divine assistance did not make the task easy, and Luke shows us a community struggling not just against outsiders but also searching for its identity.[1]

The search for identity, in all its multifaceted dimensions, is heightened in diaspora because it looks back to the familiarity of the homeland while at the same time looks forward to the transformation in the new region where roots are being laid.

---

1. Kelly, *Ecumenical Councils*, 11.

Through the lives and even folkloric tales of the Twelve and other disciples, we know that Jesus's followers ventured to the ends of their then-known world. The commemoration of their death in specific locales not only illustrates the establishment of faith communities in diaspora while spreading the gospel message, but also further demonstrates the investment of one's life in a foreign region in forming a new identity. However, the ongoing temptation was to return to the familiarity of previous worlds rather than engage the world before them. This mentality was troublesome for life in diaspora since it led to deficient theologies.[2] The inability to expand and deepen laws and customs that resonated with their changing identity became a challenge when handing on the faith through innovative expressions, especially in Christological portrayals. The ability to adapt then becomes a historical marker for the emergence of a new creation of both an individual and communal identity where the former world is not only meaningfully communicated but also reflected on in the new reality of believers.

Early Church Developments

Bernard Lonergan employs four aspects of development in his *On the Way to Nicaea*: the objective, subjective, evaluative, and finally the hermeneutical aspect. These four aspects are helpful for us to see how the church's movement coincides with the individual expression of the faith. These two movements are not in opposition to one another but in fact are needed to complement and affirm theological developments. For the scope of this paper it is important to understand that Lonergan uses the objective and subjective aspects to illustrate the movement from a biblical milieu to diaspora, from scriptural images of Jesus to dogmatic statements of Christ. The evaluative aspect is our critical reflection on this movement between the objective and subjective aspects while the

> fourth aspect [hermeneutical] arises because, inevitably, the views one holds about dogmatic development will influence one's investigation and interpretation of that development. The old axiom still remains true, that whatever is received, is received after the manner of the receiver.[3]

These four aspects, especially the hermeneutical, demonstrate the movement from the Palestinian world to the Gentile world, from the Jewish milieu to Greek-speaking cultures, and from biblical images of Jesus to

---

2. Davis, *First Ecumenical Councils*, 34.
3. Lonergan, *Way to Nicea*, 7.

philosophical/theological understanding of Christ. Commenting on Lonergan's work, Leo Davis notes,

> Explicitly the Council moved from one kind of clarity about the Son of God contained in Scripture appealing to undifferentiated human consciousness to another kind of clarity contained in dogmatic statements directed to differentiated, intellectual consciousness. But, implicitly, without their fully adverting to what they were about, they paved the way for the development of dogma.[4]

The explicit movement requires the corresponding implicit movement where the lived experience of the believers affirms the truth of the dogmatic statement as representative of the gospels. Early Christian expression of their commitment to the faith became aspects to judge the intellectual discourse over who Christ was. In short, the lives of those in a Christian diaspora mattered as much as the theological reflection occurring at the same time. The movement of theological thought must accompany the movement of a people. Through this movement a hermeneutical lens of early ecclesial communities begins to emerge.

An Authentic Expression of Church

The early ecclesial communities in diaspora had three characteristics: (1) small or scattered communities of believers; (2) suffering and sacrifice to the point of martyrdom; and (3) adaptations in the sacramental life. Future communities of faith in their development would eventually share these characteristics. In regards to the first characteristics, the early Christians formed nascent communities to support and nurture their newfound faith life. These communities came together for various reasons for nurturing the faithful, the most obvious of which was simply to draw together the initially limited numbers of believers in a specific locale in newly developing situations. Thus, one of the characteristics of life in diaspora was small or scattered communities of believers where individual faith was nurtured by examples of others and sacramental life was adapted in response to the particular circumstances found in diaspora.

Another reason for small and scattered nascent communities of faith was the sporadic persecution throughout the empire eventually culminating in empire-wide persecution of Christianity. Although, some ecclesial communities lived in relative peace, there was still ample evidence of suffering

---

4. Davis, *First Ecumenical Councils*, 71.

and sacrifice even to the point of martyrdom in living and disseminating the faith.[5] Sacrifice and martyrdom in the first couple of centuries were not unique in the initial spread of Christianity, but rather, this particular expression of Christian faith in diaspora would be one that would become a common hallmark of future faith communities.

Last, but not least, the early Christians were forced to find creative ways of living out the sacramental life. Whether due to lack of access to the Eucharistic sharing celebrated by the local bishop, persecution for public display of prayer, or residence in truly rural areas, faith life in the diaspora required adaptation to maintain and preserve the Catholic faith. Celebrations of the sacraments were not daily occurrences but depended on the ability of these small and scattered communities to gather as a church. As Joseph Martos comments on the early Christian community,

> During the first centuries . . . the form of Christian worship evolved from a fellowship meal to a ritual meal, with prayers in the general style of the earlier Jewish thanksgiving prayers but with no set words except the words of institution. It evolved differently in different parts of the empire and in the different cities within those regions, but the basic pattern was the same in all places . . . During this period also the interpretation of this sacramental action as a sacrificial meal grew more popular[.][6]

Today, we assume the later developments as the norm where ecclesial structures are visible and celebrations of the sacraments are readily available. For nascent ecclesial communities this was not the case; however, the characteristics of communities in diaspora must also be acknowledged as authentic expressions of church based on the faithful coming together in communal life in some manner, sacrificing even to the point of martyrdom, and adapting the sacramental life to continue Christ's command of becoming a Eucharistic people. Thus, we must not take lightly the developing moments of nascent communities of faith or simply romanticize these instances after a period of growth. Later retrospection must acknowledge an authentic expression of church for communities based on these three characteristics.

A Korean Community of Faith Initiated by the Laity

From the very beginning, the Christian faith was spread by the preaching of the Gospel: "But how can they call on him in whom they have not believed?

5. Kelly, *Ecumenical Councils*, 12–13.
6. Martos, *Doors to the Sacred*, 219–20.

And how can they believe in him of whom they have not heard? And how can they hear without someone to preach?" (Rom 10:14, NAB). In the case of Korea, there were no missionary activities initially proclaiming the Christian message on native soil. The Catholic faith was not planted by foreigners as found elsewhere; rather, Christianity took root in Korea through the curiosity and initiative of the natives themselves, through the faith of the laity. Through their contact with Catholics and religious texts from China, the first Korean Christians embraced the faith through their own efforts.

Similar to the early small and scattered Christian communities, the nascent communities of faith on the Korean peninsula were also small, scattered, and isolated at times because of their unique beginnings. By bringing over the faith from China and evangelizing themselves, Koreans experienced a unique event within salvation history, which nonetheless resembled the early church where the communities of faith had small and scattered beginnings. Part of this dispersion was the manner in which Catholicism entered the peninsula. The other factor creating scattered communities—especially into the mountainous areas—was the persecution to come. Like the Christian martyrdom of the first few centuries, Korean faithful refused to renounce their newly embraced faith even when faced with death because of the apparent conflict of Christianity with ancestor worship.

Martyrdom

Many early Catholics in Korea resisted societal pressures to continue the rituals required by Confucianism and instead chose to either burn or bury their ancestral tablets next to the graves of their deceased family members. These acts of defiance of ancestral worship forced governmental officials to retaliate in order to safeguard their longstanding societal traditions. By withholding ceremonial rituals that included the use of wooden tablets containing the names of deceased family members and offers of food and wine to the deceased spirit, Catholics were viewed as disrespecting, and even completely abandoning, their filial duties.

Thus, the first persecutions became a campaign to preserve Confucian customs through the eradication of the newly introduced Catholic beliefs that appeared to challenge Confucian-based society. Early persecutions resulted in either apostasy or bloody martyrdom on Korean soil as the choice between one's belief in family and one's belief in God became irreconcilable in society. All told, numerous persecutions took place throughout this early period of Korean Catholicism starting from 1785 until 1866. The last was so devastating that it reduced the Korean Catholic population by half. Over eight thousand Korean Catholics, including French missioners, gave their lives for the faith.[7] This unique event of evangelization and martyrdom scattered Korean Catholics, who thus had to adapt the ways of living out a sacramental faith life.

Adaptation

Nowhere else did Christianity spread in this manner, as missioners were invited into Korea only after the neophytes understood for themselves the need for ordained clergy in the celebration of the sacraments. After a decade of living out the faith in isolation from the universal church, the faithful in Korea became aware of the constitutive relationship between the ordained clergy and sacraments. The laity continued to "celebrate" the Eucharist without a priest even after they knew that it was not permissible. For this early Christian community, living out the communal presence as Christ's body even without a priest allowed for a true appreciation of the real presence of Jesus in sacrament of the Eucharist when the clergy finally arrived. This nascent body of believers felt it necessary to live out their faith sacramentally in the best manner they knew until their connection with the wider church through the celebrations of the sacraments was fully realized.

A Korean American Immigrant Community of Faith Initiated by the Laity

The three characteristics illustrated in the developments of the nascent Christian communities in the Levant and on the Korean peninsula are also evident among Korean immigration and religious communal encounters in the United States. Traditionally, Korean immigration to the US has been categorized in three waves. Korean immigrants in the first wave (1903–1945) were laborers seeking economic refuge, picture brides seeking social refuge, and activists seeking political refuge. The second wave, known as the postwar period, lasted from 1945–1965. Korean immigrants during this time period sought relief from the ravages of the Second World War and Korean War. From 1965 to the present, the third wave has generally been categorized as the post-1965 immigration period and is the main focus here. Many Koreans during this period left for the United States out of economic concerns and this group makes up the majority of the Korean American population today. The post-1965 wave of immigration gave rise to the communities that

---

7. Choi, *Origin of Roman Catholic Church in Korea*, 275.

we often encounter in church and society. The previous waves of immigrations did not have the religious, cultural, or social consciousness to create and sustain a religious or secular identity.

A common feature between the Korean nascent faith community of the nineteenth century and the beginnings of the immigrant faith communities of Korean American Catholics is the way the faith was nurtured by the laity. In both instances, the Catholic faith traveled from one country to another and attracted many because of the communal aspect that incorporated the spiritual as well as the cultural. Just as the universal faith initially crossed over from China to Korea by way of the laity, Korean immigrants traveled with their faith to the United States as a way of preserving both their religious identity and their cultural heritage in a foreign land. The offering of faith integrated with culture also provided those away from their homeland a sense of security beyond just the spiritual. Unlike their European counterparts, Korean immigrants were not accompanied by their own clergy. Similar to the events over a century ago, the laity carried the faith across national borders and laid the foundations for ecclesial communities in the United States before the arrival of native-speaking clergy.

Even today, most Korean clergy are missioners assigned for a brief term and treat their ministries as simply an extension of the Korean Church rather than addressing Korean Americans in their immigrant context. Thus, the immigrant laity are truly the ones who bring stability and continuity in these ethnic ecclesial communities still today. Korean American Catholic communities in their initial stages were relatively small and for those not in metropolitan areas, continue to struggle in isolated faith communities. Thus, Korean American Catholics experienced what other nascent faith community did in the beginnings of the faith journey in diaspora. However, the conditions in the United States did not provide any occasions for martyrdom. Rather, the "sacrifice even unto death" emerged in a different light for this immigrant community. Instead of laying down their lives for their immediate faith, Korean immigrants laid their lives for the future generations.

Deferred Gratification

The building of an ethnic church is a priority and necessity for the initial immigrant generation. Living in a foreign land out of necessity—whether for economic opportunities for themselves or educational advancements for their offspring—means displacement without many connections to the larger society. To provide some sort of rootedness in their community,

Christian immigrants of Korean descent seek two homes, a physical home for their immediate family and a spiritual home for their ethnic community. The former is needed for daily survival while the latter is necessary for the preservation of a cultural heritage that is integrally connected with religious aspects. Both homes carve out a place for Korean Americans in the United States and afford protection and preservation of language, customs, and practices of Korea while social and economic interactions allow the traditions of the US to strengthen this unique group of believers.

In order to create both homes in society as a method of survival and sustainability, the initial immigrant group defers much of their gratification for the future, primarily for the wellbeing of their offspring. Often, the initial immigrant group finds consolation in their decision to leave Korea once their children have reached a level of educational and financial success since the rationale to immigrate focused on these two factors. In addition, these two measures of success are so ingrained in the Korean Confucian mind-set that they are often inseparable, and thus both are required for immigrants to vindicate their decision to leave Korea, to endure long hours at their own businesses, and to live isolated from the larger English-speaking society.

This willingness to sacrifice for the next generation parallels the willingness and desires of the early Christian community in the Korean Peninsula over a century ago. The first believers risked alienation from family, loss of property or resources, and even their own lives for their faith. The belief in the Christian God was not an isolated act for these early Christians. The Catholic faith was a communal event and the reception and longevity of the faith in the lay community allowed them to sacrifice in this manner for one another and for future generations of believers. The common characteristic of Catholics in nineteenth-century Korea or in the United States today is the willingness to sacrifice for the future, a future not immediate to themselves but for generations to come. This desire for the wellbeing of future generations is also intimately connected with their sense of hope, and even the decision to lay down one's life for another.

Adaptation

Just as the initial lay community took initiative and liberties in becoming a sacramental people until the arrival of foreign clergy missioners in Korea, the faith communities of the initial immigrant groups in the United States adapted to linguistic and cultural challenges until Korean vocations reached a sustainable level for greater missionary activity. Today, the majority of Korean American Catholic communities are staffed by visiting Korean clergy.

However, early waves of the Korean American Catholics did not experience this luxury as no Korean-speaking clergy journeyed with them. Thus, creativity and adaptation was necessary for the clergy-less immigrants who built the faith communities we are accustomed to today.

Some Korean American faith communities came into being as early as the 1960s; however, most faith communities came into existence during the 1970s and 1980s. Others can trace their lineage as outgrowths of these early churches. The beginnings of these faith communities were truly creative adaptations of mainstream churches. When no Korean-speaking clergy were available, the initial Korean American Catholic groups would first participate in the English Eucharistic celebration even without knowing the English language. In addition, they would also gather separately to further their prayers, catechesis, and other religious-cultural celebrations in the Korean language. Some faith communities, especially those with large populations of Korean Americans, had Korean clergy assigned to them as an extension of their home diocese. These communities had great advantages with numerous parishioners, many resources, and priestly leadership.

Other communities who were not so fortunate to have a Korean priest assigned to them invited missionary priests who previously had served in Korea. Columban, Maryknoll, and other religious missioners served in building the early faith communities in the United States upon returning from their assignments in Korea. Their linguistic abilities and cultural familiarity were truly a bridge for those living in between two worlds. Others merged both languages as they utilized the only resources at their disposal. Local diocesan clergy prayed in English while the faithful responded in Korean. These bilingual liturgies were not the preferred method of prayer but the only experience available for immigrants making their home in the United States. Today's Korean American ministries all developed out of these initial religious and cultural adaptations much like the early Christian communities on the Korean Peninsula over a century ago.

Conclusion

The three characteristics—small or scattered communities of believers, suffering, and sacrifice to the point of martyrdom, and adaptations in the sacramental life in the beginnings of faith communities—demonstrate Lonergan's movement from the objective to the subjective aspects of faith. Although all three communities described here revealed these characteristics, it is not enough for nascent communities of faith to simply "imitate" or contain within themselves these traits. The reasons for being scattered, enduring suffering, and requiring sacramental adaptation, must be carefully assessed in regards to the evaluative aspect in order to gain a proper hermeneutical perspective. Therefore, the evaluative aspect becomes a key component in realizing the authenticity of the content of faith being lived and handed on. Without the evaluative it would be too easy for us to over-glorify nascent communities of faith because of their characteristics without making any critical evaluations of whether or not the lived reality is truly reflective of the lived reality of Jesus Christ. Thus, the characteristics of the faith life in diaspora—small and scattered communities, sacrificing even unto death, and adaptation of the sacramental life—are simply not enough. Only through an honest critique, which produces an authentic perspective on living out the faith in church and society, do these characteristics found in diaspora reveal the emergence of a new creation through their subjective expression as an authentic church.

An honest critique reveals a commonality of both Koreans and Korean Americans, that is the materially oriented concerns within the lived experience of the Christian faith. Although causes for this concern can be explained through social or religious conditioning, material accumulation beyond the poverty of the past is a primary focus for both groups and is enshrined within the spiritual realm. Certain notions of material blessings as indicators of spiritual well-being can be traced to shamanic influences on Korean belief. Similarly, the European experience of the Protestant Reformation has also influenced the outlooks of both the Koreans and Korean Americans. To critique this subjective aspect of material accumulation further intensified by the immigration experience, Brad Gregory's *Unintended Reformation* sheds some valuable light on the identification of material success as an outward expression of spiritual blessings common among both Catholic and Protestant faithful in the homeland and diaspora.

A very European model of Christianity, interpreted through the US Protestant experience, became the foundation for religious expressions. Growing initially through the evangelization and rebuilding of Korean society by both Protestant and Catholic missioners in the twentieth century, the Korean faith was greatly influenced by the European model of Christianity. In addition to being influenced by the West through evangelization, Korean Americans magnified the influences of Protestant ethos by their immigration to the United States. For Korean American Catholics to recognize their place within salvation history, a critical self-examination of these influences is needed to see if the subjective aspects of their communal life are authentic expression of the objective notions of community with its hallmark of sacrifice and adaptation.

According to Gregory, the Protestant Reformation ruptured the fabric of European society, thereby creating a void in the abilities of Europeans to answer life questions centered around one's existence, meaning, and purpose. Thus, the Reformation did not just divide Catholics and Protestants, but also unintentionally led to a society searching for answers that the church could no longer provide because of the lack of authority relegated to the Catholic Church and the relativizing of scriptural interpretation among Protestants themselves. To bridge this rupture and lay to rest the restlessness caused by Life questions—the inability to answer questions revolving around one's existence—Gregory insists that material wealth became one measure or guide in living out a purpose-driven life. Thus, material measures of the spiritual life entered into the equation in understanding one's faith, whereby material accumulation became an overarching indicator of one's spiritual wholeness. Gregory thus states,

> Anxious self-scrutiny about one's status in God's eye thus generated the Reformed Protestant "innerworldly asceticism" characterized by self-conscious hard work, diligence, self-discipline, and frugality that seemed to betoken elect status in proportion as such virtues were consistently practiced. The behaviors driven by this Protestant ethic also generated wealth and profits, especially among English Puritans, which in turn contributed to a sense of God's individually tailored providential favor.[8]

It is not by coincidence or by accident that emphasis on the material is strongly demonstrated in the lives of Koreans and Korean Americans today. Material success is very much a part of Korean and Korean American measure of not only social advancement and achievement but also in terms of religious well-being. In a shamanic culture, material or worldly well-being is a result of the spiritual harmony created by the honoring of one's ancestors. In the Protestant ethos, upon which the United States was built, hard work and individual effort creates material well-being. Having inherited both these concepts of materialism, Korean and Korean Americans have heightened their accumulation of material wealth not just to ease the painful memories of an impoverished country for most of the past century, but also to signal prosperity from individual hard work and persistence, in turn, making material gain a pseudo spirituality.

The need to evaluate critically the movement of theological thought and peoples in producing an authentic and meaningful hermeneutical perspective must be taken seriously. A modern theological reflection of the Korean and Korean American faith development as well as a postmodern

---

8. Gregory, *Unintended Reformation*, 240.

critique of a subjective aspect common in both promotes an evaluative aspect in which a renewed understanding of sacrifice of immigrants and their offspring can sometimes create an authentic as well as an inauthentic reflection of the objective portrait of Christ's own sacrifice or the martyrdom of the early church. Only in this critique does a proper hermeneutical aspect arise aligning our lives as an authentic expression of church. In doing so, a new creation of faith in diaspora is said to develop due to the emergence of a personal and communal identity grounded in the present reality and truly reflecting the lived reality of Jesus Christ and the traditions handed on.

4

Harmony in Faith:
Asian and Pacific Catholics in the United States

CECILE L. MOTUS

Population growth in the United States and in the American Catholic Church over the past half-century has been heavily rooted in immigration from Mexico and all of Latin America, Asia, the Pacific Islands, Africa, and the Caribbean. This growth is especially noteworthy in the Catholic community, having resulted both in increases in the Catholic population and in changing the array of faces in the pews and in church leadership. The presence of Asian and Pacific Catholics is especially noteworthy in these respects.

My paper is based on my experiences as a pastoral worker and ethnic ministry director. I am not a theologian nor a pastoral scholar or writer. For the last thirty years, I have been privileged to have served the Roman Catholic Diocese of Honolulu, the International Catholic Migration Commission (ICMC), and the US Conference of Catholic Bishops in varying leadership positions. My jobs were rich and gratifying experiences in diocesan, national, and international level pastoral ministries, mainly with and for Asian and Pacific people.

At the outset, I wish to clarify that the racial label "Asian" is a categorization used by the US government, including the US Census Bureau, to refer to hundreds of different groups of people living on the continent of Asia. The Vatican, other countries, and international agencies and entities use the racial label in the same manner. However, Asians do not call themselves "Asian." A Chinese does not consider herself or himself "Asian" but "Chinese." The same is true of Filipinos or Vietnamese or Indians. They do not consider themselves Asian but rather Filipino or Vietnamese or Indian. In many instances, the situation is more complex because, in a country like the Philippines, there are many distinct groups of people with their own languages, cultural norms, and traditions. The diversity is both challenge and gift.

Demographic Data

For many decades, it has been difficult to obtain hard data about the number of Catholics in the United States, and even more so, the Asian and Pacific Catholic population. In 2013, the USCCB Secretariat of Cultural Diversity in the church commissioned the Center for Applied Research in the Apostolate (CARA) at Georgetown University to study the size, distribution, and location of various Catholic populations in the country. The study, "Cultural Diversity in the Catholic Church in the United States," showed very interesting results.

Chart 1: Race and Ethnicity of U.S. Adult Catholics[1]

	Aggregate Catholic Population	Percentage of Catholic Population
Non-Hispanic white	42,512,591	54%
Hispanic/Latino	29,731,302	38%
Asian, Native Hawaiian, Pacific Islander	2,905,925	4%
Non-Hispanic Black/African America	2,091,565	3%
American Indian/Alaskan Native	536,601	1%

Who are the Asian Pacific Islander Catholics? The CARA report identified seven ethnic groups.

Chart 2: Race, Ethnicity, and Birthplace Group Estimates, 2010: Asian, Native Hawaiian, Pacific Islander[2]

Ethnicity	Estimate Population in the U.S.	Catholic Population	Catholic Affiliation%

---

1. Center for Applied Research in the Apostolate, Gray, "Cultural Diversity in the Catholic Church in the United States."
2. Ibid.

Filipino	3,416,840	2,214,112	64.8%
Vietnamese	1,737,433	483,006	27.8%
Chinese	4,010,114	340,860	8.5%
Korean	1,706,822	199,698	11.7%
Native Hawaiian/Other Pacific Islander	540,013	147,424	27.3%
Indian	3,183,063	146,421	4.6%
Japanese	1,304,286	56,084	4.3%

There are other Asian and Pacific communities in addition to the seven identified above. The 2010 census counted a total 17,320,856 Asian Americans, Native Hawaiians, and other Pacific Islanders in the general population. An unpublished survey of diocesan ministry for Asian and Pacific Islander Catholics commissioned in 2011 by the USCCB Subcommittee for Asian and Pacific Islander Affairs showed that in the eighty-eight dioceses that responded to the survey, Asian and Pacific ethnic communities were present there and were being provided some form of pastoral care like Holy Mass and/or bible study or catechesis in native languages, prayer gatherings, celebration of feasts honoring the Blessed Mother and the Child Jesus among others.

Chart 3: List of Asian and Pacific Islander Communities Provided Pastoral Care Ministries in Various Dioceses in the U.S.[3]

1 Arab	11 Hmong	21 Laotian
2 Bengali	12 Indian Kananaya	22 Marshallese
3 Burmese	13 Indian Roman Catholic	23 Micronesian
4 Cambodian	14 Indian Syro-Malabar	24 Montagnard
5 Chamorro	15 Indian Syro-Malankara	25 Pakistani
6 Chinese	16 Indonesian	26 Samoan
7 Fijian	17 Japanese	27 Sri Lankan
8 Filipino	19 Korean	28 Thai
9 Guamanian	20 Kmhmu	29 Tongan
10 Hawaiian		30 Vietnamese

Asian Pacific American (APA) Catholic populations are largest along the Pacific coast of the United States including Honolulu. CARA's diocesan-level estimates of APA Catholic populations are in Chart 4.

3. US Conference of Catholic Bishops' Secretariat of Cultural Diversity in the Church, "Asian and Pacific Catholics in the USw: 2011."

Chart 4: Dioceses with High Estimate Number of APA Catholic Population, 2010[4]

Los Angeles	358,525	Sacramento	92,447
Honolulu	163,144	San Diego	87,546
San Jose	142,663	San Bernardino	67,385
Oakland	139,228	Galveston-Houston	66,471
Orange	135,148	Chicago	66,060
Brooklyn	123,517	New York	57,867
San Francisco	117,073	Arlington	53,477
Seattle	110,184	Atlanta	46,997

The new Catholic population information resulting from the CARA study in 2013 is a significant resource for pastoral planning both at the diocesan and national levels. Of course, numbers alone do not define the significance of the presence of one or several race or ethnic groups in the US Catholic Church. The APA Catholics in the pews, rectories, convents, and parochial schools in the United States bring to mind two major mutually influential elements in their practice of the Catholic faith: 1) Catholicism itself and the varying forms brought to Asia by missionaries for the last five hundred years; and 2) the dynamic process of inculturation.

Fr. Peter Phan, the foremost Vietnamese American theologian, postulates that Catholics in every Asian country practice their Catholic faith in distinct ways. This is the result of the intersection between culture and religion. On one hand, traditional culture is purified with Gospel values, and, on the other hand, faith practices are influenced by the cultural and religious traditions of a group of people. The resulting distinct and unique ways of being Catholic have flourished in the mission fields of Asia and the Pacific Islands. Catholic immigrants and refugees have been bringing these unique gifts of faith to the United States for more than a century. Their presence has had, to a certain degree, profound effects on the Catholic Church and on American society in general.

Let us briefly examine three influential elements in the faith practices of APA Catholics in diaspora here in the United States.

4. Ibid.

Asianized Forms of Christianity

The presence of APA Catholics has transferred to the United States what many Asian scholars and theologians now refer to as "Asianized forms of Christianity." APA Catholic practices, beliefs, and spirituality mirror home country Catholicism. Dr. Anselm Min, a Korean American theologian, wrote that "ecclesial life of these communities (Asian Pacific) in the United States is a reflection of the ecclesial life in the home countries, which in turn was shaped not only by their cultural characteristics but also the kind of Catholicism that was introduced to Asian countries during the last five centuries."[5] Despite the differences, however, there are common characteristics. Catholicism practiced by most APA Catholics today is

1. Asian in spirit;
2. a source of identity and a welcoming home; and
3. anchored in devout popular religiosity.

1. Asian in Spirit

Asia is the birthplace of all world religions (including Christianity). In Southeast Asia, the main religious traditions are Confucian, Taoist, Buddhist, Islam, Animist, and Christian. Fr. Peter Phan often comments that if you scratch the surface of a Southeast Asian Catholic, you will find a Confucian or a Buddhist or an Animist, or an undistinguishable mixture of several religious traditions. Asian children are raised into traditional values and norms stemming from these spiritual traditions through many cultural events and celebrations. Family rituals and customs, folk songs and sayings, proverbs and legends espouse belief in a Supreme Being, a sense of the sacred, harmony, compassion, frugality, respect of nature and its gifts, filial piety, a sense of interdependence, and many more.

To quote Fr. Peter Phan, "Instead of frenetic activism, Asians practice love of silence and contemplation; instead of unbridled consumerism, simplicity, frugal living, and detachment; instead of physical and psychological violence, harmony and nonviolence; instead of ecological destruction, closeness to nature, respect for life, and compassion for all beings; instead of racism and sexism, tolerance and peaceful coexistence; instead of anti-family ethos, filial piety towards parents, elders, and ancestors; instead of

---

5. Min, "Pastoral Challenges of Asian/Pacific American Catholic Communities."

anti-intellectual and moral pragmatism, thirst for learning and philosophical inquiry; instead of rugged individualism, a powerful sense of solidarity."[6]

In addition, Asian in spirit means faith anchored on the value of harmony—harmony with all people, with nature, and with God who is the source of all harmony. "Harmony is the state of life God intended."[7] Asians culturally integrate rather than separate. Asians prefer "both/and" ideas rather than "either/or." They seek to pull together mind, body, and spirit. For Asians, the way to holistic integration is through dialogue because there is always more to be revealed, not just to "explain," but even more fundamentally to discover, integrate, and harmonize.

One last point undergirding the description of Catholic faith practice as "Asian in spirit" is the development of new theologies by APA theologians. Jonathan Tan, in his book *Introducing Asian American Theologies*, described a new global "intercultural theology," which incorporates Asian and Asian American resources. He wrote about APA theologians discovering theology that places no culture or theological system ahead of the other. He cited an essay written by Fr. Peter Phan entitled, "The Dragon and the Eagle: Toward a Vietnamese-American Theology," which constructed a theology out of a dialogue between Vietnamese cultural and religious traditions (as symbolized by the dragon) on the one side and contemporary US Christianity and the pluralistic US society (represented by the eagle) on the other side. Several other emerging Asian American theologies were described by Tan in his book. I encourage those interested to read the book to get a fuller sense of emerging theologies born out of the immigrant experiences of Southeast APA persons in the United States today.

The Asian spirit undergirding Catholicism practiced by Asian Americans can be an enriching factor to the American Catholic Church. It presents opportunities for dialogue and further study, leading to fuller understanding and appreciation of the uniqueness and distinctive character of "Asianized forms of Catholicism."

2. A Source of Identity and a Welcoming Home

Church as a welcoming home is not a new concept nor unique to Asian American Catholics. To many immigrant groups—including the waves of Europeans who migrated to this country some four centuries ago—the Catholic parish church is not only a place of worship. It is also a place to feel secure, preserve ethnic identity, deepen Catholic faith, and serve as a

---

6. Phan, "Asian Catholics."
7. Min, "Pastoral Challenges of Asian/Pacific American Catholic Communities."

channel for integrating into a community or a harmonic whole. Today, we still see ethnic churches or national parishes created for Armenian, Italian, or Irish Catholics. These churches provided and continue to provide communal activities, which strengthen sense of community, solidarity, the Catholic identity, cultural pride, and identity.

Similar to the pastoral needs of Euro-Americans in the past for particular ethnic ministries, APAs today have been knocking on parish and diocesan doors. Vietnamese, Chinese, Indonesian, Laotian, Samoan, Tongan, Filipino, Korean, and other APA Catholics—especially newly arrived adults—are constantly searching for Catholic parishes which wholeheartedly welcome their gift of faith and stand by them as they learn to navigate life in their new parishes.

A similar sentimental longing for belonging and welcoming has been experienced by most Filipino American Catholics. They claim that they feel more at home in a church where they can pray and sing in their Tagalog language. In many instances, Filipino pastoral needs have been sidelined because of the stereotypical impression that they do not need much pastoral care because they are fluent in English and can integrate easily into parish life. Not true! The popularity and attractiveness of family evangelization movements like Couples for Christ, Singles, Kids, Handmaids, Bukas Loob Sa Diyos, El Shaddai, and other Filipino charismatic movements are symptomatic of the need to "reroot"—reestablish ethnic connections and community pride.

In this country, most APA families have maintained their Catholic faith because loving pastors and parishes have opened their hearts and their doors to them. APA Catholics have found loving homes in welcoming parishes and dioceses that have provided them a "seat at the table" through different forms of pastoral care ministries. These include: a) parish and diocesan ethnic ministries—pastoral care that reaches out to particular ethnic or cultural groups in a multicultural or shared parish/diocese; b) missions or chaplaincies; and c) the creation of personal or national parishes which cater to the needs of mainly Chinese, Korean, and Vietnamese Catholics. I am mentioning these because these ways of ministering to Catholic groups with special language and religious traditions are practiced in most of today's US dioceses and parishes in culturally diverse populations. I am neither ranking these nor recommending one or the other.

Culturally sensitive ethnic ministries, ethnic missions or chaplaincies, and personal parishes have been valuable to immigrant Catholics and have enabled them to maintain and deepen their cultural and Catholic identity. The parishes harvest abundant fruits by "presenting the doctrine of the

Church concerning God, Man, and the world, in a manner more adapted to them so that they may receive it more willingly."[8]

Anecdotal observations have shown that APAs tend to continue active practice of their Catholic faith when they belong to parishes or dioceses that

a) offer liturgies in their first language;

b) provide language study programs for American-born children;

c) celebrate special traditional religious feasts and national holidays;

d) open facilities for fellowship gatherings and special community events where members of an ethnic community share cultural food, socialize, and share stories in their first language.

Today, to meet the longing for welcoming and belonging in a parish, the USCCB has embarked on a program to teach "intercultural ministry in shared parishes." The goal is to develop dioceses and parishes that capitalize on the enriching presence of many cultures and languages and incorporate these gifts into all aspects of parish and diocesan life—worship, music, education, leadership formation, finance, and governance. Intercultural ministry in shared parishes is a response to the call of the bishops in their 2001 pastoral letter, *Asian and Pacific Presence: Harmony in Faith,* to "build Asian and Pacific ethnic identity and community, structures of inclusion and communion with others in the multicultural local churches and with local bishops."[9]

Many examples of these moments of community and harmony are now a source of pride among APA Catholics and the dioceses to which they belong. For example, in the Archdioceses of Milwaukee, Seattle, and Washington and in the dioceses of San Bernardino and Dallas, an "Asian Catholic Day" or "Asian and Pacific Teen Rally" has been offered annually, aimed to bring together APA participants (ages six to eighteen years old) to celebrate cultural diversity, offer pastoral leadership formation including intercultural communications, strengthen APA ethnic identity, open avenues for intercultural relationships with Hispanic and other Catholic cultural groups, and plan social action activities that manifest living faith.

Moreover, in the Midwest, the Archdioceses of Chicago and Milwaukee and other neighboring dioceses have held several regional gatherings that have brought together APA youth and young adults for intercultural skills training and intergenerational dialogues. These have been enriching experiences and signs of hope for APA Catholics in diaspora.

8. Pius V, *Gaudium et Spes,* no. 62.
9. US Conference of Catholic Bishops, *Asian and Pacific Presence.*

Devout Popular Religiosity

The cultivation of popular devotions and many prayer movements is a distinguishing characteristic in APA faith practice. Popular piety or religiosity is a manifestation of genuine unabashed love for Jesus, for Mary and many patron saints, and especially for martyrs of APA origins—for example, San Lorenzo Ruiz and San Pedro Calungsod (Filipino), the Holy Martyrs of Vietnam, the Chinese Martyrs, St. Andrew Kim and the Korean Martyrs, and Our Lady of Kamalen for Chamorros. APAs celebrate special days in the life of Jesus (Christ the King, Santo Niño, and Nazareno) and the Blessed Mother. The Marian Festival observed by the Vietnamese Americans in Carthage, Missouri, every year during the week of August 15 is not only an important Marian celebration; it is considered a public celebration of Vietnamese American Catholic identity and pride. More than fifty thousand Vietnamese American Catholics attend this annual feast.

One beautiful expression of devotion to Our Blessed Mother is the "Asian Pacific Catholics for Mary" Pilgrimage in Washington, DC. While I was working at the USCCB in Washington, with the full cooperation and leadership of APA Catholic groups in the Northeast we organized an annual Marian pilgrimage to the Basilica of the National Shrine of the Immaculate Conception (BSNSIC) on the second Saturday in May. Nine APA Catholic communities participated in the first one. After eleven annual celebrations, in 2013, nineteen groups proudly brought their gifts of sacred music and various forms of prayer to the Asian Pacific Catholics for Mary Pilgrimage at the Basilica. This pilgrimage has inspired other cultural communities (African Eucharistic Congress) and Catholic movements (International Day of Prayer) to share ways of prayer that reflect different cultural values and traditions.

One significant story from this Asians for Mary pilgrimage to the Basilica is the experience of a Korean community. This community has actively participated in the celebration for two years and has been renewed by the experience. In the third year, the coordinator asked me, "Can we invite non-Catholic Koreans to this pilgrimage? I think they will be inspired by it." And they did come. A few weeks later, I was told that some of those who participated have inquired about conversion. They felt the profound presence of the Holy Spirit during the pilgrimage.

I wish to close this discussion about devotional Catholicism with what I consider a lasting legacy of Filipino American Catholics to the Church in the United States. I am referring to the novena of masses called *Simbang Gabi*. It is a nine-night novena of Masses from December 15 through December 23 observed to accompany Blessed Mother Mary in preparing for the birth of our Lord Jesus Christ on Christmas Day. An informal survey of dioceses in the United States in 2010 showed that more than two thousand parishes (some without Filipino parishioners) celebrated *Simbang Gabi*. In most instances, especially on the East coast and in California, the devotion is no longer only for Filipinos, by Filipinos. Many pastors have fully embraced *Simbang Gabi* and have made it a parish celebration incorporating Euro-Americans, Latinos, African Americans, Native Americans, and other Asian and Pacific families. I most often state that in preparation for Christmas, while others are shopping, the Filipinos are praying!

There are many more opportunities and challenges presented by the presence of Asian and Pacific Catholics in the church in this country that could bear more reflection and serious scholarly research. These will have to wait for another opportunity.

Asian and Pacific American Catholics are here to stay and will continue to impact the Catholic Church in this country with their "Asianized Christianity." Their presence is both opportunity and challenge to the local church. These varied Catholic faithful have persisted in the practice of their faith, more often without the welcoming mat from pastors and local parishioners. They have given their many gifts to the local church.

Let us continue to pray and hope for a more "permanent seat" at the table for them, along with other brothers and sisters from other cultural backgrounds. Let us pray that very soon all the many faces in God's house will learn to love each other and together continually renew the Catholic Church in the United States.

5

Passing Over:
A Theological Vision of Migration[1]

DANIEL G. GROODY, CSC

Although migration has been happening since the beginning of time, its scope and scale today is unprecedented; it is arguably one of the most defining issues of our time. With 740 million internal migrants[2] and 232 million international migrants,[3] it is a global phenomenon of dramatic proportion. A significant number of these people are particularly vulnerable, and these individuals are the primary focus of this article. In 2012, approximately 45 million migrants were forcibly uprooted, including 15.4 million refugees and 29 million internally displaced persons.[4] In 2010 alone, 42 million were displaced by natural disasters.[5] Many estimate that these numbers will increase significantly in the coming years, and by most projections, these numbers will increase exponentially in the coming years.[6]

There are various push-and-pull factors that cause people to migrate. The violations of human rights, weak juridical systems, the breakdown of the rule of law, the collapse of governments, poor economic conditions, and many other factors all contribute to the reasons why people leave their countries of origin. Amidst the disorders of the world and its social discord,

---

1. Portions of this article are drawn from Groody, "Crossing the Divide," 638–67.

2. International Organization for Migration (IOM), *World Migration Report 2011*, 49.

3. UN Department of Economic and Social Affairs Population Division, *International Migration Report 2013*, 1.

4. See UN High Commissioner for Refugees (UNHCR), "UNHCR Statistical Yearbook 2012."

5. IOM, *World Migration Report 2011*, 52.

6. IOM, *World Migration Report 2010*, 8.

migration has become a sign of our times and a profound challenge to the human conscience. For these reasons and many more, it is also a complex issue that generates controversy not only in the United States but everywhere.

My focus in this essay is to explore ways in which theology can offer not just more information about migration but a new imagination as well.[7] In particular, I would like to examine how the Passover narrative can give us a way of understanding the challenges of passing over from the dehumanized dimensions of migration to those that lead to life, justice, and solidarity. In the pages that follow, I will examine four dimensions of passover in light of the migration issue: 1) passing-over from migrant to person; 2) passing-over from injustice to justice; 3) passing-over from otherness to neighborliness; and 4) passing-over from nationalism to the reign of God. This fourfold pass-over—corresponding to the theological themes of human dignity, community, solidarity, and eschatology—is significant for our discussion of migration because it opens the road that leads us to a pass-over from alienation to communion with God and others.

Passing-Over from Migrant to Person: The Bedrock of Human Dignity

In politics, humanitarian work, and the field of migration studies, labels abound. Vigilante groups, enforcement officials, political leaders, corporations, and others often categorize people on the move as economic migrants, forced migrants, refugees, asylum seekers, internally displaced persons, victims of human trafficking, stateless people, and many other labels. Such categorizations have some proximate and utilitarian value, but they also have limits. Vigilante groups, enforcement officials, and others add to these tags dehumanizing social monikers like alien, intruder, or criminal, typecasting migrants as threats to be avoided, excluded, or deported. But those on the move, deep down, want to move beyond such labels to a space in which they can be seen first and foremost as human beings. In other words, they want to pass-over from being labeled first as migrants to being seen first as human beings.

In my own research among migrants and refugees at various borders, I often ask them to name the most difficult part of their journey. Their outer journey alone is daunting enough as they swim across canals and cross oceans, hide away in cargo ships and train cars, and endure extreme

---

7. The terms "migrant," "immigrant," "refugee," and "internally displaced person" are often used interchangeably, as I do here, although there are slight nuances in meaning. For more on the distinctions, see IOM, *Glossary on Migration*.

temperatures crossing deserts and mountains on foot. Yet beyond the physical challenges, they frequently point to the demeaning treatment and degrading stereotypes that cut to the core of their personhood. In the words of one migrant from Mexico:

> I have stowed away in baggage compartments of buses and almost suffocated in a boxcar. I almost froze to death in the mountains and baked to death in the deserts. I have gone without food and water for days, and nearly died on various occasions. As difficult as these are, these are not the hardest parts of being a migrant. The worst is when people treat you like you are a dog, like you are the lowest form of life on earth.[8]

Such stories reveal that no wound cuts more deeply than the feeling that you are not even a human being, that you are disposable, and that your life has little value, as if you are no one to anyone. Migrants struggle simply to reclaim their status as human beings, especially in the context of a society that demeans and dehumanizes them.

In the book of Genesis, we read that human beings are created in the image and likeness of God, which grounds their existence on the bedrock of dignity. Defining all people first in terms of their likeness to God grounds migration discourse in a different way than the surface labeling of the sociopolitical sphere, or worse, the degrading stereotypes used by nativist organizations, vigilante groups, and enforcement agencies. This dignity cannot be undermined or deconstructed (Gen 1:26–27; 5:1–3; 9:6; 1 Cor 11:7; Jas 3:9). It is not just another label but a way of speaking profoundly about the nature of who we are before God.

Catholic social teaching builds on this dignity by arguing that the moral health of an economy is measured not in terms of financial capital but first in terms of relational, ethical, and spiritual capital.[9] Diverging significantly from other groups mentioned above, the church in particular even reframes the whole foundation of the economic system. It sees the economy not simply in terms of the quantity of financial transactions but in terms of the quality of relational "transactions." The word "economy," (in Greek, *oikonomia*) originally meant the arrangement of a household, and the early church understood it in terms of how the world (God's household) is collectively ordered, administered, or economized.[10] In contrast to the current global economy, God's economy is based on gratuity, justice, mercy,

---

8. Quotation from personal interviews conducted by author. Notes on file in author's personal research collection.

9. US Conference of Catholic Bishops, *Economic Justice for All*, 14.

10. Mahony, "Challenge of 'We the People.'"

and sharing—not on merit, law, competition, and unbridled consumerism. Under this light, the church stresses that the economy is made for human beings, not human beings for the economy.

Catholic social teaching insists that the first concern in the immigration debate has to do with human and relational costs, not simply economic and political costs. Moving beyond the arguments of corporations, it asks how the financial system of a country enhances the dignity of every human being, especially those whose very dignity is threatened because of their vulnerable and socially insignificant status. Moving beyond the arguments of political leaders, it affirms that God—and not the state—grants rights to people. It asserts that the state's responsibility is to protect and defend those rights when they are threatened or diminished, but it does not see the state as the fundamental source or grantor of these rights. Our current legal and political system, however, continues to wrangle over the state's responsibility toward those people who cross its borders without official documentation. While vigilante, enforcement, and many political actors in this drama will continue to dispense themselves of any responsibly toward migrants, church leaders and human rights advocates will continue to insist that the God-given and essential dignity of migrants must be protected and respected, regardless of their political status.

Catholic social teaching stands in agreement with political leaders and enforcement officials by recognizing the right—and even the duty—of a state to control its borders.[11] But, going beyond that position, it also argues that when a state cannot provide the conditions necessary for human dignity, people have a right to migrate to foreign lands, even without proper legal documentation.[12] The church recognizes that unless we deal with the conditions that cause human insecurity—such as poverty, underdevelopment, human rights violations, the collapse of governments, and many others—we will never have any lasting national security, no matter how many enforcement agents we send to the border or how tall a wall we build. To argue for sovereign rights without addressing more fundamental human rights and needs outside of one's border only creates more disorder, which is our current predicament.

Moreover, while Catholic social teaching agrees with vigilante groups on the right to private property, it does not see this as an unconditional right. It acknowledges that private property can be an incentive to productivity and efficient administration, but it does not consider it an unrestricted

---

11. US Conference of Catholic Bishops, *Strangers No Longer*, 30, 36, 39, 78.
12. Sacred Congregation for Bishops, *Instruction on the Pastoral Care of People Who Migrate*, 7.

right, since the goods of the earth are meant for the benefit and development of all—not simply a privileged elite. John Paul II puts it in this way: "Private property, in fact, is under a 'social mortgage,' which means that it has an intrinsically social function, based upon and justified precisely by the principle of the universal destination of goods."[13] In other words, sovereign rights and private property rights have a place in Catholic social teaching, but these are not considered absolute rights nor even primary rights. At best, we are provisional owners (since we give up everything when we die), and therefore, we are never the final owners of any property. In this sense, only God is the final owner, which means there is a communal dimension even to all that we consider private.

As these rights claims come into conflict with each other, it is a difficult challenge to sort out the values and issues that are underneath them, and there are many different arguments about how these elements should be prioritized. If passing-over from migrant to person involves the restructuring and reordering of society according to the God of life, the dignity of the human person, and the common good, then, in David Hollenbach's words, "[th]e needs of the poor take priority over the wants of the rich. The freedom of the dominated takes priority over the liberty of the powerful. The participation of marginalized groups takes priority over the preservation of an order which excludes them."[14] While, as Benedict XVI says, the role of the church is not to replace the state, "at the same time she cannot and must not remain on the sidelines in the fight for justice."[15] No matter how we articulate our positions about migration, the arguments themselves point toward the fragmented state of our relationships—and our struggle to get them right again.

Passing-Over from Injustice to Justice: The Call to Right Relationships

From the perspective of Christian faith, every position at the border must be analyzed not simply by the standards of economic efficiency, political pragmatism, utilitarian self-interest, or national narcissism, but by the vision of the gospel, especially as it is measured by the quality of our relationships. The debate over rights inevitably leads to concerns about justice. But because so much discourse about justice in the migration debate is reduced to arguments about civil law, there is a need for critical reflection

13. John Paul II, *Sollicitudo Rei Socialis*, 42.
14. Hollenbach, *Claims in Conflict*, 204.
15. Benedict XVI, *Deus Caritas Est*, 28.

about justice that goes beyond conventional legal reasoning and toward a broader understanding. Justice, as we will consider it here, involves more than adjudicating legal infractions, bringing people to court, or appealing to a blindfolded woman with scales in one hand and a sword of retribution in the other. Space does not permit an extensive elaboration on this topic from a theological perspective, but here we will examine its connection to migration and the challenges of reconciliation. Justice, at its heart, is about creating right relationships.

In Christian theology, there are two principal notions of justice: internal justice and external justice.[16] Internal justice, which begins with God's movement toward us, deals with one's experience of justification or being put in right relationship with God through the saving work of Jesus Christ. External justice, which begins with our movement toward others, deals with the promotion of good works. Internal justice refers to God's activity within a person; external justice refers to one's response to God's grace. Internal justice relates to the first and the greatest command: to love the Lord God with all one's heart, soul, and mind (Matt 22:37–38). External justice relates to the second command, which is like the first: to love one's neighbor as oneself (Matt 22:39). It seeks humanizing activity leading to right relationships with one's self, the community, its social structures, and even to the environment.[17] God's justice, in other words, is not principally about vengeance or retribution but about restoring people to right relationships on every level of their existence and helping them become all they were intended to be as human beings created in God's image and likeness.

When it comes to immigration, people often equate the issue of justice, however, with adherence to existing law and public policy.[18] Many say that they have no problem with immigration but with immigrants breaking the law. The problem with this perspective is that it makes no distinction between various kinds of law and assumes an equal binding force for all law.

In light of the four-fold Thomistic distinction on law noted above, most migrants who cross borders without proper documentation are not simply breaking civil laws but are obeying the laws of human nature, such as the need for work, food, and dignified lives. Moreover, crossing international borders without papers in most countries is an administrative infraction, not a felony; it is not a violation of divine law or natural law, and in such cases, undocumented immigration should in no way be confused

---

16. For more on this topic, see Groody, *Globalization*, 26–27.

17. This definition is drawn in part from the excellent article by Crosby, "Justice," 579.

18. See Wilbanks, *Re-Creating America*.

with serious criminal activity or threats to national security.[19] Much misunderstanding and injustice occurs when immigrants and immigration are perceived primarily as problems in themselves rather than as symptoms of more systemic social ills and inequities.

Jesus's own ministry of reconciliation deals largely with overcoming human constructions that divide the insider from the outsider, particularly those generated by law in its various forms. He challenged the tendency in human beings to idolize the state, religion, or a particular ideology and use it as a force that excludes and alienates, even when it does so under the rationale of obedience to a greater cause. Jesus's openness to Gentiles, his approach to the Syrophoenician or Canaanite woman (Matt 15:21–28; Mark 7:24–30), his response to the Roman centurion (Matt 8:5–13; Luke 7:1–10), and many other encounters illustrate his willingness to go beyond borders and narrow interpretations of the Law in obedience to a greater law of love (Mark 12:28–34). Jesus recognized the value of the Law (Matt 5:17–18), but he also challenged people to see the larger picture of the Law and to understand its deeper meaning (Luke 13:10–17). By his words and actions, Jesus demonstrates that compassion requires a reading of the Law that gives primary consideration to meeting human needs.

Jesus's practice of table fellowship gives us a very important window into his understanding of the law in light of the kingdom of God. Through table fellowship with sinners, Jesus fulfills the message of the prophets, invites all people to salvation, and promises his disciples a place "at table" in God's kingdom (Luke 22:30). In sharing a meal with those on the fringes of society in order to create new communities, Jesus frequently crossed borders created by narrow interpretations of the Law. He reached out in particular to those who were marginalized racially (Luke 7:1–10), economically (Luke 7:11–17), religiously (Luke 7:24–35), and morally (Luke 7:36–50). His invitation to the table was good news for the poor and those deemed insignificant or rejected by society; for others, it was scandal.

In bringing scribe, tax collector, fisherman, and zealot into one community, Jesus challenged his followers to a new kind of relationship beyond humanly constructed borders, one based not on social status, the rules of a nation, or religious self-righteousness, but on a common hope for the coming of God's reign (Matt 8:11; 11:16–19). For Jesus, God's mercy could not

---

19. While "entry without inspection" has long been a criminal offense, it has traditionally been treated as an administrative violation, leading to civil deportation proceedings. In recent years, however, the Department of Homeland Security has referred for criminal prosecution increasing numbers of immigrants who have entered the country illegally and committed other immigration violations. For more on this topic, see Kerwin and Meissner, *DHS and Immigration*, 40–41.

be contained within the walls of limited mind-sets (Matt 7:1–5; 13:10–17), and he challenged people to pass-over into a higher notion of law based on God's uncalculating mercy rather than on their restricted views of worthiness and unworthiness (Luke 6:27–38).

In his ministry of table fellowship, Jesus's main focus was to help people pass-over from the slavery of narcissism, nationalism, and nihilism, and bring them (us) back again to a place of generativity, inclusivity, and right relationship with God, each other, themselves (ourselves), all of creation. This vision of justice emerges from the conviction that we are created by love, for love, and to love. Beneath the chatter and dissonance, the human heart is at work, seeking and struggling to move toward union with God and toward solidarity with each other.

Passing Over from Otherness to Neighborliness: The Challenge of Human Solidarity

Before such communion can happen, however, there has to be a fundamental shift in the way we see people who migrate. A theological perspective on migration involves more than a reflection about people moving across geographical borders: it also involves moving toward a different way of thinking and relating to all we consider as "other." As long as we see migrants as entirely different from ourselves, people with whom we have no intrinsic connection, we are diminished as human beings because we fail to see our communion with a larger body beyond ourselves. This is why the third pass-over needed in the immigration debate is the movement from seeing the migrants as "other" to seeing them as "neighbor."

We cannot move very far toward such communion and solidarity unless we are willing to try new routes of knowledge and risk new ways of relating to each other. If justice is about getting our relationships right, conversion is about removing the obstacles on the road that keep us from this interconnection. Conversion here is not about changing from one religion to another but about changing our attitudes, mind-sets, and dispositions.

In the book of Exodus we read, "I, the LORD, am your God, who brought you out of the land of Egypt, that place of slavery" (Exod 20:2). The word "Egypt" (*mitsrayim*) literally means "double straits" (a reference to upper and lower straits that form the territory of Egypt through which the Nile flows), "narrow places," or "narrow confinement."[20] Beyond the literal reading of the word *mitsrayim*, the subsequent figurative interpretations are striking.

20. See Dykstra, *Set Them Free*, 58.

In its own story of migration, Israel was delivered not only from a specific national territory but also from a narrow way of thinking. Liberation at Sinai means more than simply taking off the shackles. It involves a cognitive migration, taking on a new mind-set, adopting a new way of looking at the world, living out a different vision, and ultimately learning to love as God loves. The migration of Israel after the Exodus was meant to help Israel re-envision how to live in the world, a task that proved more challenging than the geographical migration from Egypt itself. In other words, it was easier to take Israel out of *mitsrayim* than to take *mitsrayim* out of Israel. After coming to power and becoming more prosperous, Israel frequently forgot its own migration history, forgot its heart for God in its preoccupation with empire, and consequently forgot those who came to it as strangers and immigrants.

The New Testament narrates the migration of God into the world in Jesus. The Incarnation can be seen as God's "great migration" into the broken and sinful territory of human beings, which creates legal, political, and religious controversy. In Luke's Gospel, Jesus enters the world amidst a drama involving documentation (a census of the entire Roman world, Luke 2:1–5). In Matthew's account, Jesus and his family must flee a threat that endangers their lives, making them political refugees (Herod's plot, Matt 2:13–17; a parallel to a foundational migration in biblical history, Exod 1–14). And in John's Gospel, many have trouble believing in Jesus precisely because of the place from which he emigrates (John 7:41–43, 52). In a fallen world, human beings find many compelling political, legal, social, and religious reasons to exclude—and "otherize"—the migrant Son of God.[21] The gratuity of God revealed in the Incarnation manifests that even as human beings erect barriers of every sort, God walls off no one from divine fellowship. On the journey into otherness and vulnerability, Jesus enters into total identification with those who are abandoned and alienated.

When God became a human being, it was a migration—totally—into the otherness of our human condition. In Jesus, God refuses to "otherize"

---

21. Jesus was rejected by many in his day including Herod, who feared losing his power (Matt 2:1–13); Jesus's family, who thought he was out of his mind (Mark 3:20–21); his neighbors, who failed to understand his origins (Matt 13:54–57; Mark 6:1–4; Luke 4:13–30); the rich young man, who had great wealth did not want to share it (Matt 19:16–22; Mark 10:17–22; Luke 18:18–23); the religious leaders, who envied Jesus's popularity with the people (Matt 26:3–4; John 11:47–53); Judas, who exploited Jesus for money and favor with those in power (Matt 26:14–16, 47–50; Luke 22:4–6; John 18:2–5); Peter, who feared the ramifications of association with him (Matt 26:69–75; Mark 14:66–72; Luke 22:54–62; John 18:15–18, 25–27); and the crowds, who shouted "crucify him" and did nothing to redress injustice (Matt 27:15–18, 20–23; Mark 15:6–14; Luke 23:13–23; John 19:5–7, 14–15).

anyone by integrating the human into his divine self. We can also look at the "great migration" of God in the Incarnation as one great illegal border crossing. Scripture tells us that shortly after Jesus's birth, Mary, Joseph, and Jesus fled into Egypt because of the policies of a crazed king (Matt 2:13–14). But we have no idea whether they had official permission to cross this border. Some, insisting on the holy family's licit border crossing, maintain that their migration was entirely legal. We do not know for sure. But what we do know is that when God became human in the incarnation, illegal activity was involved.

In the Annunciation, God entered Mary's womb while she was betrothed to Joseph. To be found pregnant by someone other than one's future spouse, at the very least, would put Mary outside the Jewish law. According to this law, Mary would have merited punishment by stoning. When Mary went in haste to visit her cousin Elizabeth (Luke 1:39), it was not simply because she had not seen her cousin in a long time and wanted to get reacquainted. Rather, it was because she knew if she stayed around Nazareth, she might be stoned to death!

In other words, according to our limited perceptions, the Incarnation put Mary outside the law and made Jesus not only an illegitimate child but also an illegal alien. She was illegal because she was pregnant by someone other than Joseph (namely God). Jesus was illegal in view of his law-breaking conception and alien because he really did come from another world. So then we must ask, why would God choose this time and this way to become human? God could have chosen a less scandalous and problematic time to become human, or at least, from a legal perspective, a less complicated "migration," one that many of the law-abiding religious people of his day probably would have found much more acceptable. Could this way of entering our world, however, have been the beginning of the good news, as God became illegal for all the unrighteous who are alienated from God because we have broken the law (Rom 1:18–20; 3:21–24; 13:9–10)? While this reading does not disregard the need for the law, it does point out our tendency to absolutize it. It also necessitates a more thorough contemplation of the law that goes deeper than our rational and reductive misappropriations of it.

Such a perspective also challenges those who exclude others not only on the basis of legal status but also on the basis of private rights or even national rights. It points to the need for a social, moral, and divine starting point, and it highlights the exigencies of distributive, contributive, and restorative justice that flow as a natural consequence from divine gratuity. The Incarnation should disturb us enough to move us beyond a narrow, self-serving identity into an awareness of how God reaches out to us in our sinful "otherness" and calls us to a greater identification with those considered "other" in society. The Incarnation redefines otherness by seeing strangers in terms of neighborliness. In becoming neighbor to all in the Incarnation—that is, all who live in the sinful territory of a fallen humanity—God redefines the borders between neighbors and opens up the possibility for new relationships.

The Native American Dakota wisdom tradition, in a similar vein, maintains that the longest migration of human life is from the head to the heart and back to the head again.[22] Given the acrimony of the immigration debate, it would seem that only a few accept the risks and sacrifices needed to undertake this movement toward such interconnectedness; much emotional and mental baggage often gets in the way, keeping us from moving very far into this territory. We erect walls of every sort not only at our national borders but even in our personal spaces, preferring the security of the "gated community" of our own hearts and personal opinions over the open spaces and expansive terrain that lead to the connectedness for which human beings were created. But the more we excessively protect and isolate ourselves, the more we wall others out and become aliens even to ourselves.

Passing-Over from Nationalism to the Reign of God: The Hunger for Communion

The way we perceive the other not only says something about how we see those who are different from us but also how we see our relationship to our countries of origin. It says something about our larger worldview and vision of life. The fourth pass-over on the road that leads to communion is moving from a narrow identity based exclusively on one's country of origin to a larger inclusive self-understanding in light of the reign of God and its eschatological manifestations. From a theological perspective, our national identities have some basic definitional value, but the larger question is how such an identity interfaces with our identity before God and our movement toward a more fundamental citizenship in the world to come.

This reign or kingdom of God is not a physical space, but as the Second Vatican Council describes, is a kingdom of truth and life; holiness and grace; justice, love, and peace.[23] It brings people into a different kind of social and ethical territory, because it is based not on geography or politics

---

22. "The elders say, 'The longest road you're going to have to walk is from here to here. From your head to your heart.' But they also say you can't speak to the people as a leader unless you've made the return journey. From the heart back to the head." See Walnut Ridge Consulting, "American Indian Proverbs."

23. Paul VI, *Dogmatic Constitution*, chapter 4, no. 36.

but on divine initiative and openness of heart. It leads to a different vision of the current world order, where many of the first become last and the last become first (Matt 19:30; 20:16; Mark 10:31; Luke 13:29–30). Jesus clearly taught that many of the values and metrics people employ to measure others in this world will be inverted in the next and that those excluded today will be given priority in the kingdom tomorrow. This kingdom inevitably calls people into movement, making them exiles on earth, strangers in this world, and sojourners en route to another place.[24] Because it sees in the migrant a reflection and a revelation of who it is in the world, the church seeks not only to go beyond political borders but to unite itself with those on the other side of them. As it gives expression to its interconnectedness as the body of Christ, it serves all people regardless of their religious beliefs, their political status, or their national origins.

In Phil 3:20, Paul describes Christians as living in this world but carrying the passport of another world: "But our citizenship is in heaven, and from it we also await a Savior, the Lord Jesus Christ." The author of Hebrews also speaks of the journey in hope toward a different place: "Here we have no lasting city, but we seek the one that is to come" (13:14). And in the midst of recounting the stories of the major figures of biblical history, the author writes of their faith and hope,

> All these people were still living by faith when they died. They did not receive the things promised; they only saw them and welcomed them from a distance. And they admitted that they were aliens and strangers on earth. People who say such things show that they are looking for a country of their own. If they had been thinking of the country they had left, they would have had opportunity to return. Instead, they were longing for a better country—a heavenly one. Therefore God is not ashamed to be called their God, for he has prepared a city for them. (Heb 11:13–16 NIV)

Matthew 25:31–46 speaks not only of the final judgment of individuals but of nations.[25] Scholars continue to debate who are the "least" (*elachistōn*) in this passage, but what is significant here is how they mirror the social location of so many migrants and refugees who are hungry in their homelands, thirsty in deserts they attempt to cross, naked after being robbed of their possessions, imprisoned in detention centers, sick in hospitals, and, if they make it to their destinations, often estranged and marginalized. This text implies that crossing borders makes possible new relationships, and

---

24. Pohl, "Biblical Issues," 3–15.
25. Brown, *Unexpected News*, 127–41.

it puts the verdict of judgment, in many ways, in people's own hands: the extent to which people cross borders in this life determines to what extent they will cross them in the next (Luke 16:19–31).

Conclusion:
Passing over from Death to Life

In the end, these pass-overs from migrant to person, injustice to justice, otherness to neighborliness, and nationalism to the reign of God are another way of speaking about the process of conversion and finding the road that leads to life, wholeness, peace, integration, connectedness, love, and salvation. At its core, it is also a challenge to reimagine the world in a different way and to live out of a different narrative. Because all people, whether conscious of it or not, are living out of a personal and communal narrative. These scriptural narratives help us reevaluate the prepackaged values fed to us by society and popular media, including dehumanizing narratives about migration.

What is most needed in the immigration debate is not simply more information but a new imagination, a new way of scripting how we see this issue and how we see our relationship to it. Such a process entails choosing to live out a different story and live out a different value system from that of contemporary society, one that passes-over into a gospel-based vision of one's life. Such an exchange is not just a process of substituting one narrative for another but a transformation process whereby we exchange an enslaving narrative that disconnects and isolates us for a liberating one that connects and unites us. The road to life entails discerning which of these narratives enslave us and which help us become truly free, all the while knowing that final liberation will come only at our own resurrection.

Reading the current reality of migration in light of the Passover narrative reminds us that we are, in fact, built for communion; it is our fundamental task in life. Borders have some value in protecting the well-being of a people, forming a cultural identity, and managing the resources of a country. But when they become barriers that keep us from realizing our fundamental interconnectedness and interdependence, our broader responsibility to our brothers and sisters in need, and a larger call to hospitality to those who suffer, then we lose not only a sense of ourselves, but also our basic calling in this life. When we come closer to this goal, we come closer to the communion we are called to share. But when we move from this vision and build walls which alienate and exclude, then we not only deprive those in need, but we lose touch with our deepest selves and have deported something of our very own souls.[26]

---

26. Hing, *Deporting Our Souls*.

6

"One Does Not Live By Bread Alone..." (Matt 4:4): The Relational Turn of Theologies of Migration in the Twenty-First Century

GIOACCHINO CAMPESE, CS

The "irruption of the migrants"[1] in the Christian theological scene is a fact that is confirmed by the abundance of articles and books that have been published on this issue since the beginning of the twenty-first century especially from biblical, ethical, pastoral, systematic, and missiological perspectives.[2] We have argued elsewhere that while theological reflection has made great progress in this field (because in many contexts the phenomenon of human mobility is impacting the Christian churches), much is still to be done, especially in terms of integrating this theme into mainstream theology, which is often too busy with abstract topics or simply does not consider migration as an important or relevant issue.[3] Here, rather than offering a review of the numerous themes that have been touched on by theologians who have written on the theme of migration in the last decade, we would

---

1. I use "migrants" as a general term to refer to the more vulnerable categories of people on the move, such as economic migrants, refugees, asylum-seekers, and displaced people. I use the expression "irruption," comparing it to the "irruption of the poor," which has been made popular by Latin American liberation theology in Campese, "Irruption of Migrants," 3–32. In this chapter, the terms "migration" and "human mobility" are used as synonyms.

2. The most complete bibliography in this field is the one offered by the Center for Migration Research (CSERPE) run by the Scalabrinian missionaries in Basel, Switzerland. It is available online at http://www.cserpe.org/theology.htm. The Scalabrini International Migration Institute (SIMI) based in Rome is working on updating this bibliography and creating a digital library on the theology of migration.

3. See Campese, "'But I See that Somebody is Missing,'" 71–91.

like to focus especially on an aspect of this reflection that is fundamental, not so much for the future of this discipline, but most importantly for the future of societies and churches that are facing the issue of human mobility: the centrality of human relationships.

This gives us the opportunity to explain the title of this essay, which has been taken from Matt 4:1–11, the famous passage about the temptations of Jesus in the wilderness at the very beginning of his public ministry. The quote from Matt 4:4 has been chosen to underscore one of the main temptations that our societies and churches are facing in terms of the way they deal with migrants and refugees: it is the temptation of considering migrants simply as bodies that need our assistance or, to use a religious term, our "charity," as bodies to be fed and clothed; it is the temptation of paternalism and an attitude of superiority; it is also the temptation of short-term commitment. Bread alone is not enough, says Jesus, and his response to this temptation shows the way toward the integration and full recognition of the humanity and agency of the migrants, who are crucial to the future of society and church. What is most important is that this track, the one that highlights human relationships as a key theme in the theology of migration, has been taken by scholars who work in this field since the beginning of the twenty-first century and as time goes it is receiving even more consideration.[4] In our view, this shows that theologians who are reflecting on migration are not only becoming more aware of the primary relevance of this theme, but that they are also listening more attentively and intently to the voices of migrants and refugees.

This chapter is divided in three main parts. In the first, we will sketch some of the elements of the contexts of migration, which have led us to the decision to focus our attention on the issue of human relationships as a fundamental aspect of the complex reality of migration. The contexts to which we will refer are mainly the United States and Italy, chosen because of our direct experience and knowledge. The second part will take a critical look at some of the pastoral and theological responses to the phenomenon of migration, particularly within the Roman Catholic Church. In the third and final part we will see how some theologians who are studying human mobility are taking what we call "a relational turn" and how Pope Francis is contributing to this discourse, one that is fundamental to developing a constructive and healthy Christian practice and thought on migration.

---

4. One of the first works to deal with these issues has been Groody, *Border of Death, Valley of Life*.

The Contexts

In inviting US bishops and cardinals to a mass to be celebrated on April 1, 2014, in the border town of Nogales, Arizona, auxiliary Bishop of Seattle and Chairman of the US Bishops' Committee on Migration Eusebio Elizondo said, "The US–Mexico border is our Lampedusa. Migrants in this hemisphere try to reach it, but often die in the attempt."[5] Pope Francis's momentous trip to the tiny Italian island in the middle of the Mediterranean Sea, at the very border between Africa and Europe, has achieved at least two things: it has called people and churches' attention around the world to the reality of the borderlands where the tragic human side of migration can be experienced, and it has contributed decisively to make the connection between the US–Mexico border and the Mediterranean border explicit. Unfortunately, the most striking trait that these two borders have in common is death. Thousands of migrants have died at the US–Mexico border since 1994 when successive US governments have decided and maintained that the better strategy to control migration, or to better show that migration is under control, is to militarize and "securitize" their southern border.[6] Almost contemporaneously the same strategy was prevailing in the Old Continent where the European Union began promoting the cooperation of its member states in terms of migration, asylum, and border security. Frontex, the European agency for the management of its external borders founded in 2004, is one of the major outcomes of this cooperation that is ensuring the process of militarization and "securitization" of what is now called "Fortress Europe."[7] Italian journalist and blogger Gabriele del Grande reports that since 1988, and despite the recent rescue operations run by Frontex, more than 21,000 people have died at the European borders.[8]

Lampedusa has become, especially thanks to Francis' visit and powerful homily,[9] the symbol par excellence of the mortal risks the migrants have to go through in order to reach what they consider their "promised land." In this sense, the US–Mexico border and the Mediterranean Sea come together to tell the stories of the numerous and overwhelming difficulties migrants find in their journey. At the same time, these borders become a powerful hermeneutical lens that allows a view of the phenomenon of migration from

---

5. Coday, "US Bishops to Celebrate Mass."

6. For a theological reflection on the US–Mexico border, see Campese, "¿Cuantos más?," 271–98; Ahn, Chiu, and O'Neill, "And You Welcomed Me?,'" 303–22.

7. See its official website at http://frontex.europa.eu/.

8. See the blog by Gabriele del Grande entitled precisely "Fortress Europe," at http://fortresseurope.blogspot.it/.

9. Francis, "Homily in Lampedusa."

the margins, that is, from where migrants and refugees usually live and are made to live by the people and the government agencies that have the responsibility of the political and social management of this issue. In fact, the migrants, after having overcome the obstacles of the geographical borders, have to overcome the obstacles that society, politics, and mass media put in their way and that very often force them to live a life at the margins. Also in this case we must acknowledge that Pope Francis's insistence on the presence of the church at the geographical and existential peripheries of our world is right to the point.[10]

We know that the majority of migrants do not cross the Sonoran Desert on foot or the Mediterranean Sea on rundown boats, but in most of the cases arrive by land or air in the United States or Europe with valid documents, and many of them become undocumented when their visas expire. The fact that migrants have not crossed a sea or a desert does not mean that their lives are any easier. Discrimination, exploitation, marginalization, insecurity, fear, scapegoating, and violence are not just abstract concepts, but words that describe the existence of many migrants in the United States, Europe, and elsewhere. Take the case of countless women who work as domestic care workers working with children and elderly people often in thankless and abusive environments while sending money to and worrying about their own children and families in their countries of origin. There have been many cases of these care workers' being tortured and physically and sexually abused by their employers, especially in the Middle East where often the laws allow them to treat these women as slaves. Farmworkers exploited by their employers experience a similar plight, often living in unhealthy and inhuman conditions in dilapidated and makeshift settlements at the very margins of our societies. Recently, journalistic investigations both in the United States and in Italy have uncovered the issue of sexual exploitation among women immigrant farmworkers in these two countries.[11] One should also remember the situation of asylum-seekers—children, women, and men who, while waiting for the response to their request for political asylum, are often "parked" in overcrowded reception camps where they live in unhygienic conditions and are treated as numbers and not as human beings. While here we are referring specifically to what is happening in the Italian context, we realize that similar situations can be found around the world. This is why we found very relevant the observations of Mary Jo

---

10. See especially Francis, "Address to the Ecclesial Convention."

11. On this issue, see the June 25, 2013 PBS documentary "Rape in the Fields" and its updates online at http://www.pbs.org/wgbh/pages/frontline/rape-in-the-fields. On the Italian situation, see the investigation conducted by journalist Antonello Mangano online at http://www.terrelibere.org/.

Leddy who, starting from her direct and vast experience with asylum seekers and refugees in Canada, affirms that this geographical and social separation is compounded by the separation promoted by bureaucracy, which she describes in this way: "We realized that, in spite of the best intentions, many social policies keep the newcomers from meeting ordinary citizens. Taxpayers pay money to the government that in turn pays social workers to help them. In the process the taxpayers and the clients never meet each other, never see each other face to face."[12] Particularly tough are the circumstances of young immigrants living and studying in countries which do not recognize them as legal residents or as citizens, even if they were born there, and therefore are legally robbed of the opportunities that all young people must have to build the present and the future of any society.

Recently, a brilliant and very emotional documentary entitled *Abrazos* has laid open another dimension of the plight of the migrants, a dimension that is so obvious and at the same time is mostly overlooked. In *Abrazos*, Guatemalan-American filmmaker Luis Argueta tells the stories of different Guatemalan families in Worthington, Minnesota, who because of lack of documentation are not able to visit their families back in Guatemala. This means that parents have not seen their sons and daughters who have migrated to the United States for over twenty years; that grandparents have never met their grandchildren; and kids have never met their siblings and other members of their extended families. Thanks to the heart of a group of people coordinated by Lisa Kremer and organized under the nonprofit organization Familias Juntas, born in the context of a Roman Catholic parish community, a group of US-born kids of Guatemalan immigrant parents are given the opportunity to visit their siblings, grandparents, and extended families in Guatemala. *Abrazos* follows the journey of these people emphasizing the primary importance of human and family relationships, of being able to have and "embrace" your family, and underlining the injustice caused to people involved in migration processes that do not allow them to have a normal family life.[13]

The obstacles and injustices that migrants and refugees have to face are mostly due to the fact that for different reasons they are not considered as normal human beings. Their situation as strangers in an environment that is not originally their own puts them is a situation of social, legal, political, cultural, and even religious vulnerability. Prejudice and hostility toward them are a sad reality within our societies, and it seems that the recent economic crisis arouses further negative attitudes because when local

---

12. Leddy, *Other Face of God*, 82.
13. See the documentary's official website: http://abrazosthefilm.com/.

people lose their jobs they sometimes tend to blame immigrants who they see as their competitors in the best case and as those who steal their jobs at worst. The outright racist and violent anti-immigrant language that has been used in our societies by some politicians and pundits—who have built their careers by constantly demeaning the migrants—often fuel the negativity toward migrants. This poison injected in our societies has somehow made public opinion tolerant or indifferent toward hateful and malevolent expressions and behaviors against migrants.[14] It is alarming to see how often people do not react against or even justify xenophobic and racist expressions and conduct. This gloomy environment that more often than not surrounds migrants and hinders human contacts with the local communities has been defined by Susanna Snyder as the "ecology of fear."[15] And when fear prevails over more constructive ways to deal with people, the first victims are the migrants who begin to be referred to and treated not as human beings, but as "aliens," some kind of not completely human creatures that threaten the normal processes of daily social life.

Two final observations are in order regarding the analysis of the reality of migration that we have been providing here. The first bears on the need of a "farsighted" approach to migration, an approach that looks realistically at its complexity and its consequences in the present and the future. For years now governments and politicians have been debating about how to manage irregular migration or to change the laws regarding citizenship especially for immigrant children and children of immigrants, but nothing has been done while, in the meantime, they and the mass media keep focusing on the latest immigration emergency. The provocative but "farsighted" remarks by Swedish writer Henning Mankell must be read in this context. He affirms that Lampedusa is the symbolic center of Europe because it is precisely in what happens around and in this tiny island at the borders between the Old Continent and Africa that the future of Europe is decided. In other words, it is through the attitudes and political strategies implemented in and around Lampedusa that one can understand what kind of society Europe wants to be.[16]

The problem is that most people do not grasp and see the significance of this. After centuries and decades migration flows in Italy, Europe, the United States, and other Western countries, immigration is too often not

14. I speak about these negative attitudes and language in Campese, "'But I See that Somebody is Missing,'" 73–78. See also the analysis offered by Italian sociologist Maurizio Ambrosini in Gandolfi, "C'è un'indifferenza cattolica?," 557–59.

15. See Snyder, *Asylum-Seeking*, 85–126, where this theologian provides an in-depth analysis of the roots, elements, and consequences of the "ecology of fear."

16. Nausner, "Alla Luce di Lampedusa," 342–43.

yet seen as it should, that is, a constant in the history of humanity and a structural element of our globalized world. Instead, it has become common to treat it as a "perpetual emergency," that is, a "problem" to be tackled the moment it appears, but with no thought for the fact that the "immigration emergencies," such as the arrival of tens of thousands of asylum seekers every year in Italy, are becoming normal; a normality that needs to be properly managed. The way governments address the issue shows the "short-sightedness" of their approach that leads also to a short-term commitment, which is focused on just solving the immediate problem with food, clothing, and a temporary shelter. The question is that the "problem" cannot be solved immediately because more often than not societies are not facing a "temporary" presence because many migrants for different reasons arrive and settle down, even if they frequently express the intention to go back to their countries. The management of the emergencies such as the landings of thousands of migrants and asylum seekers on the European coasts shows the fallacy of a short-sighted approach: governments and sometimes also public opinion tend to show a more sympathetic and compassionate attitude toward these people in the short term, but in the long term indifference, resentment, and more or less explicit exclusion begin to emerge. This first-aid or Band-Aid solution is easier, but less demanding in terms of time and effort, less adequate in the long term, and maintains those who receive migrants in a position of superiority that is typical of this approach. Here, in our opinion, surfaces the colonial mentality that still lingers on in the Western world, a mentality for which it is right to help these "poor people" rescuing them from the dangers of deserts and seas, giving them food, clothing, and a provisional shelter, but it is extremely difficult to implement strategies that facilitate their inclusion within society because ultimately they are not considered as equals. On top of this inability to deal properly with the long-term issues of migration, compounded by colonial attitudes, the migrants keep on reminding host societies that, as an eloquent banner carried during an immigrant rally in Italy read: "We are not here just to eat and sleep."

The second observation is about the resilience and power of the human spirit that moves people—those who migrate and those who host them—to share values, material, spiritual resources, and to welcome each other's differences in an effort to build a community together. The tenacity of the human spirit surfaces and inspires people in the most unlikely situations and contexts. A recent example of this is the witness of Save the Children photographer Giles Duley who was interviewed about his interaction with the Syrian inhabitants of the refugee camp of Za'atari in the Jordanian desert in which live one hundred thousand people, half of them younger than eighteen years old. Duley says that, in this camp he has met persons—kids, mothers, fathers, families—who try to live a normal life in exceptional conditions, and not refugees, a term that we often use to create a distance between "us" and "them."[17] This is to reiterate that, often, material assistance can separate people and that a constructive and positive approach to migration must include the basic elements of human life such as respect, healthy relationships, family, friendship, and community. Borrowing the words of the title of the 2000 movie by Ken Loach on the struggle for the rights of janitors (mostly immigrants and members of minorities) in Los Angeles, all human beings, and so also immigrants, need *Bread and Roses*.

Pastoral and Theological Responses to Migration

Mankell's choice of Lampedusa as the symbolic center of the Europe to come has to be read together with the already mentioned and emblematic trip made by Pope Francis to this island. Both people, from different perspectives, come to the same hermeneutical conclusion: human reality, and not just the reality of migration, has to be read from the margins, from the peripheries because it is from there that it can be interpreted more correctly and profitably for the future of humanity.[18] Starting from this viewpoint we will discuss in what follows some of the pastoral and theological responses to migration. The first is taken precisely from the homily of Francis on the occasion of his visit to Lampedusa. There the Argentinian pope, who had spoken of the tragic deaths of migrants as a "painful thorn in my heart," described and denounced what he called the "globalization of indifference,"[19] an attitude that does not belong only to a society that is gotten passively used to the deaths of migrants, but has spread also among Christians. From a pastoral viewpoint, it is fundamental to start by saying that the Roman Catholic Church, together with other Christian churches, is without any doubt one of the institutions more involved in the care and support of migrants around the whole world. This statement could be easily proven by the endless list of people and structures dedicated in this church to the care of migrants. Yet, there is also no doubt that the church exists within particular contexts and when these contexts are flooded with negative images of migrants, then it is inevitable that this negativity, the "ecology of fear," could influence also the views and behaviors of Catholic believers. So it happens that Catholics get accustomed to the death of migrants to the point of not

---

17. See Baduel, "Quei Bimbi in Bianco."

18. On the importance of this hermeneutical stance, see also Spadaro, "Wake Up the World!"

19. Francis, "Homily in Lampedusa."

being bothered by these tragedies, of not feeling responsible for the migrants who are dying, and of losing the capacity to cry and grieve (as Pope Francis would suggest).[20] The indifference toward the plight of migrants and refugees does not only involve the lay members of the church, but also its pastors, bishops, and theologians. In fact, besides a practical indifference there is also a theological indifference that has already been addressed elsewhere also in terms of exclusion.[21] To be fair, and as we have stated right at the beginning of this essay, there has been an important progress in this field in the last fifteen years, but it is also true that often the migrants are not detected by the Catholic theological radars, especially the radars of most of the great academic institutions and some local churches. Two of the reasons behind this theological indifference are: (1) a theology that is used to dealing with doctrinal issues and does not let itself be challenged by the most pressing issues of their times, such as the phenomenon of human mobility today, and (2) a theology that is still Eurocentric, imprisoned in the intellectual boundaries, the way of interpreting, and expressing reality imposed by the Western world. Gerrit Noort makes the latter point in his missiological reflection on the presence of migrant churches in the Netherlands: "Despite the fact that, since 1997, much academic research has been done on the emerging migrant churches and the implications for the shape of Christianity in a multicultural society, and though intercultural hermeneutics has become more important in the theological discipline, systematic theology remains largely untouched by theology from the global South or from migrant churches."[22] On this issue, one sees appeals for a theology that includes and reflects the great and beautiful diversity that makes Christianity come from many sides: from liberation, postcolonial, and feminist theologies; from that recent branch of Christian studies known as World Christianity; and from European and North American theologians who have understood the necessity of this transformation.[23] The point is that theology in the Western world can no longer continue to elaborate a culturally homogeneous discourse on God and the world because in a world and in a church that becomes more global such a discourse is an anomaly that must be overcome.[24] Postcolonial, liberation, and inclusion issues are not just characteristics of the theologies from the global south, but must be part

20. Ibid.

21. See Campese, "'But I See that Somebody Is Missing,'" 79–81.

22. Noort, "Emerging Migrant Churches," 13.

23. See, for instance, Sobrino, *El Principio-Misericordia*; Nausner, "Alla Luce di Lampedusa," 341–56; Johnson, *Quest for the Living God*; Walls, "World Christianity," 235–40; and Colzani, *Missiologia contemporanea*, 8.

24. See Nausner, "Alla Luce di Lampedusa," 354–55.

of any theology that tries to be a meaningful discourse about God today in our globalized world.[25]

A second response is hostility, and also in this case the anecdotal evidence shows that the environment of fear that has been created around the issue of migration has spread from society to the church generating at times a climate of aversion toward newcomers. Unfortunately, many of us have witnessed and heard of episodes in which migrants have been turned away from our local churches and their charitable agencies simply because they belong to the wrong nationality and skin color or because they are undocumented. Disparaging and offensive remarks about migrants have been made also during Eucharistic celebrations, the highest moment of communion with God and our brothers and sisters. This hostility has also found some kind of theological expression in the work of a former Roman Catholic priest (now an Episcopalian priest), Dominique Peridans. In an essay written a few years ago, Peridans criticizes both the official position of US bishops on migration as found in the document *Strangers No Longer: Together on the Journey of Hope*[26] and the work of one of the most prominent representatives of the theology of migration in the United States, Daniel Groody,[27] accusing them of "fideism."[28] However, what is worrying is not so much the somehow anomalous theological reflection such as the one by Peridans, but rather the working theology that guides the daily practice and common language of many Christians who treat migrants as a problem and a threat. That is something that needs the churches' attention so that the "ecology of fear" does not become the normal environment in which Christians, both migrants and those who receive migrants, deal with this issue.

The third response is what we will call the "first-aid" or "doing charity" approach, which has deeply influenced both Christian practice and thought. Italian sociologist Maurizio Ambrosini has noticed that this is becoming a common course of action especially in the case of significant and sudden emergencies: people respond generously and quite willingly to circumstances such as the arrival of hundreds of children, women, and men in a broken-down boat in Lampedusa or elsewhere, but after a few days they would like the problem to disappear, not counting on the fact that migration

---

25. Snyder, *Asylum-Seeking*, 212.

26. This pastoral letter is a joint document of the US Conference of Catholic Bishops and the Conferencia del Episcopado Mexicano issued in 2003. The text is available online at http://www.usccb.org/issues-and-action/human-life-and-dignity/immigration/strangers-no-longer-together-on-the-journey-of-hope.cfm.

27. Peridans refers in particular to Groody, "Crossing the Divide," 638–67.

28. See Peridans, *What Are They Thinking?*, 5.

is not a "nuisance" that suddenly goes away.[29] Practitioners and theologians of hospitality have underlined some of the shortcomings of this way of acting and thinking;[30] it separates the givers from the receivers; it hinders a real encounter and relationship among people; it requires just a short-term commitment; and it understands itself as unilateral assistance. Also, Jon Sobrino points to the problems that an understanding of solidarity as one-sided humanitarian help or almsgiving could cause.[31] In this framework, there is no space for mutuality and reciprocity: the "givers" are supposed to materially and intellectually help the "receivers" who are so poor and wanting that they can only hope on the benevolent assistance of their givers. This approach is the by-product of a colonial and Eurocentric legacy that not only maintains the gap between the "civilized" and "uncivilized" but does not project a future in which somehow people coming from different backgrounds can live together on equal terms. From this perspective, the European material and spiritual colonizers will always be on the "giving" side and the "poor" un-evangelized and uncivilized people from the global South on the "receiving" side. In the same way, today people from the global South arriving in the Western world are treated as needy people, as "poor," as bodies to be fed, clothed, and given shelter. Using a traditional spiritual terminology, migrants do not just have bodies, they also have souls. Or, to paraphrase the expression of Swiss playwright Max Fritsch, we would like to consider migrants just as workers, but what we got is human beings.

In the ecclesial context the result of this approach is the inability or the great difficulty in being church together.[32] Martha Frederiks and Nienke Pruiksma, in their study of how migration has affected the structure and identity of the Roman Catholic Church and the Protestant Church in the Netherlands, come to the following conclusion: while it is true that both churches have recognized the presence of immigrants, they have not yet become truly multicultural churches because Christian immigrants are not given equal opportunity to participate in the shaping of the future of the local church.[33] In other words, Christian churches generally welcome and take care of the material needs of Christian immigrants, that is, they give assistance to immigrants, but just as recipients of "hospitality" and "charity" and not as equal partners that could and will contribute to a renewed vision

---

29. See Gandolfi, "C'è un'indifferenza cattolica?," 557–58.
30. See, for example, Pohl, *Making Room*.
31. See Sobrino, *El Principio-Misericordia*, 213.
32. The working group of the Federazione delle Chiese Evangeliche in Italia (Federation of Evangelical Churches in Italy) that deals with the issues of migration is called "Being One Church Together." See its website at http://www.fedevangelica.it/.
33. Frederiks and Pruiksma, "Journeying toward Multiculturalism?," 151.

of the church in a world that is undergoing, also thanks to migration, a process of great transformation. A similar situation is found in Italy where Ambrosini observes that there is the awareness within the church of the now permanent and significant presence of immigrant families, but still they are not recognized of co-protagonists of public and ecclesial life. The passage from what he calls the "first-aid code" to the "life together code" has not yet occurred. Church life mirrors what happens in society at large: it is emblematic that even in the pastoral councils of parishes and dioceses where the immigrant population is numerous, the presence and participation of immigrants is very sporadic. This is not the result of a positive will to discriminate, but is the result of the lack of understanding that with the massive presence of immigrants the situation is changing and calls for collaboration, for sitting together around the table and planning the present and the future with, and not only for, everybody.[34]

The fourth response can be simply described as the option for ethnic churches and ethnic theologies. It is definitely not our intention to offer a comprehensive overview and assessment of these realities that deserve much more consideration and study than what we could do here in a few sentences. For our purpose, it will suffice to say that both ethnic churches and ethnic theologies clearly have advantages and disadvantages. For example, national parishes and ethnic chaplaincies or centers must be credited for having helped immigrants around the world to maintain their faith in often hostile, unsympathetic social and church environments and to have facilitated their integration within society and the ecclesial community without renouncing their peculiar cultural and religious heritage. At the same time, there is no doubt that these solutions also present some potential and real downfalls that go from the formation of parallel Christian communities, which often have little interaction with other ethnic communities and the local church in general, to their being able to cater to the needs of the first generation migrants, but finding it difficult to understand and meet the needs of their children. The so-called "ethnic" theologies have emerged in a post-Vatican II environment in which we have witnessed the proliferation of theologies from the global South and from the oppressed groups, such as women and indigenous people. It is thanks to these theologies that we have learned the fundamental lesson of the centrality of context for any theology. Stephen Bevans, who has written one of the classic works on this theme, reminds us that there is no such a thing as a theology that is not contextual.[35] Ethnic theologies have brought to the table the voices of those who were thought

---

34. Gandolfi, "C'è un'indifferenza cattolica?," 558.
35. See Bevans, *Models of Contextual Theology*.

to be mute or too dumb to say something intelligent and relevant about God and church. These voices have revived the catholicity of the church and are helping to break up the hegemony of Western theology in Christian discourse. However, at the same time ethnic theologies can fall into the trap of isolation and lack of communication with other theologies because of an ill-conceived "incommensurability" among different perspectives, which results in groups doing "their own thing" from their own experiences and viewpoints without making the effort to dialogue with Christians who have different experiences and ways of thinking.[36] Churches that do "their own thing" without worrying about the rest of the worldwide church are not catholic; and in the same way theologies that are concerned only about "their own people and issues" without worrying to communicating with other theological discourses are not catholic. And most importantly they do not reflect the "catholicity" of the Christian God, who, as Anselm Min points out, is not a tribal God and thus cannot be properly communicated by a tribal theological discourse.[37] The cultural and religious plurality that becomes ever more evident in the contexts in which we live demands from us the effort to go well beyond "our own" and demands the necessary intercultural practical and theoretical skills that can help us to live our present and build our future together, bridging the cultural, political, social, and religious gaps that divide people from one another.

The Relational Turn:
From First Aid to Friendship and Convivencia

It is not our intention here to discuss in detail what is bringing about this relational turn,[38] but just to highlight, as our starting point, what we consider the most important of these factors: the experience with migrants. Recently, Pope Francis has reminded the church that Christian faith is not a "lab faith," but a "journey faith," that is, a faith that is lived in history, in the human journey, in the encounter with real people and their issues at the geographical and existential frontiers of our world. Theological reflection must reflect this fundamental dimension of the faith by not taking the problems into the "theological laboratory" where they are often transformed into artificial experiments, as Pope Francis observes, but by dealing with them in

---

36. This insight comes from within the field of ethnic theologies, which shows that they are well aware of this danger. See Phan, "Introduction," xxvi–xxvii.

37. See Min, *Solidarity of Others*, 138.

38. We have emphasized the importance of this issue in Campese, "Theologies of Migration," 167–88.

the real context in which they emerge.[39] The relational turn comes mostly from the experience and reflection of ministers and theologians who have being working for and with vulnerable migrants and refugees for years in "dangerous locations," such as national borders, urban peripheries, migration camps, and settlements "in the middle of nowhere" where people live in miserable conditions while working in agricultural fields. These locations are places in which Christians who want to minister with migrants are literally forced "to get dirty and muddy," to accept and face the messiness of the reality of migration and the feelings of anger, disgust, and hopelessness that arise from these situations. These locations have the power to make ministers feel powerless vis-à-vis situations of chronic exploitation, injustice, misery, and death. But at the same time, these locations break through the incredible hope, strength, and tenacity that characterizes the human spirit and the religious faith of the migrants.[40]

It is in these frontiers, where the great complexity of the phenomenon of migration can be experienced and from what we define "healthy powerlessness" vis-à-vis the challenges of this complexity, that the right questions are born. The right questions are not primarily "what do we have to do?" or "what can we give?" but first and foremost, "who do we want to be with?" and consequently, "who do we want to be as a Christian and human community?" Eleazar Fernandez reinforces this insight by maintaining that the presence of migrants challenges us not only with the question, "What is to be done?," but also with more essential questions such as "who are we, what do we hope for, and where do we go?".[41] In other words, the right questions are not so much about "doing," but about "being"; they are not so much about the body, but the heart. The experience with migrants and refugees teaches in fact that what really wounds them is not so much the lack of food and clothing, but that they are not respected and treated properly as human beings.[42] And even charity and material assistance can become offensive if they are done with no respect toward their dignity as human beings. The heart comes first, a heart whose beauty and intensity can be better observed and understood particularly in the migrants' popular Catholicism, during the celebrations of their devotions, such as the Virgen de Guadalupe for

39. Spadaro, "Interview with Pope Francis."

40. Among the theologians who have explicitly referred to the messiness of the reality of migration that is characterized by sin and grace, we mention here Snyder, *Asylum-Seeking*; Leddy, *Other Face of God*; and Osborne, "Migrant Domestic Careworkers," 1–25.

41. Fernandez, *Burning Center*, 218. Here, Fernandez is quoting from Ruiz, "Diaspora, Empire, Solidarity," 50.

42. Groody, "Spirituality of Migrants," 147–48.

Mexicans or the Señor de los Milagros for Peruvians, in which they show the depth of their humanity and faith.[43] Daniel Groody has observed that the heart is not just the site of feelings, as we usually understand it, but that "the biological-symbolic site of wisdom and knowledge and a metaphor for the whole of one's conscious, intelligent, and free personality. The heart integrates and informs all aspects of a person, including the mind, will, and emotions."[44] Hence, the human heart cannot survive by bread alone, but needs to be nourished by attention, compassion, understanding, and tenderness. In other words, the heart needs caring and just human relationships. And any effort to deal with the reality of migration, even to bring about social justice where there is little or none, that does not begin with and involve the heart, is bound to be a failure.

This relational perspective was powerfully expressed in the field of Christian mission by the members of the so-called "younger churches" in a famous speech by Indian Anglican cleric V. S. Azariah during the World Mission Conference in Edinburgh in 1910: "Through all the ages to come the Indian Church will rise up in gratitude to attest the heroism and self-denying labors of the missionary body. You have given your goods to feed the poor. You have given your bodies to be burned. We also ask for love. Give us friends!"[45] From these words, it is clear that the generous giving, self-giving, and sacrifice of Western missionaries were much appreciated by the people who were evangelized by them, but they were not sufficient. Azariah expresses the need to go beyond a unilateral view of mission that highlights the financial and moral superiority of the Western "givers" in comparison to the "poverty" of the recipients of their missionary work. To ask for friendship means to demand just and healthy human relationships and, therefore, to reclaim the human dignity of the "receivers." In the same way, the migrants and refugees today do not ask just for food and clothing; they do not just want people who speak for and dedicate their lives to them. They want friends; they want to establish meaningful friendships that are able to bridge across the multiple social, cultural, religious, and national boundaries that divide people from each other. Without these encounters and relationships on equal terms, it will be impossible to recognize in each other God's presence and grace and discern God's workings in our midst.

For migrants and refugees, people who for different reasons have been uprooted from their own land, communication and relationships are crucial:

---

43. Cruz, "New Way of Being Christian," 101.

44. Groody, *Border of Death*, 8.

45. This quote from Azariah is taken from Robert, "Cross-Cultural Friendship," 100.

with their families back in their countries of origin, with fellow countrymen and women who are going through the same experience of immigration, with any other person who would like to share and celebrate with them their lives, values, faith, and food. The church must become a privileged site where this *convivencia* is patiently built up and made possible. In this sense, the migrants become the protagonists of the redefinition of the church not just as the place of liturgical celebration and national identity, but as the human and faith community where catholicity becomes a reality, where human relationships can break through the borders and walls that divide people and make them enemies (Eph 2:11–22), where the God of all nations in Jesus Christ and by the power of the Spirit makes people believe and behave as brothers and sisters regardless of nationality, culture, social status, religion, and gender. To this end, it is important to add that Trinitarian theology must become a main resource for a theology of intercultural relationships and *convivencia*. In her stimulating book on the Trinity, Catherine LaCugna first of all emphasizes the practical dimension of Trinitarian theology, affirming that "the doctrine of the Trinity is ultimately a practical doctrine with radical consequences for Christian life."[46] She then continues, describing this practical aspect precisely in terms of relationships using the concept of the Trinitarian communion that expands to the whole of humanity and creation. "Indeed, Trinitarian theology is par excellence a theology of relationship: God to us, we to God, we to each other. The doctrine of the Trinity affirms that the 'essence' of God is relational, other-ward, that God exists as diverse persons united in communion of freedom, love and knowledge."[47]

Given both the relational nature of God and the relational essence of migrant humanity, it should not come as a surprise that different theologians writing on migration, and who have had a direct experience of ministry with migrants, have been putting (as far as we know for the most part independently from each other) the theme of relationship at the center of their reflections. This fundamental issue has been referred to in terms of encounters at different levels (at the grassroots, with powers, in worship, and in theology) and, in particular, as "one-to-one, embodied relationships," which are the lifeblood of the ecology of faith because it is through these encounters that stereotypes can be broken down and mutual support can start:[48] from a more ethical perspective, as "kinship across the borders" that is based on a rich understanding of solidarity (incarnational, institutional,

---

46. LaCugna, *God for Us*, 1, 377.
47. Ibid., 243.
48. Snyder, *Asylum-Seeking*, 198.

and conflictual);[49] as "neighborliness," which "means looking out for each other, sharing a common space; it involves proximity. It involves face-to-face relationships that go beyond the faceless world of the political, and the intimate and private world of family and friends";[50] as "theology of connectedness" by developing multicultural relations;[51] as cross-cultural and cross-religious friendships/relationships based first of all, as it has been underlined by LaCugna, on the doctrine of the Trinity as most intimate friendship/relationship among Father, Son, and Holy Spirit; and on Jesus of Nazareth's example in terms of friendship/relationship that was particularly expressed in his table fellowship with everybody, even with the most marginalized and negatively labeled members of society such as the strangers;[52] and on the fundamental missionary dimension of relationships with migrants who are rebuilding their lives in a new context.[53] Theologians who have dealt with the theme and practice of hospitality have reached similar conclusions. Christine Pohl, for instance, affirms: "Communities that practice hospitality discover that one of the most precious resources they have to share with people is their fellowship and friendship. More than offering services to 'those' in need, they welcome people into a common life."[54] Relationships in the context of migration are the indispensable way to integration, inclusion, sharing—*convivencia*—which is not living in the same building and neighborhood, often without even exchanging a simple word of greeting, but about the quality of life together, about enjoying and celebrating life together. It is fundamental to focus on relationships on equal terms in a context in which, too often, these are made impossible by formidable obstacles among such as the bureaucratic systems and Western colonial paternalism.

There is no doubt that today this "relational turn" has found a determined and intelligent supporter in Pope Francis who, in his preaching and writing, has emphasized the "affective dimension" of evangelization since the very beginning of his Petrine ministry. During the homily of the mass of the official inauguration of his papacy on March 19, 2013, Pope Francis twice exhorted Christians not to be afraid of goodness and tenderness. For him, goodness and tenderness are not about superficial emotions, but signify the

---

49. Heyer, *Kinship across Borders*, 114–23.

50. Leddy, *Other Face of God*, 93–94.

51. Noort, "Emerging Migrant Churches," 15–16.

52. See especially Luke 7:33–50; 14:1–24; 15:1–2; 19:1–10; and others.

53. Campese, "Mission and Migration," 247–60. The idea of cross-cultural friendship in the context of migration has been inspired by Robert, "Cross-Cultural Friendship," 100–107.

54. Pohl, *Living into Community*, 170. See also her compelling study on hospitality in Pohl, *Making Room*.

capacity and willingness to care for and protect each other and creation.[55] Most importantly, tenderness points to the greatest gift of God's infinite love for humanity and the whole creation: "Every human being is the object of God's infinite tenderness."[56] And Jesus, the Son of God, is for Pope Francis the incarnation of God's tenderness who "by becoming flesh, summoned us to the revolution of tenderness."[57] This "revolution of tenderness" to which we have been called must transform us into people who wake up from the slumber of indifference and become capable of weeping and grieving for our migrant brothers and sisters, to become compassionate people, people who are able to reestablish caring human relationships where indifference, fear, suspicion, and even hate exist toward migrants and refugees.[58] Is it by mere chance that the "affective dimension" of evangelization is being highlighted in our times? Is it just because the pope is Latin American and, by culture, more interested and passionate about these issues? Or is the Spirit guiding us, also through the message of Pope Francis, to rediscover what is one of the core centers of the Christian mission, a dimension that often takes a second or third place in comparison to what are considered more "theological/rational" and "political/strategic" issues? Perhaps we have forgotten that a successful process of evangelization, today as in the past, happens in the daily relationships and communication among people. It is in the simple dynamic of human communication and relationships, and not particularly through sophisticated missionary programs and strategies, that the Good News of the Reign of God needs to be proclaimed and witnessed to today.[59]

We conclude this chapter by proposing the reflection of Antonio Torresin, an Italian parish priest, a reflection that shows some of the theological and ministerial implications of a "relational turn," of the rediscovery of the "affective dimension" of Christian mission in the context of migration and specifically in terms of hospitality.[60] Torresin observes that there are two main aspects to hospitality: to give hospitality and to ask for and receive hospitality. In church ministry and also in theological discourse, more attention has been focused on giving hospitality as a moral virtue and practice, but this is a unilateral view that often conceals the power game that

---

55. Francis, "Homily for the Beginning of the Petrine Ministry."
56. Francis, *Joy of the Gospel*, 274.
57. Ibid., 88.
58. See Francis, "Homily in Lampedusa."
59. Recently, Italian theologian Severino Dianich has insisted on this "person-to-person" dynamic as the main "structure" of evangelization. See his *La Chiesa Cattolica verso la sua Riforma*.
60. What follows is taken from or inspired by Torresin, "La Parrocchia Ospitale," 8–13.

is being played wherein the person on the receiving end is more or less explicitly considered inferior to the person who is giving. Torresin says that the less explored and more original dimension of hospitality, a dimension exemplified by Jesus himself in the Gospels, is to ask to be welcomed by the people we encounter in our journeys. This means to take a risk, especially for Christians who have been used to giving hospitality because they put themselves in the hands of "strangers" who can either receive or reject them. Putting oneself in that position means to choose to become vulnerable and dependent on the person for whose openness, generosity, and hospitality one is asking. Christians who are in charge of hospitality rarely take the risk to be on the receiving end. Yet, the rewards of becoming vulnerable to another person's hospitality are rich indeed. We will underscore three of them. First, we realize that our God does not just give hospitality, but receives also the gift of hospitality, as can be seen, for instance, in the famous passage in which Abraham welcomes the three pilgrims by the oaks of Mamre (Gen 18); God stands by the door and knocks, ready to share food with whomever opens the door and lets God into his/her life (Rev 3:20); and Jesus himself, in Luke 19:1–10, asks to stay at Zaccheus' house, and this act of hospitality allows God's grace to enter in this chief tax collector's life and transform it. In other words, the Trinitarian God wants to be our guest and to listen to our stories, problems, hopes, and deepest yearnings. The Trinity wants to make communion with humanity. Second, we cannot establish full and sound human relationships with migrants and refugees just by meeting them on our terms and turf. Christian communities have to make the effort and take the risk of familiarizing themselves with migrants by asking permission to enter their homes, where they can fully express their spirit and heart. Third, in order to meet migrants on equal terms on their turf, Christian communities must often renounce the tendency to go into somebody's home with the intention to help and solve their problems, usually with a bag of food or clothing. This "performance anxiety," as Torresin calls it—the anxiety of "doing" something—stands in the way of true knowledge of each other. Christian communities must approach migrants and refugees with their own vulnerable humanity, offering them the best gift: their friendship, their long-term commitment to *convivencia*. It is a difficult path to follow but the only one that keeps the community open to newcomers and does not allow differences to separate people from one another.

We human beings cannot live by bread alone, "but by every word that comes from the mouth of God" (Matt 4:4). All of us, migrants and non-migrants, need words of friendship, encouragement, consolation, hope, solidarity, healing, courage, faith, and sometimes reproach. Christian communities must come to understand that God's words will also reach them through the mouths of migrants and refugees, through the gift of their lives and values. This will happen only if we put at the center of Christian reflection and practice healthy human relationships based on equality and sharing, not so much "things," but especially heart and spirit.

7

The Love of Many Lands: Theology, Multiplicity, and Migrant Identity

Matthew John Paul Tan

Introduction

This short work will focus on the challenges facing the Catholic migrant, and will give particular attention to the topic of multiplicity as the fulcrum of these challenges. In an age of growing insecurity, the migrant has now become one of a class of outsiders that has become demonized, excluded, or even *included* in exploitative ways. What is different about this work on multiplicity is that it parts company with those that engage this problem as a purely social or a cultural problem. This work seeks to go further by treating migrant identity, and the experience of multiplicity in migrant identity, as a theological issue. Indeed, this paper will assert that giving theological consideration to migrant identity and the multiplicity therein would be able to furnish possibilities that social or cultural analysis might overlook.

The launch point for the theological consideration of multiplicity and its tie with migrant identity can be found in Book II of Augustine's *Confessions*, a line of which reads: "I have been fruitlessly divided. I turned from unity in You, to be lost in multiplicity."[1] This article would return to give this line explicit consideration, though the reader might notice echoes of it reverberating through what follows immediately below. In substantiating the giving of theological consideration to the issue of multiplicity within migrant identity, it would be necessary to make two inquiries after elaborating on the contours of the problem of multiplicity. The first inquiry will briefly

---

1. Augustine, *Confessions* 2.2.1.

engage social and cultural theory in its modern and postmodern variants, and highlight the salient aspects of multiplicity in migrant identity, which can become problematized. The second inquiry will, having acknowledged the salience of those insights, also highlight some of the conceptual shortcomings brought to light by both theoretical inquiry and the experience of the migrant. This second inquiry will then consciously take a theological turn, to show how Augustinian theology, particularly as articulated in the theology of St. Bonaventure, could fill in the conceptual gaps on the issue of multiplicity in migrant identity that social and cultural theory generates.

It must be noted that this inquiry is preliminary and will be by no means exhaustive. The aim of this paper is merely to identify and elaborate on one concrete element of the migrant experience that can act as a pastoral pressure point within the Catholic Church, particularly as migrants begin to show a greater prominence in many churches in the West. Moreover, in identifying such a pressure point, this paper does not intend to treat the issue of multiplicity as a problem to be overcome. Rather, this paper hopes to be the first step in reframing the debate about the place of migrants in the church and in society at large by looking at the migrant as an icon of the church which images a divine reality, rather than looking at them as a distortion of that reality.

Problematizing Multiplicity

As mentioned above, the first task of this paper would be to set out the contours of the problematique of multiplicity in migrant identity. Migrants generally face two burdens in their country of residence. The first is that they are not born in the country of residence, and in varying ways, this permanently marks the migrant as an outsider. Secondly, because they are not born in the country of residence, the allegiances of the migrant always remain a live question, particularly in times of societal stress. To put it bluntly, the constant question to the migrant in such times pertains to whether the migrant as an outsider living in the midst of the native-born is a patriot or a traitor. What complicates matters is that many migrants often make no attempt to prove their patriotism in such binary terms. Instead, many migrants celebrate their previous belonging. It can be at very quotidian levels, such as through food or language, or in terms of allegiances to the symbols or institutions of the country of origin, be they flags, political and social organizations, or systems of law.

In response to such celebrations of multiple belonging, very often assertions are made that migrants undermine the social fabric, engendering disunity and dissension". To put it crassly, many argue that it is bad enough that outsiders are taking the jobs of the native-born, and now ask out loud if social cohesion must be surrendered as well. This line is often used by all manner of political entrepreneurs, and happens everywhere from the most liberal democracy to the most dictatorial regime.

In order to problematize these dynamics surrounding the issue of multiplicity, the question must be asked: how and to what extent can any political community resolve the challenge of multiplicity in the migrant? Answering this question is a massive undertaking that would be beyond the task of a short article, since a whole array of secondary questions will flow from it that must be addressed in their turn. Therefore, the task set by this article will be more modest, and will pertain specifically to the question of the contours of a political theory that could in turn equip such a *polis* to engage such a challenge.[2]

Multiplicity and Social Theory

The Cosmopolitan Solution

Attention must now move to how social theory has sought to tackle the issue. At the risk of sounding reductionistic, social theory has often framed the key challenge of multiplicity as a tension between the one and the many, between the part and the whole. Of key importance here is Kristen Johnson's *Theology, Political Theory, and Pluralism*,[3] which meticulously tracks the genealogy of these attempts, two episodes of which are relevant to this work.

The first attempt at resolving the issue of multiplicity that Johnson identifies can be broadly termed liberal cosmopolitanism, which tries to solve the problem of multiplicity by positing an order in which everyone can belong, regardless of their background, so long as they conformed to a single, ostensibly universal standard by which it is possible, in the words of John Rawls, for "deeply opposed though reasonable comprehensive doctrines . . . [to] live together and all affirm the political conception of a constitutional regime."[4] Liberal cosmopolitanism tried to solve the tension of multiplicity by emphasizing the one (the one here being the standard of reasonableness) over the many. In such a schema, multiplicity amongst

---

2. The question of whether and how a *polis* needs to be configured to institutionalize the theory has been bracketed out, with this work focusing solely on the theory. The *institutional* contours of the *polis* are an important question, but will have to be the task of another work.

3. Johnson, *Theology, Political Theory, and Pluralism*.

4. Rawls, *Political Liberalism*, xviii.

migrants is solved by the insistence on uniformity, which usually involves funneling all public expressions of migrants through a common vocabulary, whether it is in terms of emphasizing what is common in each individual regardless of origin, creed, and geography,[5] or more commonly in terms of demanding conformity to a civic code. This civic code is often enforced through a common language or common schema of civic practices, or what Rawls calls a "superordinate plan ... to which the aims of all individuals and associations are subordinate."[6] What is interesting is that such a process of conformity can be applied even within nations that are ostensibly multicultural. Indeed, Stanley Fish has identified a problem with multicultural projects founded upon an insistence on tolerance defined as unqualified acceptance of any cultural practice as valid and equal. The pressure point for such polities, argues Fish, is located in the instant those being tolerated show signs of intolerance within a multicultural society. In such a circumstance, both the persistence and the condemnation of the intolerance would result in the undermining of the principle of tolerance.[7]

The migrant also faces the inverse of the above problem when governments, regardless of political stripe, in affirming the multiculturalism of the polity, nonetheless couch this multiculturalism in terms of an overriding insistence that migrants assimilate into the polis and abiding by ostensibly national values (whether such values be "Australian," "French," or "American"). The problem becomes acute when such values are often left either poorly defined or even given no content at all. The migrant is often left wondering what such values may be, but when such quintessentially national values are brought up in the discourse—usually in times of national stress—the migrant always falls short of fully abiding by them precisely because their origins, and thus their loyalties, are located in places outside of the polity of residence. Thus, when a migrant decides to express his or her love for the land of her birth, very often that loyalty can only go so far as the cosmetic and the culinary.

Ultimately, it is the migrant's country of residence that determines what is a reasonable amount of loyalty to a migrant's country of origin. What is more, the boundaries for such loyalties will very often shift, and at the impetus of the polity of residence when it is opportune. For the cosmopolitan, a migrant's multiplicity of national loyalties is seen as a dilution of loyalty to the country of residence, or at the very least running the risk of upsetting the hierarchy between one's own particular aims and the more universal

5. Taylor, "Politics of Recognition," 25–74.
6. Rawls, *Theory of Justice*, 463.
7. Fish, *Trouble with Principle*, 1.

aims set by the "superordinate plan" of the *polis*, to put it in Rawlsian terms. By contrast, the native-born citizen is given a superior status over the migrant because they deem themselves unbound by the burden of multiple loyalties. By extension, the native born are able to assume the magisterial position of determining the standards to which migrants must conform. It would seem that the problem of multiplicity is met with chauvinism from within the cosmopolitan solution.[8]

The Postmodern Solution

Johnson identifies an alternative to the chauvinism in the cosmopolitan solution to the problem of multiplicity, which can be broadly termed the postmodern solution.[9] In contrast to the cosmopolitan demand for conformity of all loyalties to a universal superordinate loyalty to the country of residence, postmodern responses have balked at the emphasis on such uniformity. This is because, for the postmodern, what is universal already involves some appeal to a culturally contingent identity structure and what Chantal Mouffe calls "an ensemble of contingent practices."[10] Instead of asking how the parts can be made to fit into a national whole, the postmodern position is more interested in two other questions. The first is: if the contingent identity shapes what is universal, what is the number of parts or constituents to that identity? The second is: what are the implications if there is more than one constituent part?

The first question is relatively easy to answer for the postmodern. The idea of a single identity is an illusion, a highly persuasive illusion, but an illusion nonetheless. Rather than appeal to an illusory unity, the postmodern solution suggests that the starting point to the challenge of multiplicity lies in the recognition that "we are in fact always multiple and contradictory subjects" and "inhabitants of a diversity of communities (as many, really, as the social relations in which we participate and the subject positions they define)."[11] Moreover, rather than regard this starting point as a problem to be solved, as it is in the cosmopolitan solution, the postmodern position celebrates multiplicity as the very *engine* of political life.[12] Thus, the real solution is not learning how to be tolerant toward the migrant's difference,

---

8. Hage, *White Nation*.

9. Johnson refers to this as "agonistic" or "post-Nietzschean" political theory. See Johnson, *Theology, Political Theory, and Pluralism*, 84–139.

10. Mouffe, *Return of the Political*, 145.

11. Ibid., 20–21.

12. See for instance Honig, *Political Theory*, 117.

but how to find the means to engage, respect, and even embrace multiplicity within a single polity. Given this complexity, the task for postmodern theory is to find ways in which one dominant mode of belonging can adapt to accommodate other modes of belonging at the same time.[13]

Engaging multiplicity in this vein becomes a twofold task. The first aspect of this task is an institutional one, where politics must maintain a constant vigilance against fetishizing the institutional status quo as somehow natural and given, as well as search for points of difference in the social fabric and ensure that those differences become part of the social fabric and not eliminated. This means finding ways in which migrant communities, their customs and systems of law can become incorporated into the overall life of any given *polis,* and not just relegated to ghettos, museums, or case studies in a textbook.[14] The second—and arguably more important—task is finding ways of honoring within the civic body the multiplicity in each and every citizen, since multiplicity within the republic is because of a multiplicity within each individual citizen.[15]

The topic of the multiplicity of self has been given an exemplary treatment in the thought of Gilles Deleuze and, after him, William Connolly. Deleuze worked on the assumption that lived life at the individual and communal level always exceeds any kind of political ordering. In a book called *A Thousand Plateaus,* co-authored with Felix Guattari, Deleuze used two botanical categories to signify two different kinds of politics. The first is a conservative arboreal or "tree-like" politics and the second was a seemingly more radical rhizomic alternative, where different networks of connections become possible within any point in the rhizome. Following Deleuze, William Connolly called for a movement away from the arboreal manner of engaging multiplicity, that is, by funneling what is drawn at the roots through a single filtration system in the trunk. According to Connolly, the trouble with liberal cosmopolitanism is that they appear to affirm plurality, while insisting on conformity in reality, with the elements that do not conform being dismissed as abnormal.[16] In an arboreal regime, the migrant would have to give up his ability to live out the full extent of his belonging in one community in order to live in another. In keeping with the general trajectory of the postmodern position on multiplicity, Connolly argues that arboreal politics hide behind a myth of a cohesive identity, and it is a myth because such identities are in reality composites of an array of other

---

13. Ibid., 39.
14. See for instance Connolly, *Ethos of Pluralization,* 28.
15. Honig, *Political Theory,* 117.
16. Connolly, *Ethos of Pluralization,* 90–91.

contingent identities. Because of this contingency, Connolly stresses that there is nothing permanent about any one composite of identities. Rather, they converge only for a brief time and disappear, since the "energies, and remainders that circulate through every cultural configuration . . . are not captured by their self-identification."[17]

Also, such composites only work when each constituent part does not melt into any single larger institutional form. For a composite identity to work, every constituent must maintain its own integrity and work in tension with other constituents.[18] Our identities are thus tapestries of constantly changing composites, and Connolly says that such a pluralistic reality is respected not by the *polis* conceived as a tree, but as a rhizome. For Connolly, a civilizational tree maintains its integrity as long as its horizons remain static and borders tightly controlled, while the rhizome constantly pushes against such boundaries in unpredictable ways. To tie this back to migrants and multiplicity, the postmodern position, especially its Deleuzian variant, allows the migrant's to display multiple loyalties since no one loyalty can originate from a single point of origin. Going further, it should be noted that the plurality and contingency that come with self-identification is not just an idea arrived at cognitively in the mind of the migrant, but a lived, embodied reality. Multiplicity is occurring not only in the way one *thinks* of one's belonging, but is also bound up in the way one's *body* is caught up and moved within the social body. If there is anything that a migrant can count on, it is that belonging, whether singular or multiple, is a practice aimed at the body. This can be in terms of the clothes one wears, the social bodies the migrant binds his body to, to whose body the migrant's cleaves in marriage, the marking as an outsider via verbal and physical assault, and so on. The flux implied by this array of bodily practices means that everybody, migrant or native-born, is not a static unitary category. The self-expression of any one identity will always, in the words of Maurice Merleau-Ponty, "assume segments derived from another."[19] The postmodern solution to multiplicity, in sum, is suspicious of the notion of a cohesive civic identity because to be a subject in any civic body is to be unavoidably multiplicitous.

We can see the promise in the postmodern position in going beyond liberal cosmopolitanism through its greater appreciation of multiplicity. Be that as it may, such an appreciation should not obscure one major drawback. This lies in the fact that the postmodern position overcomes the weaknesses of the cosmopolitan solution to multiplicity, not by overcoming the

17. Ibid., 98–9.
18. Ibid., xvi. See also Benhabib, *Claims of Culture*, 5.
19. Merleau-Ponty, "Eye and Mind," 168.

dichotomy between the part and the whole, but by repeating that dichotomy and then inverting the priorities that liberal cosmopolitanism champions. Johnson identifies that the postmodern solution, exemplified in voices like Connolly's, presume that "unity and difference, solidarity and diversity, and the universal and the particular must stand as irreconcilable opposites."[20] While correct in identifying the illusory whole within the cosmopolitan solution and in critiquing the aggrandizement of that illusory whole over the part in the name of unity, the postmodern position itself can be critiqued for doing nothing more than championing the incomplete part over the whole in the name of diversity, on account of the sheer contingency and dialectical nature of any identity marker. This is problematic for the experience of the migrant's real struggle with multiplicity because, to borrow from Charles Mathewes, the postmodern position's insistence that every part lives in tension with one another comes at the price of "refusing all imaginative possibilities of some sort of ideal absolute harmony."[21] Ultimately, the postmodern position does a disservice to the migrant by dismissing the possibility that the migrant may desire to achieve some sense of harmony within one's own identity, or at the very least closing off any creative avenues that make such a harmonization possible.[22]

The Response from Theology

Multiplicity and Coincidence

Though by no means exhaustive, the above has indicated the limitations by which social theory alone can engage the challenge of multiplicity within migrant identity. At this juncture, this work submits that Christian theology could go further than either the cosmopolitan or postmodern positions on the issue of multiplicity, because it has been an issue that Christian theology has been engaging from its earliest days. It might disconcert some, however, when they consider that the starting point of treating multiplicity was its link to sin. Origen of Alexandria, for instance, used the maxim of "where there is sin, there is multiplicity."[23] In a similar vein, Maximus the Confessor spoke of the fruit of sin as "the one nature [being] shattered

---

20. Johnson, *Theology, Political Theory, and Pluralism*, 124.
21. Mathewes, "Faith, Hope, and Agony," 137.
22. Johnson, *Theology, Political Theory, and Pluralism*, 132.
23. Origen's ninth homily on Ezekiel states it thus: *ubi peccata sunt, ibi est multitudo*. Cited in de Lubac, *Catholicism*, 33.

to a thousand pieces."[24] This claim is based on the ancient Christian assertion that sin is fundamentally a form of separation where, in the words of Cyril of Alexandria, "Satan has broken us up." Separation, as Henri de Lubac argued, is synonymous with a "breaking up" of a unity into the multiple, and with this sin-induced multiplicity come schism, heresy, and dissension, against which the antidote is the virtuous pursuit of oneness.[25] Augustine takes up this theme and carves an inroad in which he ties multiplicity not to identity, but to love. With his famous beginning to his *Confessions* "our hearts are restless until they rest in thee," Augustine makes a fundamental anthropological claim that we are driven by love before anything else, and sin has redirected our love from God to other things. In that redirecting of our loves, Augustine writes that he "turned from unity in You to be lost in fruitless multiplicity."[26] Lost in sin, each seemingly whole person has been rendered into what de Lubac called "so many cores of natural opposition."[27]

It is submitted that using the keywords of "love" and "sin" can help unveil why multiplicity in migrants are framed as a problem by political entrepreneurs, and an indicator as to the scale of the problem that migrants are perceived to pose to the native-born. In this Augustinian light, we can see that the criticism by political entrepreneurs of a migrant's love for multiple polities is a kind of civic attempt at critiquing the multiplicity of loves brought about by sin. And in a civic parallel to Origen's point that the antidote to multiplicity is singularity through the help of virtue, the implicit claim of such entrepreneurs is that the vice of multiplicity of loves of polities is cured by the virtue of a singular and exclusive love of the country of residence, known more colloquially as "patriotism." The migrant, insofar as he is a patriot of multiple countries, is seen as a secular kind of sinner in the manner similar to Augustine's equation of sin with a multiplicity of loves.

We see from the above that theology in an Augustinian key can provide a lens for diagnosing the problem associated with the challenge that multiplicity poses in civic discourse. However, it must be noted that Augustinian theology can go also go further in providing an inroad that both the cosmopolitan and the postmodern positions miss, which focuses on the

---

24. *Quaestiones ad Thalassium*, 2. Cited in Ibid.

25. To continue the section from Origen's ninth homily stated above: *ubi peccata sunt, ibi est multitudo, ibi schismata, ibi haereses, ibi dissensiones. Ubi autem virtus, ibi singularitas, ibi unio, ex quo omnium credentium omnium erat cor unum et anima una.* ("Where there is sin there is multiplicity, there is schism, there are heresies, there are dissensions. Where there is the help of virtue, there is singularity, there is union, and from that all the believers are of one heart and one soul.") Cited in Ibid.

26. Augustine, *Confessions*, 2.1.1.

27. de Lubac, *Catholicism*, 34.

relationship between the part and the whole. Before going into this point, it must be noted that like the postmodern theorists, Augustinians would see multiplicity as an inescapable part of the human condition. Unlike the postmodernists, however, Augustinians would also see multiplicity as a disruption to the human condition. While postmoderns are content to leave the self fragmented, the Augustinian would be reluctant to call this a "solution." Indeed, the Anglican theologian Graham Ward reminds us, following Augustine, that to merely say "we are multiple" is to abandon the migrant to "endless dissemination" and eventually dissolution.[28] In other words, while acknowledging that the migrant is multiplicitous, the migrant cannot be content with merely being left as so many fragments with no hope of harmonization of these fragments.

Before going on to how Augustinian theology can resolve the impasse left by the postmodern solution, a side note is required here. In acknowledging that multiplicity is an inescapable human condition (if not fundamental), theology shows that the multiplicity of the Catholic migrant can be seen not merely as problematic but also iconic. The migrant, in his or her embodied experience of multiplicity is an image of the church in a number of respects. The first aspect is negative, in that the framing of the migrant as a secular sinner because of his or her outward multiplicity externalizes and makes apparent an internal reality which effects *both* the migrant and the native-born. The multiplicity of the migrant in this Augustinian sense is a symptom, one of the many out-workings of our brokenness as a result of sin. Furthermore, this is a symptom that is not unique to the migrant. The native-born thinks that migrants are the only ones with a problem of multiplicity simply because that multiplicity is the most visible. Therefore, if everyone is marked by multiplicity, as Augustine claims we are, it means that the multiplicity externalized by the migrant should bring to our attention subtler multiplicities within each of us that we remain unaware of. What the migrant does is make the native-born face up to this hidden multiplicity. As the icon brings hidden realities to the level of our gaze, so should the migrant cause each of us, particularly the native born, to gaze into and interrogate our own hidden multiplicity, whether it is in our hidden love of mammon over God, love of country over Christ, or making our love of country dictate how Christ is to be loved.[29]

At this point, one may be forgiven for thinking it problematic to be talking about migrants as icons of sinfulness. Indeed, it will be problematic if sinfulness is all that migrants are good for theologically. One could easily

---

28. Ward, *Cities of God*, 95.
29. On this last point, see Budde, *Borders of Baptism*.

talk about the migrant status of the church, which *Lumen Gentium*—the Second Vatican Council's Dogmatic Constitution on the Church—explicitly affirms.[30] The question that needs to be asked, however, is how multiplicity figures into this migrant status, and how theology can expound on this multiplicity in a way that overcomes the limitations of the cosmopolitan and postmodern positions.

To continue with the Augustinian rubric, it is submitted that the founder of the church, Jesus Christ, has sought to engage the problem of multiplicity by transforming it, from the fruitless multiplicity of Augustine's *Confessions* to a fruitful, redemptive multiplicity. To this, this paper will draw upon the thought of another theologian in the tradition of Augustine, namely the medieval Doctor of the Church St. Bonaventure of Bagnoregio. It may be argued that Bonaventure differs greatly from the fourth-century Bishop of Hippo. Though the extent of Bonaventure's continuation of Augustine's legacy cannot be exhaustively explored here, it is argued that both doctors are bound by their common assertion of the centrality of love in the economy of salvation, and flowing from that there is also a common reliance on centrality of love in either dispersing a union or drawing the many into a unity. Where the differences arise are the result more of emphasis than on the substantial content of their respective claims.

Central to this consideration is Bonaventure's take on the ancient theme of the coincidence of opposites, in which everything has an opposite with which it is both in tension and intimately united via a mediator. While Christianized versions of Heraclitus's philosophical trope are found elsewhere, Bonaventure grounds his take on the coincidence of opposites on the patristic positing of Christ as the Divine *Logos,* or the reasoning behind all of creation. For Bonaventure, the Divine *Logos* was not extrinsic to creatures. Rather, since it is through the *Logos* that all things were made, it was the very ground of every creature's existence and an integral part of each creature's structure. Bonaventure expresses this unity by looking at the *Logos* as the Word, for which every creature that can exist and ever will exist is but an articulation of that Word. This intimate union of every creature to its opposite via the mediation of the Word is possible because, as Bonaventure expresses it in his *Soul's Journey to God*, within Christ one sees at once "the first and last, the highest and the lowest, the circumference and the center, the Alpha and the Omega, the caused and the cause, the Creator and the creature, that is the book within and without."[31]

---

30. The document noted that, paralleling Paul's second letter to the Corinthians (2 Cor 5:6), the church "journeys in a foreign land away from the Lord" as an "exile." See Paul VI, *Dogmatic Constitution*, 6.

31. *Itinererium Mentis ad Deum*, 6.7. Cited in Delio, *Simply Bonaventure*, 88.

Bonaventure is able to locate this coincidence of creaturely opposites in the *Logos* because he regarded the *Logos* as the crucial mediator that holds the Trinity in a Triune equation. For Bonaventure, the *Logos* was not simply one monad within the Trinity, but is a person who by its nature inheres to another person in an intimate relationship.[32] More specifically, the *Logos* is for Bonaventure a person that brings into itself two other, seemingly polar opposites, the Father, who is all generator, and the Spirit, who is all generated.[33] The means by which this happens is the mutual co-inhering of the persons in the Trinity via a dissemination of love. It is this notion of the *Logos* mirroring both the Father and the Spirit which explains why the *Logos*, in becoming man in the person of Jesus Christ, reveals to all who encounter Him the fullness of the Triune God. Moreover, the *Logos* does not reduce or eliminate the particularities of either generator and generated to fit into a homogenized unity. For Bonaventure, unity in the *Logos* presumes the integrity of both Father qua Father and Spirit qua Spirit, since the *Logos* is but the inhering of both Father and Spirit in their fullness.[34]

Bonaventure's defense of the *Logos* as the coincidence of opposites can make very promising inroads to the challenge of multiplicity and migrant identity, insofar as the migrant's multiplicitous loves can be said to mirror the Trinitarian co-inhering of one divine person in another. We must remind ourselves here that the *Logos* is at once the coincidence of opposites and the ground of being for every creature. If, through sin, every creature is marked profoundly by a multiplicity of loves, then this multiplicity, so long as it is anchored in the *Logos*, will no longer be necessarily constituted as the "cores of natural opposition" mentioned above. In the *Logos*, each constituent love is no longer merely the opposing element of another constituent love, for the *Logos* seeks a return to unity what sin had fragmented into the multiple. Augustine said as much in a sermon on Psalm 58, in which he spoke of how God, through the *Logos*, "gathered up the fragments from every side ... and welded into one what had been broken."[35] In the *Logos*, each constituent identity is now united with other constituent identities, for each constituent presumes the other rather than opposes the other. In Bonaventuran terms, each constituent in its own way expresses the one infinite plurality of ideas within the *Logos* that other constituents also express. Moreover, though each constituent is transformed in the *Logos*, it is not

---

32. Ibid., 40.

33. Ibid., 44–47.

34. For greater detail on this, see Cousins, *Bonaventure and the Coincidence of Opposites*.

35. Cited in de Lubac, *Catholicism*, 36, footnote 35.

required to surrender its integrity in order to be harmonized in the *Logos* or to one another. In so being transformed in the *Logos*, each constituent arrives at a greater integrity. In Augustinian terms, each constituent love in the migrant becomes more itself the closer it gets to the *Logos*.

One Eucharistic Multiple

While the co-inhering of opposing constituent identities participating in the co-inhering of the Trinity in a Triune unity may sound good in theory, there remains the question of a concrete practice that forms the concrete locus in which this co-inhering of an identity to the *Logos* is actualized. To this, attention will turn to a practice not easily associated with immigration, namely the practice of the Eucharistic liturgy. More specifically, following the lead of Graham Ward, attention will be given here to the breaking or fraction of the Eucharistic bread, where the one bread, now the one Body of Christ, is broken, distributed, and consumed by the congregation. Ward articulates an understanding of the Eucharist at this juncture—an understanding articulated most explicitly in the Anglican Sarum Missal—in which the dispersed particles of the Eucharistic host do not disappear into the particulars of the recipient. Rather, the dispersal becomes the means of a greater communion of the many recipients into the one Eucharistic Body of Christ as "subsequent other bodies come to share in it."[36]

It is argued that, in a Eucharistic light, one can see multiplicity—the migrant's and the native-born's alike—not merely as a problematique hopelessly lacking a solution. Rather, multiplicity can be seen as redemptive insofar as it—and the body that bears it—is sacramentally abiding in the multiplicity of the broken body of Christ truly present in the Eucharistic bread.[37] No longer will the migrant's constellation of constituent identities be working in tension with each other and facilitating the "endless dispersal," as is the case in the postmodern position. When participating in the Eucharistic logic of breaking, distribution, and communion, the fragmentation of the body becomes not a dissolution but an expansion, what Graham

---

36. Ward, *Cities of God*, 152.

37. It must be stated that this work takes for granted the doctrine of the real Eucharistic presence of Christ in the bread and the wine. The success of Eucharistic practice to render fruitful the problem of multiplicity hinges on the strong sacramentality that this doctrine embodies. While it would be impossible to exhaustively explore the issue of sacramentality here, it will be submitted that were the Eucharistic presence be merely symbolic, the ontological divide between the Eucharistic elements and the Body of Christ would be too great to make any meaningful ontological connection between the Body of Christ and that of the migrant, which receives the Eucharistic elements.

Ward calls an "expansion *en Christo*."[38] This is because the Body of Christ, while broken, nonetheless was not dispersed. This is prefigured in the rather ironic fulfillment of the prophecy that even though the body of Christ was broken on the cross, "not one of his bones shall be broken."[39] For Ward, the severely wounded body of Christ did not disperse into nothingness. Rather, the wounds became the means by which His body expanded in order to take in His creatures and give new life, to become the basis of a new act of creation. Indeed, it is interesting to note that in his essays on the six days of creation, Bonaventure spoke of a new creation, what he called a "Seraphic Order," emerging to replace the current order. However, such an order is not won by conquest, but by the suffering flesh of the Mystical Body of Christ.[40] More explicitly, Delio notes a sermon on the stigmata of St. Francis of Assisi, in which Bonaventure asserted that the "flesh of those who have made the journey of love in union with God," or more specifically, the wounds of that flesh, form the gateways by which that the new creation, located in Christ, enters into this world.[41]

The important stage in the Eucharist that ties what is going on in the Body of Christ to what is going on in the body of the migrant occurs at the point of the reception of the Eucharist. Having spoken of the extension of Christ's body above, Ward goes on to speak of the importance of Christ's "handing-over" of his own body at the Lord's supper, first to the disciples, then to the world, as that all-important catalyst to the process of the dissemination of Christ's Body.[42] In making the link between the Body of Christ and the body of the recipient, Ward relies on a sermon by Gregory of Nyssa, in which he says that when Christ's Body "is in ours, [the former] translates and transmutes the whole into itself."[43] In other words, at the point of reception of the Eucharist, the multiplicity of the migrant becomes transmuted into the extended singularity of Christ's Body.

Multiplicity becomes not a disappearance of the migrant's body but a participation in the extending pluralization of Christ's Body. In being united in the Body of the *Logos,* the *logos* as the extension of the migrant's body become life giving in two interconnected ways. First, insofar as the body of the migrant is transmuted into the Body of the Eucharistic Christ, the

---

38. Ward, *Cities of God*, 106.
39. John 19:36.
40. *Collationes in Hexaemeron* 20.15. Cited in Delio, *Simply Bonaventure*, 153.
41. Ibid., 154.
42. Key to this is the passage in the Synoptic Gospels in which, at the Lord's Supper, Christ takes bread, names it "my Body," and couples it with the exhortation for his disciples to take it.
43. See *The Great Catechism*, 37.x. Cited in Ward, *Cities of God*, 270, footnote 15.

outward wounds of the migrant that in turn form his identity, be they the wounds of xenophobic assault or the wounds of separation from compatriots from the country of birth, become iconic of the wounds that reside within each and every person, migrant and native-born alike. The wounds, the outward sign of opposition to the migrant, can become the very site for coincidence, a forging a unity where all are united in their own unique forms of woundedness. Secondly, if we were to take Bonaventure's observation in the *Hexaemeron* seriously, the union of wounded bodies in the Eucharistic Body of Christ is also life giving in opening the pathways toward a new creation beyond the confines of the world we see. Ward alludes to the possibilities of this participation in bringing about this new order in the special vocation of the Eucharistic body of the recipient, and by extension, the migrant. In the saving pluralization of Eucharistic Body of Christ, the migrant's pluralistic body is no longer a centrifuge of fragments waiting to disperse into nothingness. Rather, in the same way that the dissemination of the Body of Christ assembles possibilities that may never have existed, the body of the migrant in the *Logos* can be seen as realizing the unfolding of a new creation in its "offering a space for the meeting and mapping of other specified bodies" and thereby becoming a coincidence of possibilities that may never have existed before.[44]

Conclusion

This article has defended a Eucharistic rubric by which it sought to show how "the Christian doctrines of the incarnation and creation stand opposed to closed immanentalist systems [and] . . . stand opposed also to the endless deferral and unquenchable grief for a lost body."[45] More specifically, it sought to show how, when it comes to the migrant's love of many lands, the *Logos* stands as the counterpoint to the dichotomy within contemporary politics of either smooth uniformity on the one hand or splintered fragmentation on the other. When this dichotomy is overcome in the *Logos*, the migrant's love of more than one nation is no longer seen as merely a means of disintegrating the *polis*. Rather, it is precisely through the migrant's affiliation of the land of origin that greater affiliation to the land of residence blossoms. Instead of enmity, the migrant's love of many lands can embody a bridge for greater amity between nations, as they mirror the coincidence of opposing elements in the *Logos*.

44. Ibid., 95.
45. Ibid., 106.

This is not achieved by a greater centrality to the migrant's ties to the *polis*, but via a greater centrality to the migrant's ties to Christ. This means that Christ is more than an optional add-on in resolving the impasse of a migrant's love of many lands. This article has asserted that the *Logos* is the indispensable linchpin of a transformation of that multiplicity of loves from something that dissolves into something that redeems. It is only in Christ and in his Body that the migrant can become an icon that knocks our pretensions to a false stability and unity both within the Church and within the *polis*, and it is only in Christ that multiplicitous love can be transformed from a cacophony to a symphony. The migrant's multiplicitous body—indeed all bodies, since all bodies are multiplicitous—when anchored and expanded within the context of the Eucharistic Body of Christ, can become (in its attempts at harmonizing participation in social, cultural, and civic bodies) a portal for others to see the unity of the new heaven and new earth.

8

Becoming a Multicultural Church in the Context of Neo-Nationalism: The New Challenges Facing Catholics in Japan

MARK R. MULLINS

Introduction

The close relationship between patterns of immigration and the spread of the Catholic Church is well documented in many places—the United States, Canada, and Australia, for example—but it has been largely irrelevant for understanding similar developments in Japan until very recently. The arrival of migrant laborers from Catholic countries began in the 1980s and, over the course of several decades, has contributed to the emergence of diaspora religious communities within the church in Japan. This has created an unanticipated growth in the Catholic population and created new challenges for a minority church that, for the past half century, has focused on the task of "inculturation" and what it means to be a "Japanese" church.

This essay briefly sketches the historical context for understanding the recent impact of the new migrant workers and the Japanese Catholic efforts to transform the church into a multicultural community that welcomes their contributions and full participation in parish life. In addition to our consideration of the "pastoral" response within the church, we will also examine the "prophetic" response of the Catholic bishops to the current situation outside of the church. The new effort to create multicultural parishes is being initiated at a difficult time; that is, when the larger Japanese society is being shaped by neo-nationalistic movements and political initiatives, which are pushing public institutions to adopt policies that only support a narrow essentialist Japanese identity and provide little social space or support for cultural and religious minorities. We will consider how the Catholic Bishops' Conference of Japan and the Japan Catholic Council on Justice and Peace have been critically addressing this larger context as they seek to create a more inclusive community and hospitable environment for immigrants within both church and society.

Overview

The Catholic Church has a long history in Japan that stretches back to the Society of Jesus and its early mission to Japan, initiated by Francis Xavier in 1549. After a very successful period of evangelization—now referred to as "the Christian Century"—the political authorities identified the transplanted faith as an "evil religion" (*jakyō*) and incompatible with Japanese tradition and values. The government issued a nationwide ban on the Catholic religion in 1614, which was followed by three decades of intense persecution. Priests were expelled and followers who refused to renounce their faith faced arrest, torture, and martyrdom. Some followers sought to preserve their faith secretly in underground or "hidden" communities (referred to as the Kakure Kirishitan), and a number of these communities survived the period of national isolation (*sakoku*) that stretched from 1635 until Japan was forced to reopen its doors to the West in 1858.

The second wave of Catholic mission to Japan began in 1859 with the arrival of Société des Missions Etrangères, a missionary society from France. Missionaries from many other religious orders soon followed. Recovering some members who had reemerged from the "hidden" communities, the church grew significantly over the course of several decades. Increasing nationalism and the empire-building aspirations of the Japanese government, however, soon created a difficult situation for both the Catholic and Protestant missionary enterprises due to their relationships and loyalty to "foreign" religious institutions and governments. By the late 1930s, the growth of Christian churches of all denominations was brought to a virtual halt under the difficult wartime atmosphere and conditions.

The third wave of Catholic mission began at the end of World War II, when the Supreme Commander of Allied Powers, General Douglas MacArthur, welcomed the return of both Catholic and Protestant missionaries throughout the Occupation period with the understanding that they would contribute to the rebuilding of war-devastated Japan. MacArthur was convinced that the "democratization" of Japan would require "Christianization," and he used the resources of the Occupation Forces to facilitate and support the postwar missionary movement in various ways.

In the postwar free-market religious economy, the Catholic Church managed to grow, and many of its institutions—schools, social welfare, and medical facilities—became widely recognized for their contributions to Japanese society. Today the Catholic Church in Japan claims a membership of 444,441, some 993 parishes, 848 religious houses and missionary institutions, forty-two medical facilities (including twenty-three hospitals), 605 social welfare facilities (nursing homes, daycare facilities, orphanages), and 850 educational institutions (including twenty-one universities, sixteen junior colleges, 114 high schools, and 103 junior high schools).[1] There are some 350,000 students enrolled in the Catholic schools, so the social influence and impact of the church clearly extends beyond the number of those who actually pursue baptism and church membership.

Although Christianity is often labeled as a "Western" religion, this broad category tends to obscure the multicultural and multinational nature of the missionary movement since the mid-nineteenth century. The Catholic faith has been spread in Japan by some eighty-five religious orders from fifteen different national headquarters. These diverse cultural expressions of the faith have been institutionalized by religious orders in schools and parishes across Japan. Of course, "foreign" priests and religious are not the only significant actors in the development of the Church in Japan. In fact, over the decades there has been a gradual but significant shift from the church being a foreign missionary enterprise to one being led largely by Japanese priests and religious. Today, in fact, there are twenty-seven Japanese bishops leading the church; also, some 452 of 499 diocesan priests are Japanese; 410 of 896 religious are Japanese; and 880 of 1,422 priests are Japanese. In short, Japanese Catholics have also been active agents in the reception and reshaping of this transplanted faith, especially since the Second Vatican Council (1962–1965).

The church in Japan, like many local churches around the world, has focused a great deal of effort on "inculturating the Gospel" over the past half-century. This has involved the de-Europeanization of various aspects of the faith and an effort to create new cultural forms more compatible with Japanese religious sensibilities and felt needs.[2] Even though the Western and Eurocentric nature of the church has often been offered as a major reason for the slow growth in Japan, the various efforts in inculturation (or "Japa-

---

1 This data is drawn from Catholic Bishops' Conference of Japan (CBCJ), *Statistics of the Catholic Church in Japan 2012*.

2. For more details on these experiments in inculturation, see Mullins, "Between Inculturation and Globalization," 171–77.

nization") have not proved to be particularly effective in attracting more Japanese to the faith. With only 444,441 members, the church remains a small minority in Japan. Even when combined with the membership of Protestant and Orthodox churches, the total Christian population of 1,920,892 constitutes only 1 percent of the population.

Various indicators gleaned from annual statistics suggest that steady decline rather than growth will likely characterize the church in the decades ahead.[3] Between 1995 and 2012, for example, the enrollment in Sunday schools and catechism classes has dropped significantly. For the elementary or primary school age children, the number has declined from 20,077 to 13,779, and for the high school age bracket, from 11,472 down to 3,167. Similarly, the number of infant and adult baptisms combined has declined from 10,803 to 5,694 during the same time period. Average mass attendance has also dropped by over 35,000 for Sundays, some 43,000 for Easter, and over 82,000 at Christmas.[4] The decline in the number of priests—from 1,758 to 1,422—provides another indicator of institutional decline and suggests a leadership crisis is on the horizon. In 2005, there were already reports of a number of "priestless parishes" where laity were conducting liturgies on Sunday.[5] Since there are now 1,841 parishes, religious houses, and mission centers and only 1,422 priests, it means that there are at least a few hundred places without a full-time priest, and many parishes must share priests who circulate among them. Needless to say, these figures are closely related to the basic demographic realities shaping all social institutions in contemporary Japan—a low birthrate and aging population—which means many other religious organizations and various public and private social institutions are similarly struggling with patterns of decline.

Diaspora Catholics and the Pastoral Response of the Church in Japan

It is in the context of these rather gloomy signs of decline that the church has been overwhelmed with a wave of new migrant workers—many from predominantly Catholic countries like Brazil and the Philippines—who

---

3. These annual statistics are provided by the Catholic Bishops' Conference of Japan and available online at http://www.cbcj.catholic.jp/jpn/.

4. The figures for foreign language masses are not included here.

5. According to a report in the *Japan Catholic News* (no. 1103, February 2005), there were already twenty parishes in the Diocese of Sendai in Northern Honshū that were without a resident priest. Given the continued decline in the number of priests, this is undoubtedly becoming a serious problem in many other dioceses as well.

often seek out the church as a familiar place of support in the new and unfamiliar environment. Since the late 1980s, the number of foreign workers arriving in Japan has steadily increased to partially make up for the shrinking Japanese workforce and shortage of laborers needed for the less attractive jobs widely known as the three Ks—*kiken* (dangerous), *kitanai* (dirty), and *kitsui* (demanding)—usually associated with factory work, construction, and domestic jobs. The highest concentrations of these migrant workers are in Yokohama, Nagoya, Tokyo, Saitama, Kyoto, and Osaka, which are also the areas where many Catholic parishes have suddenly found themselves with many new non-Japanese parishioners.

The Catholic Bishops' Conference in Japan has not included this influx of non-Japanese Catholics in the annual statistical reports, but the Catholic Commission of Japan for Migrants, Refugees, and People on the Move began to gather data on this new type of parishioner and reported that the number had dramatically increased between 1996 and 2005, with foreign parishioners now exceeding the number of Japanese members (see Table 1).[6] By 2005, in fact, the percentage of non-Japanese members had reached 81 percent for both the Dioceses of Nagoya and Saitama, 69 percent for both Kyoto and Yokohama, 47 percent for Sendai, 46 percent for Niigata, and 45 percent for Tokyo. While the non-Japanese parishioners come from many different countries—China, Vietnam, Korea, and Peru, for example—the two major sources of migrant workers are Brazil and the Philippines, two countries where the Catholic Church has dominated religious life for centuries.

Table 1. Japanese and Foreign Membership, 1996 to 2005.

	Japanese Members	**Foreign Members**
1996	436,543 (58%)	317,185 (42%)
2001	441,906 (52%)	406,972 (48%)
2005	449,925 (46%)	529,452 (54%)

In 2011, the number of Filipinos in Japan was 220,882.[7] Many of these are domestics or production workers; since 2005 the number coming as entertainers has declined, and the number coming as caregivers and nurses is gradually increasing as Japan adjusts some of the requirements to work in this field in order to address the needs of Japan's aging population.

6. The Catholic Commission's report and these statistics were made available online some years ago, but are no longer preserved on the site (http://www.jcarm.com/).

7. See International Organization on Migration, *Country Migration Report: The Philippines*, 55.

Since over 80 percent of the population in the Philippines is Catholic, it is understandable that many workers look for a supportive parish community soon after their arrival in Japan.

Although the percentage of Catholics in Brazil is lower than in the Philippines, and has declined markedly from 95.6 percent in 1910 to 65 percent in 2010,[8] the church has still been a significant influence on Japanese immigrants to Brazil since they began arriving in 1908. It is not surprising that increasing numbers of Japanese converted to Roman Catholicism as they adapted to life in Brazil given the Church's prominent position in that culture. Over the course of several generations, the Japanese community in Brazil grew to over a million, and many descendants of the early Japanese migrants, referred to as *Nikkeijin*, began the process of reverse migration to take advantage of better employment opportunities in Japan from the 1980s. By 2001, in fact, some 250,000 *Nikkeijin* had returned to Japan.[9] Since many came from families that had converted to Catholicism after migrating to Brazil, it is understandable why many would find their way to churches in Japan as a familiar place and a source of community support.[10] Although on a smaller scale, a significant number of migrant laborers from Peru (50,000) and Vietnam (40,000) have also found their way to the church in Japan, adding to the cultural and linguistic diversity.

Under these new circumstances—globalization and the increased presence of Catholics from various countries and cultures—Cardinal Peter Seichi Shirayanagi has recognized that the church in Japan can no longer be preoccupied with inculturation, stating that "we are no longer permitted to think only of how we can make it our size." "Just as Christ's love drove him to forego his divine privilege," he further explains, "so we too must at times put aside our identity as Japanese. We are entering an era in which we must accept as it stands a church community composed of parishioners of many cultures and many tongues."[11]

Here I can only highlight a few aspects of the pastoral response to the needs of immigrants and the impact of diaspora communities on the larger Japanese Church. First, one can observe that serious efforts have been made to provide religious services in multiple languages in parishes across Japan.

8. See Pew Research Center, "Global Catholic Population."

9. Quero, "Worshiping in (Un) Familiar Land," 26.

10. Our concern here is primarily with the impact of immigrants on the Catholic Church in Japan, but it is important to recognize that many other forms of religion—Protestant sects, Pentecostal movements, and new religions—have also accompanied immigrants from Latin America to Japan. For a broader comparative perspective, see Quero and Shoji, *Transnational Faiths*.

11. Tran, "Toward Multicultural Church Communities," 29.

Foreign language masses are particularly concentrated in Saitama, Tokyo, Yokohama, Nagoya, and Osaka.[12] In 2005, for example, the Saitama Diocese conducted twenty-six masses in English, fourteen in Spanish, twelve in Portuguese, seven in Tagalog, four in Korean, four in Vietnamese, and one in Chinese. Although the number of foreign language masses has declined slightly since then, close to seven hundred were conducted each month in 2012.

Second, the church has also established other institutions to address the needs of migrants. The Catholic Tokyo International Center (CTIC), for example, was established in 1990 to provide support for migrants and refugees in multiple languages. Located in the Meguro Church, it provides various support services—legal advice and counseling, for example—for migrants and refugees in multiple languages (Japanese, English, Tagalog, Portuguese, Spanish, Chinese, and Italian) and helps disseminate information about foreign language masses in parishes throughout the Tokyo and Chiba areas.[13] The Maryknoll mission work has also expanded to include pastoral care of large Latino populations in the Kyoto Diocese, and in Tokyo, a Philippine Migrant Workers Center is operated in the Maryknoll house. The Maryknolls also maintain the Kalakasan Migrant Women's Empowerment Center in Kawasaki, just outside Tokyo, which ministers to migrant women who have been victims of domestic abuse, providing crisis intervention and counseling, and operating programs to help their bicultural children flourish in the midst of difficult circumstances.[14] Even the Fukuoka Diocese on the island of Kyushu in southwestern Japan offers masses in Spanish and English, and through the Minoshima Pastoral Center provides special programs and care for migrant workers, particularly Peruvians of Japanese background.

Third, the church has made serious efforts to incorporate new cultural expressions of the faith and affirm the contributions of the newcomers to parish life. While many of these migrant workers share the Catholic faith with Japanese parishioners, they bring to Japan very different cultural traditions and expectation about how that faith should be practiced and celebrated. Hugo Quero,[15] for example, reports on a new Brazilian-inspired parish that was recently established in Jōso, part of the Diocese of Saitama just outside of Tokyo, where a large number of Brazilian *Nikkeijin*

12. For the number of foreign language masses for each diocese, see Mullins, "Between Inculturation and Globalization," 184.

13. See the CTIC homepage, http://www.ctic.jp.

14. For information on the Kalakasan Center, see the homepage, http://kalakasan.com.

15. Quero, "Worshiping in (Un)Familiar Land."

are concentrated. With the cooperation and joint fundraising of both local Japanese members and migrant workers, the parish was able to build and consecrate a new church building in 2009. Some six hundred individuals attended the consecration ceremony and the dedication of the church "to Our Lady of Aparecida, a popular Brazilian devotion," which affirmed the important place of the *Nikkeijin* in this new parish community. The multicultural nature of the community is also apparent in the fact that a Brazilian priest is serving this parish and additional pastoral care is being provided by three sisters of the Daughters of Jesus—one Japanese, one Filipino, and one Brazilian.[16] Quero also reports on a relatively successful multicultural parish initiative launched in Hamamatsu in 1995. Under the leadership of Father Higa, the church there formed the Hope Group (Grupo Esperança) to address the needs of a number of migrants concentrated in this industrial area. Over the course of a couple of decades, a multicultural and multilingual parish has been created and attracted migrants who attend the services conducted trilingually—either in Japanese, Portuguese, and Spanish or in Japanese, Tagalog, and English. While one might think this kind of service would be frustrating and a disappointment to each language group, over six hundred people attended the first mass and over three hundred the second one during the Easter festivities. According to Quero, these experiments of integrating very different groups in multicultural parishes across Japan is ongoing, and much remains to be sorted out since "different spiritualities and different theologies" are encountering each other "within the same confessional church."[17]

The rapid pluralization of the membership base over the course of two decades has presented new challenges to the church in Japan. As we have seen, some serious efforts have been made to provide pastoral care and respond to the various needs of the migrant workers and their families, but it is apparent that the resources of this minority church have been stretched to

---

16. This development is highlighted in *Catholic Weekly,* "New Joso Church to be Evangelization Center for Multi-Cultural Communities."

17. Quero, "Worshiping in (Un) Familiar Land," 33–34. For additional studies and concrete examples of the situation in these contemporary parishes, see the special issue on "Migrants and the Catholic Church in Japan" of the *Journal of Sophia Asian Studies,* edited by Takefumi Terada, professor of anthropology at Sophia University, Tokyo. It includes interviews with a priest working in Filipino Catholic communities, a report on the activities of the Catholic Tokyo International Center, a study of Japanese Brazilian migrants in Japanese parishes, and a study of the issues facing the second generation of bicultural children in the Church. The articles and interviews in this special issue are available online at http://digital-archives.sophia.ac.jp/repository/search?f.3=2008-12-27&kw=%E4%B8%8A%E6%99%BA%E3%82%A2%E3%82%B8%E3%82%A2%E5%A D%A6&vt=&lang=en#refine.

the limit. The church is receiving some assistance from priests and religious from the Philippines, Brazil, and nearby Korea. This support is greatly appreciated, but it is widely recognized that priests will need to be retrained and seminarians educated overseas so that Japanese will be better prepared to provide pastoral care and services in the languages of the immigrants in Japan.[18]

During the two decades that the church has been undergoing internal pluralization, Japanese society as a whole has been increasingly shaped by a nationalistic government that has passed legislation promoting policies of homogenization and an essentialist version of Japanese identity. It is this larger social context that we must consider—particularly the resurgence of neo-nationalism—in order to understand why the leadership of the Catholic Church has embraced a new prophetic role in contemporary Japanese society.

The Resurgence of Nationalism in Post-1995 Japan

It is widely recognized that 1995 represents a watershed moment in modern Japan due to several events that occurred in close succession, which combined to create a national sense of social crisis.[19] On January 17, a major earthquake—7.3 on the Richter scale—struck the Osaka-Kobe area and caused major damage to the infrastructure of this densely populated urban center, leading to the loss of over six thousand lives. Less than three months later, members of Aum Shinrikyō, a new religious movement founded in the mid-1980s, launched a sarin gas attack on several lines of the Tokyo Metro subway system on March 20, which resulted in thirteen deaths and over five thousand injuries due to exposure to the poison gas. Lastly, August 15 of that year, which marked the fiftieth anniversary of the end of World War II, was accompanied by many commemorative events and widespread debate about how Japan's imperial past should be remembered and taught in the public schools. Recall that Japan has faced an even larger crisis moment since then with the triple disaster of 2011—earthquake, tsunami, and nuclear accident—which has left the nation reeling as it attempts to address major social, health, and economic problems.

---

18. This point has been emphasized by Fr. Kaoru Kawaguchi, former director of the Catholic Tokyo International Center; see Kawaguchi, "Interview Record 2," 128.

19. Here, I am drawing on material from my more detailed analysis of the relationship between social crisis and the resurgence of nationalism; see Mullins, "Neo-Nationalist Response to the Aum Crisis."

The widespread sense of social crisis that spread as a result of these disasters also created an environment in which the political interests and agenda of neo-nationalist leaders and groups have found a more receptive audience and their initiatives are gaining traction. The overall goal of these religious and political groups is to reverse the process of "imperialist secularization" brought about during the Allied Occupation of Japan, which largely removed the influence of Shinto values and institutions from public life. While conservative religious groups and politicians have sought to restore such Japanese traditions to the public sphere since the end of the Occupation, it has only been in the context of the post-1995/2011 crisis situation that these neo-nationalist initiatives have gained some traction. Over the past two decades, leaders of the national government—largely administrations of the Liberal Democratic Party (LDP)—have renewed the efforts to (1) restore state support for Yasukuni Shrine, a controversial site dedicated to the war dead and Class-A war criminals; (2) revise the Fundamental Education Law in order to restore the emphasis on patriotism; and (3) revise the postwar "Peace" Constitution (1947)—particularly Article 9—so that Japan can truly become a "normal nation" again.[20]

The Prophetic Response of the Catholic Bishops

Many Catholics, other religious minorities, and secular intellectuals are concerned that these "restoration" efforts are incompatible with the Constitution of Japan (1947), which guarantees its citizens the "right to life, liberty, and the pursuit of happiness" (Article 13), the freedom of religion, and the clear separation of religion from the state (Articles 20 and 89). The Catholic bishops have been critically engaging these developments in public life in an effort to ensure that Japanese society becomes a just and hospitable environment for all people.

Over the past three decades, the Catholic Bishops' Conference of Japan and the Japan Catholic Council on Peace and Justice have issued numerous statements of protest to the government regarding efforts to renationalize

---

20. It is important to recognize that many LDP Diet members have long been closely associated with the Association of Shinto Shrines and its political arm *Shinseiren*—established in 1969, and more recently with the newer political group Nippon Kaigi ("Japan Conference"), established in 1997. The number of LDP politicians affiliated with this Shinto political association has steadily increased over the decades: in 1984, there were only forty-four Diet members claimed by this association, but this had grown to 204 by late 2013 (which represents 28 percent of the Diet membership). The leadership of the LDP today, in fact, essentially promotes the shared values and goals of these two organizations.

Yasukuni Shrine and to promote official visits by the prime minister and government officials, and to the more recent legalization of the *Hinomaru* (national flag) and *Kimigayo* (national anthem), approval of revisionist history textbooks for public schools, revision of the Fundamental Education Law, and the proposal of the Liberal Democratic Party to revise the Constitution (particularly Articles 9, 20, and 89).[21] Pastoral letters addressing these issues have also been distributed widely to the faithful, as the bishops are concerned that the church be careful not to embrace the government's agenda as it did in the 1930s and 1940s. Their stance today is based on critical self-reflection and a belief that the church failed to perform its prophetic task during the difficult circumstances of the wartime period. Here we can only briefly consider a few concrete examples of the critical response of Catholics to legislation surrounding Japan's national symbols, public education, and proposed revisions to the Constitution of Japan, particularly in relation to their concerns for the life of diaspora communities and the rights of religious minorities.

National Symbols and Public Education

Following Japan's defeat and subsequent Occupation in August 1945, the use of the flag and anthem was restricted and discouraged until January 1949, when the Supreme Commander of Allied Powers rescinded the restriction and General MacArthur announced in his New Year message that the Japanese people could once again freely use the flag and anthem.[22] It was in 1958 that the Ministry of Education first instructed public schools that it was "desirable" for the flag to be raised and the anthem sung at official school events (entrance and graduation ceremonies). Under these "soft" guidelines, however, compliance rates were not too impressive. There was considerable opposition from members of the teachers' union, Nikkyōso, and other social critics to the use of these national symbols in the schools, since they had once been used for the mobilization of both teachers and students in wartime Japan. Although the Ministry of Education issued instructions in 1989 mandating that the flag and anthem be used in all entrance and graduation ceremonies, many teachers and some schools refused to comply.

---

21. Catholic Bishops' Conference of Japan, *A Compendium of Official Statements*. Some of these official statements and documents are also available online at http://www.cbcj.catholic.jp/jpn/doc/doc_bsps.htm#syukyo and http://www.cbcj.catholic.jp/jpn/doc/cbcj/061102.htm.

22. Cripps, "Flags and Fanfares," 81. This section on conflict over the use of flag and anthem in public schools draws on my earlier study; see Mullins, "Japanese Responses."

It is important to note here that the Hinomaru and Kimigayo had never been officially approved as the nation's flag and anthem by any government administration. Some officials and politicians thought that the problems surrounding use of these symbols could be resolved if they were "officially" acknowledged by passing legislation in the Diet, Japan's national bicameral legislature. It was during the administration of Prime Minister Keizō Obuchi that this was finally achieved in 1999.[23] At the time this legislation was being debated in the Diet, the Prime Minister assured all concerned that freedom of conscience would be protected and no coercion would ever be involved in public institutions if the bill passed.[24]

Many religious leaders and public intellectuals remained unconvinced and continued to raise serious concerns about the proposed legislation. The Catholic Council on Justice and Peace, for example, sent a letter of appeal to Prime Minister Obuchi on March 12, 1999, which expressed opposition to the government's rushed efforts to legalize the flag and anthem. According to the council's interpretation, the Hinomaru is a symbol of Japan's military aggression and invasion in Asia. Likewise, the lyrics of the Kimigayo express praise for the emperor as the ruler of Japan, which violates Japan's postwar constitution that placed the government clearly in the hands of the people. Rather than approving these as the symbols of the nation, the letter urged government representatives to consider a new flag and anthem that would reflect the principles of peace and democratic values that are foundational to Japan's Constitution.[25] Months later, just four days before the legislation was passed, the Japan Catholic Council on Justice and Peace and several

23. Even though the bill was passed by the Diet, it did not actually represent the view of the majority of Japanese on this issue. When the national flag and anthem legislation was being debated, for example, an opinion poll conducted by the *Mainichi Shinbun* (July 14, 1999) found that 43 percent were in favor of official recognition of the *Hinomaru* as the national flag, while some 52 percent were opposed or in favor of a more careful debate and discussion; similarly, 36 percent were in favor of official recognition of *Kimigayo*, while some 58 percent were opposed or in favor of more serious debate.

24. For the original Japanese record of Prime Minister Obuchi's explanation on June 29, 1969, see http://sdaigo.cocolog-nifty.com/kokkikokkasingirokushoroku.pdf.

25. The March 12, 1999 appeal regarding Hinomaru and Kimigayo and other official statements introduced here are contained in the following publications of the Catholic Bishops' Conference of Japan, or available online at the sites indicated: *Katorikku Kyōkai no Shakai Mondai ni Kansuru Kōteki Hatsugenshū* [A Compendium of Official Statements of the Catholic Church on Social Problems]; *Nihon Katorikku Shikyō Kyōgikai Iya-bukku 2008* [The 2008 Japan Catholic Yearbook]; http://www.cbcj.catholic.jp/jpn/doc/doc_bsps.htm#syukyo; http://www.cbcj.catholic.jp/jpn/doc/cbcj/061102.htm; http://www.jccjp.org/jccjp/zi_liao_shi.html; http://www.cbcj.catholic.jp/jpn/doc/cbcj/140703.htm; and http://www.cbcj.catholic.jp/jpn/doc/cbcj/131226.htm.

Protestant bodies issued a joint declaration addressed to the prime minister, other representatives of the Liberal Democratic Party, and to the Kōmeitō Party—which was a part of the LDP coalition government—to express their strong opposition to the legalization initiative.[26] The declaration states that if the legislation is passed, it will undoubtedly lead to coercion and a violation of the individual rights and freedoms that are protected by the constitution. In particular, it expressed concern for public school teachers who may be forced to provide leadership in the ritual use of the Hinomaru and Kimigayo against their will.[27]

As it turns out, their concerns were justified. Before the end of the year, the Ministry of Education reaffirmed its instructions to require all public schools to use the "legal symbols" for official events, such as entrance and graduation ceremonies, and worked closely with school boards to see that the rules were enforced. The passing of this legislation clearly strengthened the position of politicians and educators who felt it was their duty to have all teachers and staff lead students by example in singing the national anthem before the flag for important school ceremonies. Even before the intensification of "guidance" from the Ministry of Education, a number of teachers had already been disciplined for failing to comply with the 1989 guidelines. The situation only became more difficult for teachers after 1999.

For those enforcing the Ministry of Education policy, the primary concern is to preserve the social harmony of the school community and promote patriotism and pride in country. Those teachers refusing to participate are viewed as selfish and excessively individualistic. For the small minority of teachers—whether members of the more critical left teachers' union (Nikkyōso) or Christians—the new policy is a clear sign of Japan's rightward shift and represents a return to the wartime educational policy of coercion. While those imposing the new patriotic rituals do not regard them as "religious," and some who participate may gain a sense of well-being and

---

26. For the English version of the declaration against the legalization of the flag and anthem (*Hinomaru Kimigayo no Hōseika ni Kōgi suru Seimei*), see National Christian Council of Japan, "Position Statement." The Protestant groups involved in the August 9, 1999 declaration were the ecumenical National Christian Council of Japan (Nihon Kirisuto Kyōgikai), the Japan Evangelical Association (Nihon Fukuin Dōmei), the Reformed-Presbyterian Church (Nihon Kirisuto Kyōkai), and the Reformed Church in Japan (Nihon Kirisuto Kaikakuha Kyōkai).

27. The Catholic Church also expressed concern about the use of the national symbols in their own private schools. In a May 15, 2000, letter to the Education Committee of the Japan Catholic Bishops' Conference, the Japan Catholic Council on Justice and Peace appealed to members of the Education Committee not to uncritically incorporate these national symbols into official school events, but reflect on the impact of their possible use in light of the Gospel. This letter also noted that many Catholic schools were already using these symbols in contrast to most Protestant private schools.

Japanese pride through the experience, others forced to participate regard them as oppressive and linked to the wartime civil religion that required public school teachers to participate in rituals of respect toward the Imperial Rescript of Education, singing of the national anthem, and shrine visits.[28]

In a wide-ranging epistle to the faithful in 2004, the Bishops' Committee for Social Concern offered critical reflections on the problems that have emerged in the Tokyo public school system since the Hinomaru and Kimigayo were made "official," drawing particular attention to the situation of non-Japanese:

> This year in the capital city of Tokyo, teachers who did not stand during the raising of the national [Red Sun] flag and the singing of the [You Are Eternal] national anthem, were given punishments, and those children who took the same actions were given a warning. In the Convention on the Rights of the Child, Article 12, it states, "the child who is capable of forming his or her own views [has] the right to express those views freely in all matters." In Article 13, "the right to freedom of expression," in Article 14, "freedom of thought, conscience and religion," are praised. It can be said that these latest responses by the Tokyo government put unjust pressure on the children, are a tightening of management control, and are an infringement of their human rights. The forced use of the "Red Sun" flag and the "You Are Eternal" anthem *directly affects the identity of multicultural children and those children with a foreign nationality*, [same Treaty Article 8], and is a serious problem that cannot help but cause divisions in the classroom.[29]

The pressure on teachers and staff to comply with the Ministry of Education's instructions with regard to flag and anthem increased with the revision of the Fundamental Education Law, passed by the Diet on April 28, 2006, which "restored" patriotic moral education as a central component of public education. The movement to revise the education law can be traced back to discussions that began in the 1960s, but it was Prime Minister

---

28. Today, there are over seven hundred plaintiffs (teachers or staff) at various stages of appeal with district courts and the Supreme Court to either reverse or prevent future disciplinary action for non-compliance. To the dismay of the plaintiffs, the Supreme Court ruled on May 30, 2011, that it was not a violation of the constitution for a principal to instruct and require teachers and staff to stand and sing the Kimiyayo in front of the national flag at school ceremonies. It appears that disciplinary action against teachers in public schools is likely to continue and, perhaps, increase.

29. "In Order to Make Peace Set Your Heart to that of a Child," the 2004 letter addressed to "All Our Brothers and Sisters," is included in *The Catholic Bishops' Conference of Japan Yearbook 2008*, 74. Emphasis mine.

Shinzō Abe, a well-known nationalistic leader, who finally pushed the legislation through the Diet.

While Abe and his supporters firmly believe that this has laid the foundation for restoring a "beautiful Japan," the Catholic Bishops' Conference maintains that the individual rights guaranteed by the constitution are being violated by the strict enforcement of the revised Fundamental Education Law. In fact, the chair of the Social Committee points out that the revised law has provided the basis for a radical shift in the educational system from one that seeks "to nurture individual character to one aimed at cultivating individuals who will comply with the policies of the state."[30]

In response to the government's promotion of the new education law, Catholic representatives raised a number of concerns. Daiji Tani, Bishop of Saitama Diocese and Chair of the Committee for Refugees and Migrants, for example, appealed to the government for more consideration to be given to the educational needs of the increasing number of non-Japanese children and children of mixed marriages, but to no avail.[31] The chair of the Catholic Schools Educational Committee also expressed grave concerns that the revised Fundamental Education Law would eventually allow for state intervention and interference in private schools and, ultimately, lead to the restriction of individual rights and freedom of religious expression.[32] In addition, he raised the possibility that the new law would eventually have an impact even on some 800 private Catholic schools and their 240,000 students, which would further weaken the clear separation of the state and religion. The chair of the Social Committee of the Japan Catholic Bishops' Conference, likewise, criticized the new law and argued that the view of education it advances will prove to be an obstacle for educating students appropriately for the future of Japan and international society.[33]

---

30. This viewpoint appears in a letter from the Chair of the Social Committee of the Japan Catholic Bishops' Conference to Prime Minister Shinzō Abe and Bunmei Ibuki, the Minister of Education, Science, Sports and Culture, dated November 2, 2006. This letter is contained in the 2008 yearbook edited by the Catholic Bishops' Conference of Japan (Katorikku Chūō Kyōgikai 2008, 298–301) and is available online at: http://www.cbcj.catholic.jp/jpn/doc/cbcj/061102.htm. A comparison of the old and new laws—with the changes highlighted—is available on the Ministry of Education's home page: http://www.mext.go.jp/b_menu/kihon/about/06121913/002.pdf.

31. See his April 21, 2006 letter addressed to Prime Minister Koizumi, included in *The Catholic Bishops' Conference of Japan Yearbook 2008*, 289.

32. See his September 26, 2006 letter to Prime Minister Abe and Ministry of Education, included in *The Catholic Bishops' Conference of Japan Yearbook 2008*.

33. See his November 2, 2006 letter to Prime Minister Abe in *The Catholic Bishops' Conference of Japan Yearbook 2008*, 298–301, and online at http://www.cbcj.catholic.jp/jpn/doc/cbcj/061102.htm.

Constitutional Revision and Religious Freedom

Given the impact of legalization of the flag and anthem in 1999 and the revision of the Fundamental Education Law in 2006, Catholics and other religious minorities are particularly concerned about the plans of the Liberal Democratic Party (LDP) to revise the postwar Constitution. This has become a serious issue since the return to power of the LDP in December 2012, after several years of leadership by three successive prime ministers from the Democratic Party (DPJ). Shinzō Abe, the leading advocate for constitutional revision, who began his second tenure as prime minister in December 2012, has resumed this agenda. The sweeping victory of the LDP and its allies in the July 2016 election means that by most counts the current government now has the required two-thirds majority in both the lower and upper houses of parliament to push ahead with plans to revise Japan's pacifist constitution. There are still major challenges, however. The main coalition partner, Kōmeitō, is supported by members of Sōka Gakkai, a large Buddhist and pacifist religious organization, so proposed scrapping of Article 9 is still likely to face serious opposition in the Diet.

The Japan Catholic Council for Justice and Peace and the Catholic Bishops' Conference have long seen the protection of Article 9 as one of their key responsibilities, a conviction shared by other Christian churches as well as representatives of other religious traditions. The church has issued a number of statements (1986, 1995, 2005) regarding its own war responsibility and failure to fulfill its prophetic role during the war, and has apologized to neighbors in Asia for the suffering it caused. It recognizes the current constitution as a safeguard against repeating such a painful history. Since Prime Minister Abe's return to power, he has reinterpreted Article 9, and his Cabinet has pushed through new security legislation, which will allow for the exercise of a right to collective self-defense. The Catholic Bishops' Conference issued a strongly worded critique of this reversal of the long-held interpretation of the Peace Constitution and Abe's plans to revise this article:

> We, the Catholic Church, are convinced that it is false to think that national security can be ensured by military buildup and the use of force. This is a dangerous idea that aggravates distrust among nations and shatters peace. Moreover, the backtracking on the principles of the Peace Constitution at this moment obstructs the easing of tensions in East Asia so that dialogue and trust among nations will be beyond our reach. Peace is built solely on respect for the dignity of all. Peace can be built only

by sincere reflection upon history and apology for past conduct followed by forgiveness.[34]

Catholics and other religious minorities are also concerned about the impact of proposed revisions of Articles 20 and 89, which guarantee religious freedom and the clear separation of the state from religion. At a bishops' meeting in 2006, the year after the LDP issued its draft for a revised constitution, a question came up for discussion that brought all of the concerns surrounding these Articles into focus: "What will we do if our children are forced to participate in shrine visits (*jinja sanpai*) again?" In light of this question and the potential danger to religious freedom, the bishops felt compelled to call a special meeting to address these issues. In 2007, they published the results of their study and deliberation as *Shinkyō no jiyū to seikyō bunri* (*Freedom of Belief and the Separation of Church and State*). According to the analysis of Bishop Tani in this volume, the LDP's proposed revision to these articles softens the clear separation of state and religion with the addition of a significant qualifying phrase: the state would be prohibited from providing public support for religious activities that "transcend customary practices" (*shūzokuteki kōi*). The bishop argues that this would allow the government to redefine certain practices as "customary" rather than "religious," which would then permit the government to provide financial support for the controversial Yasukuni Shrine as a site of "customary practices," and even allow public educational institutions to require staff and students to participate in these social rituals. Given the impact of the new legislation passed on flag and anthem (1999) and education (2006) over the past two decades, religious minorities have a legitimate concern over the potential expansion of coercion that could result from the proposed revisions.[35]

Conclusion

Acknowledging the church's failure to fulfill its prophetic role during the wartime period, the bishops in recent years have critically engaged neo-nationalistic trends in an effort to protect the rights of the individual religious minorities and to promote public institutions that are hospitable environments for migrant workers and their children. It would be misleading,

34. Catholic Bishops' Conference of Japan, "Statement of Protest."
35. See Catholic Bishops' Conference of Japan, *Yearbook 2008*. For a detailed treatment of these concerns, see the chapter by Bishop Tani in *Shinkyō no jiyū to seikyō bunri*: "Jimintō shinkenpō sōan o kenshō suru [An Examination of the LDP Draft Constitution]."

however, if we did not acknowledge that the critical stance and political engagement of the bishops and other official representatives is not fully supported by the church at large. Japanese Catholics are deeply divided over these public issues.[36] Some members hold to a pietistic or apolitical faith and frown on the public engagement by church representatives, while others actually support the agenda of the LDP and neo-nationalists considered above.

Some of the best-known Japanese Catholics and political figures, in fact, include two LDP Diet members—former Prime Minister Tarō Aso and Eriko Yamatani—who both fully support the current government's position on patriotic education, constitutional revision, and the Yasukuni Shrine. Both are now serving in the cabinet of Prime Minister Abe, who is widely recognized as one of the most nationalistic political figures in postwar Japan. Yamatani is known as a regular contributor to a Catholic radio broadcast, but at the same time represents the far right of the Liberal Democratic Party. She is an active member of Shinseiren, the Shinto-related political group, and regularly appears as a speaker at their study meetings and gatherings held across the country. She has also served as the chief secretary of a group of Diet members who support Yasukuni Shrine visits and is a strong advocate of "official visits" to the shrine by the prime minister—actions which continue to cause major problems for Japan's international relations. In recent years, she even maintained her reelection office within the precincts of a Shinto Shrine (Katori Jingu), in Chiba Prefecture. Although a Catholic, she clearly holds to the view of shrines as "non-religious" civic institutions, a view the Catholic Church adopted under duress from 1936 to 1945.

The well-known Catholic novelist and writer, Ayako Sono, and her husband, Shūmon Miura, are also strong supporters of the LDP government's position on patriotic education and the Yasukuni Shrine.[37] These public figures could very well have more influence than the prophetic Japa-

---

36. For a more detailed analysis of the divisions within the Catholic Church today and the complicated history of the relationship with Shinto and shrine rites, see Breen, "Shinto and Christianity," "The Danger is Ever Present," and "Popes, Bishops, and War Criminals," as well as Mullins, "How Yasukuni Shrine Survived the Occupation."

37. It is worth noting that in the case of Ayako Sono, support for Yasukuni represents a fundamental change. In a 1985 article, she advocated that a new religiously neutral war memorial site be built as an alternative to Yasukuni (See Sono, "I Will Visit Yakusuni Shrine."). She developed her early position while serving as a member of the committee formed by Nakasone's government to review the issue of Yasukuni *sanpai* by prime ministers and other government officials. By 2005, however, she had joined other neonationalists and declared "I will visit Yasukuni" (see Sono, "I Will Visit Yasukuni Shrine."). Her husband, Miura, is the editor of the 2005 *Yasukuni jinja o tadashiku rikai suru tame ni*, a volume in which he expresses his own appreciation for Yasukuni Shrine as a Japanese Catholic.

nese bishops, who these days tend to offer a critical perspective on these controversial issues that is closer to the position of many Protestant leaders.

The Catholic Church is clearly in the midst of a major period of transition in Japan. It has been transformed through its embrace of diaspora communities in recent years and responded positively in many ways to the needs of foreign workers. A number of practical difficulties remain, however. In many parishes, there are clear tensions between older Japanese members and new non-Japanese members surrounding their different expectations, particularly with regard to the use of sacred space, church facilities, and financial matters. Given the low birthrate and declining population in Japan, it is likely that the country will continue to rely on migrant workers to keep the economy functioning, which could maintain the flow of non-Japanese Catholics into parishes across Japan. The church in Japan could very well be revitalized by these new immigrant Catholics, that is, if they are able to transcend their differences and find a way to combine their resources and work together. Given the divided nature of this minority church and the fact that the total number of foreigners comprises only 1.6 percent of Japan's population, it seems unlikely to this observer that the multicultural vision articulated by the Catholic bishops will gain widespread support in the foreseeable future.

9

Diaspora as Mission?
Toward a Theological Interpretation of the Experience of the Cuban Catholic Community in South Florida

ONDINA CORTÉS, RMI

The Cuban Diaspora

Since colonial times, some Cubans have chosen or been forced to live away from their homeland to escape national upheavals, to prepare the various wars of independence, or for reasons of economy and education. In the nineteenth century, Cuban communities developed in Key West, Tampa, and New York.[1] Prominent figures of Cuban history spent most of their adult lives in exile. Such is the case of Venerable Félix Varela, who ministered among New York immigrants and became vicar general of the Diocese of New York in 1837. He was not the only Cuban patriot of the nineteenth century to find himself in exile in the United States. Renowned Cuban patriot José Martí lived the last fifteen years of his life in New York.[2]

However, the longest and largest exodus in Cuban history began soon after the triumph of Fidel Castro's Cuban Revolution on January 1, 1959. Since then, close to a million and a half people, about 10 percent of Cuba's population, have left the island. The majority of these immigrants

---

1. Pérez, "Cubans in the United States," 127–37.

2. Between 1871 and 1959, over 220,000 Cubans lived in the United States, and many of these came as exiles at various points in time. Pérez, "Cubans in the United States," 128.

have settled in Miami. Sociologists Portes and Stepick,[3] among others, have shown how Cuban and succeeding immigrants not only adapted to their new home in Miami, but profoundly transformed it.[4] The Cuban diaspora has had a significant impact on the life of the Catholic Church, particularly in South Florida. Conversely, Catholicism has played a crucial role in the development of this community's corporate identity. Catholic hermeneutical and theological resources have played an important role in the community's discourse and theological self-understanding. One central resource is the preeminent symbol of Our Lady of Charity, patroness of Cuba and icon of the exile's national identity, fertile with a sense of freedom and reconciliation.

To understand the Cuban exile experience, one must look at the distinct waves of the Cuban migration. Each wave, with its particular characteristics, has affected the social, political, economic, and religious makeup of South Florida. The first wave of Cubans, approximately 250,000, arrived by plane and boat from 1959 to 1964.[5] Although among this group were some of the top military and political leaders of the defunct Batista government, it mostly included those affected by nationalization and the Agrarian Reform, as well as those concerned about the revolution's turn to communism, the loss of Catholic schools, and the move to reduce religious practice. Also during this time period, 14,000 children were sent alone by their parents to the United States, as parents feared communist indoctrination of their children and losing their parental rights.

The second wave of Cuban migration took place from 1965 to 1973, and brought 260,500 people to the United States on twice-daily flights called "freedom flights."[6] About half of these people were resettled in different parts of the country.[7] Middle class families disproportionately constituted the demographics of this wave.[8] By this time, Catholic Church membership in Cuba had decreased due to government imposed restrictions on religious institutions and direct and indirect measures against those who declared themselves Catholic.[9] However, once in the United States, Cubans sought to

---

3. Portes and Stepick, *City on the Edge*.

4. On this subject, see Pérez, "Cuban Miami," 83–108; see also Stepick, *This Land Is Our Land*.

5. García, *Havana USA*, 13.

6. Pérez, "Cubans in the United States," 130.

7. Most of them quickly found their way to Miami, the "capital of the exile."

8. García, *Havana USA*, 38.

9. Crahan, "Cuba," 87–112.

be involved in church in a variety of ways. It was during this time that most Catholic Hispanic movements developed in Miami.

In 1980, during the so-called "Mariel Crisis," close to 125,000 Cubans left the island. Exiles were permitted to go from the United States to pick up their families at Mariel Bay, but were forced by the government to bring other people. Those whom the government considered "antisocials" or "scum" (mental patients, homosexuals, and convicts[10]) were placed on boats and sent to the United States. This migration was young, mostly men, and more racially mixed than the previous ones. They had grown up in communist Cuba and, for the most part, had not received any religious formation.

The serious economic crisis that Cuba faced after the dissolution of the Soviet Union prompted a new wave of immigrants. In 1994, close to 200,000 *balseros,* or rafters, crossed the Florida Straits in makeshift rafts, and many died on the way. The ones intercepted at sea were taken to the US military base in Guantanamo, where they stayed for about a year or more until they were allowed entry in the United States. By the 1990s, the Catholic Church in Cuba had emerged from its silence. Many people returned to the church and younger generations were introduced to the faith. Still others had no church contact or practiced Afro-Cuban religions or *Santeria.* Since the arrival of the *balseros,* another 300,000 Cubans have come, mainly through a quota system established to discourage illegal migration. Many continue to come via third countries or overstaying after a visit.

Earlier waves of Cuban immigrants considered themselves exiles or what has been termed "victim diaspora,"[11] implying they left for political reasons. More recent waves self-define or are perceived by other Cubans as economic migrants, and thus, they generally prefer the term of "diaspora," which in recent scholarship and popular use is more widely applied.[12] Cuban exiles in general, but especially earlier waves, did what they could to retain their cultural distinctiveness, since "loss of culture also meant

---

10. While some people in prison had committed serious crimes, others had been convicted for buying or selling food in the black market, for seeking freedom of expression through the arts, or other actions considered subversive. Pedraza, *Political Disaffection,* 153–54.

11. See Cohen, *Global Diasporas,* 39–59.

12. The classical use of the term referred to a coerced migration, usually for religious, ethnic, or political reasons, as in the Jewish experience. Later diaspora studies identified diasporas as groups with a history of dispersal, a collective identity, memories of an idealized homeland, desire for eventual return, and resistance to assimilation. Safran, "Diasporas in Modern Societies," 83–99. More recent scholarship has expanded the concept further to include multiple causes for dispersal (victim, but also labor, trade, and de-territorialized diasporas). See Cohen, *Global Diasporas.*

disintegration of traditional identity and claim on the homeland."[13] However, they also integrated very well into the social, political, and economic life of the United States, thus, reflecting a transnational character.[14] Cubans in the United States are actually more likely to call the United States home than immigrants from any other Latin American country.[15] This ability to integrate, but not to assimilate, has also characterized the attitude of Cuban Catholics toward the Catholic Church in South Florida.

The Impact of the Cuban Diaspora on the Catholic Church of South Florida

The Cuban exodus radically changed the life of the Catholic Church in South Florida. This large and continuous migration posed multiple challenges to the Catholic community. It led the church to open new spaces and expand its offerings. However, the exiles not only came with their needs, but enriched this church with their gifts.

The original massive exodus prompted the US government and the Catholic Church to join forces in creating a variety of programs: resettlement programs, refugee services, special educational programs, and the like. Over time this set of offerings changed. Just to cite some examples, during the early days of the exile, the Catholic Church developed many emergency assistance programs, cared for unaccompanied minors, and helped resettle the refugees throughout the United States. The Mariel Crisis caught the church off-guard, but soon church facilities were turned into shelters to welcome the young men who were arriving and had no family in the United States. More recently, during the *balsero* crisis, priests traveled to the US military base in Guantanamo to offer spiritual assistance to the people interned in the camp. Also, the Archdiocese of Miami opened a program called *Centros Varela* to prepare the newly arrived children to enter the public school system the following year.

At the pastoral level, this overwhelming presence of non-English speakers begged a response. The majority of those who arrived in the early waves were Catholic.[16] As a result, many parishes in Miami began to cel-

---

13. Poyo, *Cuban Catholics*, 2.

14. Fernández, *Cuba Transnational*, xv.

15. More than half (52 percent) of Cuban-born persons in the United States consider the US their "real homeland," as compared to Mexicans (36 percent), Central and South Americans (35 percent), and Puerto Ricans (33 percent). *Pew Research Center*, "Cubans in the United States: Fact Sheet," 4.

16. In 1960, about 75 percent of the population of the island was Catholic. See

ebrate masses in Spanish, "though these masses were [often] conducted in the parish halls"[17] to avoid altering the mass schedule of the English speaking community. By 1962, ten parishes had mass and confession in Spanish.[18] These numbers grew as new parishes were founded throughout the diocese. Also, Catholic schools opened, sometimes staffed by the religious sisters who had come from Cuba. From 1958 (when the diocese was created) to 1963, the number of parishes nearly doubled, from 51 to 94.[19] However, incorporation into the life of the local Church did not come easy. It was not only the language barrier but also the culture barrier that led these immigrants to feel as foreigners also in the Catholic Church. They were coming from smaller, close-knit communities, and found churches cold and impersonal. However, they did not attempt to create national churches, but rather slowly integrated in the local parishes and created new programs to serve the needs of this population. With the growing Hispanic population, many of these parishes have become "in effect national parishes."[20]

Many of the exiles belonging to the first waves had been active in the church in Cuba, formed in Catholic schools, trained as leaders in Catholic Action groups. Soon these Catholic lay leaders, often with the support of Hispanic priests who had been expelled from Cuba, began to look for pastoral responses to the needs of families and youth. They founded lay organizations or movements, some of which existed in Cuba or elsewhere; others were created to address a variety of issues. In 1962, *Cursillos de Cristiandad* was founded in the Archdiocese of Miami; in 1963, *Movimiento Familiar Cristiano* for married couples; in 1971, *Encuentros Familiares* to minister to whole families; in 1973, *Impactos* for families with small children, *Camino al Matrimonio* for marriage preparation, and *Encuentros Juveniles* to evangelize teenagers. The Second Vatican Council's call for lay involvement in the mission of the church confirmed these initiatives, and they very much reflected the creativity and excitement of the church at that time. These programs benefited all Hispanics in the diocese.

Later waves also included Catholic leaders who had remained in the church despite the repression; some had been imprisoned, or sent to forced labor camps. Some recognized liturgical musicians, singers, and composers came in these later waves. Their music is not only played in Miami, but in

---

Stepick et al., *Churches and Charity*, 18.

17. Poyo, *Cuban Catholics*, 94.

18. Ibid.

19. Many of the new parishes were created to accommodate the growing Hispanic population. See Archdiocese of Miami, *Historia de la Arquidiócesis de Miami*, 10.

20. Matovina, *Latino Catholicism*, 51.

Cuba. However, the majority of the members of later waves were in need of basic formation and sacramental preparation.

In sum, the Catholic Church of Miami grew in numbers, but most importantly, it was enriched with priests, sisters, and Catholic leaders who now invested their talents and gifts in their new church community.

What Has Catholicism Offered the Cuban Diaspora?

The previous section identified some concrete ways in which the Catholic Church welcomed and helped the Cuban diaspora transition. A somewhat less obvious contribution concerns how resources within the Catholic faith have informed key themes of this community's diasporic discourse and experience. A theological interpretation of the experience of the Cuban Catholic community helps elucidate this nexus and shows how the exile community appropriated critical hermeneutical and theological resources and codes from the Catholic tradition for its self-understanding and projected action.

A Sense of Mission

The first hermeneutical resource is mission. In light of their baptismal commitment, Catholic exiles transformed their experience of expatriation into an opportunity to evangelize—a call to mission. In the words of a Cuban lay leader, "We need to convince ourselves, this minority that we are, that God has permitted this exile for something more, and perhaps, until this something is accomplished, the return to Cuba will remain remote."[21]

Jesus' mandate to evangelize all peoples[22] is a mandate to cross borders, to leave one's comfort zone and even one's country to bring the Good News of the Kingdom to others. In some way, Jesus creates dispersion, diaspora. The apostles and early disciples eagerly went to the "ends of the earth," reaching places as remote as India and Spain. In the letter of James and the First Letter of Peter, the recipients of the letters are identified as members of the dispersion or diaspora. While Cuban Catholics did not intentionally leave their country to evangelize in the United States, many have come to find purpose in their experience of exile through their commitment to evangelization and engagement in the service of others. This hermeneutic

---

21. Interview with Miguel Cabrera cited in Poyo, *Cuban Catholics*, 219.

22. "Therefore, go and make disciples of all nations" (Matt 28:19). *NRSV Bible, Catholic Edition*, 1993.

of diaspora, which Fernando Segovia[23] and Ada Maria Isasi[24] pioneered at a scholarly level, began in the hearts of simple Cuban exiles who tried to understand what God was asking of them: Why were they in exile? What did God want them to do in exile?

The interpretation of exile as an opportunity for mission was central to the teachings of two exiled bishops: Bishop Boza Masvidal, auxiliary bishop of Havana who was expelled from Cuba in 1961 and lived the rest of his life in Venezuela, and Bishop Agustin Román, expelled from Cuba as a priest, with Boza and 130 other priests.[25] Román became the founder of the Shrine of Our Lady of Charity in Miami and, later, the first Cuban bishop of the United States. Through his initiative, Cuban exiles in different parts of the world joined in a reflection on their diasporic experience in 1995.[26] Their final document concluded: "having been renewed in the Spirit, we will announce Jesus Christ and with creativity and generosity become missionaries of life and hope."[27]

Exodus as a Time of Conversion

A second critical theological code is the Exodus, which is also present in the exile's interpretation of dislocation. Cubans in exile have drawn a clear parallel between the Jewish Babylonian exile and the Cuban diaspora. In light of this reflection, Cubans are to discover "in the events of their history the saving action of God" and see this experience as an opportunity to purify their sins—self-sufficiency, arrogance, rancor, and idolatry in all its forms.[28] The loss of the homeland experienced by the exiles accentuated the eschatological longing for the "permanent home." In church and daily life, they often sing the song *Un Pueblo que Camina*: "*Somos un pueblo que camina y juntos caminando podremos alcanzar, otra ciudad que no se acaba, sin penas ni tristezas, ciudad de eternidad.*"[29]

---

23. Segovia, "Toward a Hermeneutics of the Diaspora," 57–74.

24. Isasi-Díaz, "'By the Rivers of Babylon,'" 149–64.

25. Clark, *Religious Repression in Cuba*, 11.

26. This came to be known as CRECED: Comunidades de Reflexión Eclesial Cubana en la Diáspora (Cuban Diaspora Ecclesial Reflection Communities).

27. Comunidades de Reflexión Eclesial Cubana en la Diáspora (CRECED), *CRECED Final Document*, 416.

28. CRECED, *CRECED Final Document*, 204–10.

29. "We are a people on a journey. Walking together we will reach another city which does not end, where there is no suffering, nor sadness, an eternal city." The author is Emilio Vicente Mateu, OCP; the translation is my own.

Our Lady of Charity

But by far, the most important theological resource that Catholicism in its Cuban expression offers the exile community is the Marian devotion to Our Lady of Charity, patroness of Cuba. This Marian symbol is rich with codes embedded in its history, tradition, and popular devotion that mediate particular values and a sense of identity.[30] In a semiotic understanding of symbols, these codes "help us to elicit the message that is borne by the sign."[31] Codes contain the "structure of cultural mechanisms on the ground of which we see something as referent to something else."[32] These codes are embedded in people's consciousness. The devotion to Our Lady of Charity has played a critical role in the forging of a Cuban exile identity. In fact, it has mediated this identity through faith.

Our Lady of Charity in Cuba

The origin of the image and the devotion in Cuba dates back to the year 1612,[33] when royal slave Juan Moreno and two Indian brothers, Rodrigo and Juan de Hoyos, were searching for salt in the Bay of Nipe. A storm came up over the waters, and after the storm passed, they found a small statue (about fourteen inches high) floating on the waters with the following inscription: *Yo soy la Virgen de la Caridad* ("I am the Virgin of Charity"). Later on, a shrine was built on the hill town of *El Cobre* (near the copper mines), where the image remains to this day.[34]

One of the codes that emerged through the devotion to Our Lady of Charity was to associate her with the quest for freedom and the rights of the disenfranchised. In 1783, the royal slaves of *El Cobre* asked the King of Spain to grant them their freedom. They claimed to be inspired by their "Queen and Mother" for whom they built a temple.[35] One hundred years before the

---

30. The role of Marian devotion in the maintenance of cultural identity is not exclusive to Cubans. Mexicans clearly conflate national identity with the Marian devotion to Our Lady of Guadalupe. The popular sense is that to be Mexican is to be *Guadalupano*. See Elizondo, *Guadalupe, Mother of the New Creation*.

31. Schreiter, *Constructing Local Theologies*, 50.

32. van der Ven, *Ecclesiology in Context*, 106.

33. Based on the document found in the *Archivo de las Indias*. More information is available at http://www.listindiario.com/ventana/2010/9/3/157472/La-Caridad-del-Cobre-Simbolo-de-Cubania.

34. This shrine was rebuilt many times until the one standing today was completed in 1927. Larrúa-Guedes, *Historia*, 738.

35. Ibid., 290–91.

abolition of slavery in Cuba, 1,065 slaves were granted their freedom, an event associated with their devotion to *Nuestra Señora de la Caridad*.[36] For obvious reasons, this devotion continues to inspire those who struggle for freedom and human rights.

Another code that developed around this devotion is her connection with Cuban national identity. During the Cuban War of Independence from Spain in the latter part of the nineteenth century, this devotion of the copper slaves and eastern Cuba became a national icon of identity.[37] The rebels, known as *mambises*, attached the image of Our Lady of Charity to their clothing or hats[38] and invoked her protection in battle. In their experience, Our Lady of Charity—*La Virgen Mambisa*—was one of them, with them, and on their side. She functioned as a symbol of both national identity and the struggle for freedom.[39] Our Lady of Charity has been recognized by the Cuban government[40] as a national symbol, along with the flag, and the national hymn.

A final code that derives from this devotion is how she brings together all Cubans. Popular iconography depicts her with multiethnic Cubans in the boat beneath her. These three men were believed to be a Spaniard, a black, and an Indian.[41] In the popular imagination, she embraces all Cubans, regardless of race, social class, or ideology.

Our Lady of Charity in Exile

For the Cuban exile community, she also functions as both the intercessor for the freedom of Cuba and national icon of their identity. Through the devotion to Our Lady of Charity, Cubans make sense of their exile experience and express their diasporic nationalism. As Tweed says, they "symbolically construct a common past and future, and their shared symbol bridges the homeland and the new land."[42]

---

36. For a well-documented history of these slaves and their devotion to Our Lady of Charity, see Díaz, *The Virgin, the King, and the Royal Slaves of El Cobre*.

37. Portuondo Zúñiga, *La Virgen de la Caridad del Cobre*, 23-24.

38. Ibid., 180-84.

39. Larrúa-Guedes, *Historia*, 435.

40. Paradoxically, until 1991, this government defined Cuba as an atheist state.

41. The original document relating her story, which was found some decades ago in the *Archivo de Indias*, identifies the men on the boat as two Indians and one black slave.

42. Tweed, *Our Lady of the Exile*, 84.

On September 8, 1961, two years after the beginning of the Cuban exile, an estimated twenty-five thousand Cubans gathered at the Miami Stadium to honor Our Lady of Charity.[43] A duplicate of the original statue had just arrived from Cuba, smuggled out with the help of the Panamanian embassy in Havana. This was the first event that brought the diasporic community together, helping it reconnect to the homeland and their hope for freedom.

The celebration of Our Lady of Charity has been taking place in Miami ever since. Thousands gather to honor the Mother of Jesus, to connect to their cultural roots, to reaffirm their Catholicity, and to pray for the freedom of Cuba. This religious-patriotic event brings together different generations, as Cubans continue to transmit to their children and grandchildren their love for the homeland. An *ermita* (shrine) in honor of Our Lady of Charity was built in 1973. This shrine is first and foremost a place of religious encounter and the focal point of the devotion. As diaspora theories affirm, "for a diaspora to be able to live on by transmitting its identity from one generation to the next, it must as much possible have places for periodic gatherings of a religious, cultural or political nature, in which it can concentrate on the main elements of its iconography."[44]

At the Ermita, faith intersects with nationalism. A mural behind the image on the main altar depicts the highlights of Cuban history. This is not only a place of prayer and devotion but a place where Cuban exiles find the spiritual support to face a myriad of situations, especially those linked to their homeland. Our Lady of Charity functions as a bridge that unites Cubans in the island and exile. She is not "Our Lady of the Exile," nor *El Cobre* alone; she is mother of all, Our Lady of Reconciliation. In Miami, this devotion also cuts across races, social classes, and even degrees of orthodoxy, as the shrine attracts Cubans with varying degrees of faith affiliation from the active practicing Catholics to those who are involved in Afro-Cuban syncretic practices, such as *Santeria*.

The Ermita in Miami unites Cubans in a number of ways. The location of the Ermita by Biscayne Bay allows pilgrims to look over the ocean and imagine that the land and the people left behind are just beyond the horizon. One very real way in which these two populations are joined together is that every Saturday night the mass celebrated in Miami is transmitted live to Cuba through Radio Martí. People who attend experience a real connection to people on the island, not only through prayer, but through the radio waves. The Ermita is the place where many newly arrived Cubans first

---

43. Ibid., 32.
44. Bruneau, "Diasporas, Transnational Spaces and Communities," 37.

encounter the Catholic Church in the United States and begin the difficult process of integrating their Catholic experience of their homeland and this new environment. Cubans who came in previous exile waves welcome recent arrivals through programs organized at the Ermita to assist the new exiles with their basic needs as well as initial Catholic formation or sacramental preparation.

Conclusion

There is no doubt that the Cuban diaspora—along with other migrations, mainly Hispanic and Haitian—has revolutionized the Catholic Church in Miami. All archdiocesan programs and offices offer their services in English and Spanish and are culturally sensitive to the Hispanic population (and Haitian). Cuban Catholics have found in the church the inspiration and support in their long journey of exile. The experience of diaspora has helped them expand their Catholicity to global dimensions, as Cubans share in community with people from many different countries in the multicultural reality of Miami. Catholicism in its rich cultural expressions has been, and continues to be, a lens whereby this diaspora can interpret its experience of displacement and finds direction as they continue to integrate in their new home, while maintaining their heritage.

10

Diasporic Devotions

DORIAN LLYWELYN, SJ

On a windy hilltop on the edge of the small south Chilean city of Punta Arenas stands a small, modern, and aesthetically unremarkable church. It is the home of a modern, life-sized statue of the suffering Jesus, the eighteenth-century original of which is found some 1,500 miles away, in the remote Pacific archipelago of Chiloé. Over the past thirty years, collective devotion to the image of Nuestro Padre Jesús Nazareno[1] has developed both in popularity and complexity, to the point that the annual Jesús Nazareno procession has become an important fixture in the liturgical calendar and public life of the city.

As I begin this exploration of the devotion, a word about the approach is in order. The classic dictum of Albertus Magnus, that "grace builds on nature," provides the theological method of this paper. My essay considers the complex strata of geography, history, and socio-ethnic aspects of the Jesús Nazareno cult.[2] These considerations ground the theological meaning of this particular devotion as an expression of the collective faith of one diaspora community. I hope, too, along the way to persuade the reader of the value of devotional spirituality as not only an expression of belief but as an important *locus theologicus*.

The Shrine—the Santuario de Jesús Nazareno—is located in Barrio 18 de Septiembre, a neighborhood that is socially as well as geographically somewhat marginal in the life of the city. In common with the inhabitants

---

1. Referring to Jesus as "Father," while not classically Trinitarian as an expression, is found in many expressions of Latin American Catholicism, and in Filipino Catholicism, too.

2. I use the term in its technical sense, evidently, to mean a system of formal religious veneration and its associated adherents.

of many such areas throughout the country, the people of the barrio suffer from poor housing and roads, disproportionately high unemployment, drug and alcohol abuse, and concomitant social problems. Ethnocultural factors as well as socioeconomic class play their part in this marginality. As is the case in many other parts of Chile, Punta Arenas has a population of largely European origin: Croatian, Basque, and German surnames are comparatively common in the city. However, most of the devotees of the image, and many of the inhabitants of the barrio, are Chilotes—recent immigrants and their second- and third-generation descendants, whose ancestral roots are in the far-off islands of Chiloé. Not infrequently darker-skinned and shorter than Chileans who have a greater proportion of European ancestry, Chilote phenotypes can give evidence of their mestizo generic heritage. Historically, the Chilote community, both in their home territory and in the mainland diaspora, has been somewhat looked down upon: *Chilote* can still be something of a byword for "backward" or "bumpkin" amongst other Chileans. Even until recently, Chilotes on the mainland sometimes masked their own origins out of a desire to blend into the successful and aspirational mainstream of Chilean society.[3]

Caguach: The Homeland

Many strands of history, both secular and religious, are woven into the skein of devotion to Jesús Nazareno at the Santuario. In 1567, the Spanish crown claimed the Chiloé archipelago as its own, but during the colonial period, it maintained only a minor, military presence in the islands (one claim I heard made by one member of the Santuario community is that all Chilotes are descendants of just thirty Spanish soldiers). The collapse of the Spanish empire during the Napoleonic wars gave rise to a Chilean independence movement and a civil war, with the new republic of Chile being finally established in 1826. Notably, the inhabitants of the archipelago resisted republican rule, being the last holdout of Spanish allegiance. This stance suggests that cultural conservatism has continued to characterize Chiloé and the Chilotes over the centuries. Isolated as it was from the mainland, communications between the archipelago and faraway Santiago were naturally difficult. Moreover, ongoing wars with the indigenous Mapuche and Huilliche peoples of the southern frontier of the republic, even into the late nineteenth century, occupied the attention of Chile's leaders in the

3. Much of the background information concerning Chilotes in Punta Arenas comes *viva voce* from Fr. Miguel Velásquez, the rector of the Santuario, in informal interviews I conducted in June 2012.

capital. These political and geographical factors made Chiloé almost a forgotten outpost of the country for most of the nineteenth century and into the twentieth century, too.

In the 1830s, Darwin had visited Chiloé as part of his five-year journey around the world. Finding it a "most forlorn and deserted place," he was surprised at the absence of money, and what he saw as a primitive level of agricultural development.[4] On the islands, in the natural cycles of fishing, forestry, and agriculture of a traditional rural society, lived out under harsh conditions, timeless social habits continued largely unchanged for most of the nineteenth century and beyond. Life in Chiloé even today is a rich social fabric, one that continues to cherish its traditions of shared agricultural labor and communally organized celebrations that have a notable emphasis on hospitality and festive meals. It is, according to one commentator, "a distinct enclave, linked more to the sea than the continent, a fragile society with a strong sense of solidarity, a deep territorial attachment,"[5] and a distinctive folk culture.

What is surprising about Darwin's accounts is the absence of any reference to Chiloé's artistic culture. As early as 1608, Jesuits had arrived on the archipelago setting up a system of circulating missions and developing a unique style of wooden churches of renaissance and baroque inspiration, many of which still survive and which are now recognized by UNESCO as World Heritage Sites. Under the tutelage of the Jesuits, native craftsmen developed a still-extant tradition of woodcarving that combines European baroque with indigenous features and motifs. Images of Christ, Mary, and the saints had been an essential part of evangelization efforts in the Spanish Empire from their very beginnings. In his study of religious life in colonial New Spain, William Taylor describes a "culture of immanence." This was part of a religious world that it held in common with Catholic Europe, one in which "images were the main bridge to the power and blessings of divine presence."[6] In varying degrees, this cultural gestalt extended to all Spanish colonial territories.

The arrival of the Jesuits coincided with the period of Tridentine reform, amongst the characteristics of which was a culture of devotionalism. In the Americas, the missionary strategy of the Jesuits involved "enriching European faith with indigenous symbols" and incorporating "unique

---

4. Darwin's brief accounts of Chiloé are found in chapters 13 and 14 of *The Voyage of the Beagle*.
5. Rohter, "For Some on Island."
6. Taylor, *Shrines and Miraculous Images*, 56.

elements of imagination and creativity."[7] The religious soil of Chiloé was already tilled and fertile, able to accept the cult of images, and to give that devotional spirituality its own local flavor.

Following the suppression of the Jesuits in 1767, the Chiloé missions were taken over by the Franciscans, who brought with them from Spain a statue of the Jesus of the Via Crucis, the Jesús Nazareno. Very similar images are found throughout former Spanish imperial territories, in Latin America and the Philippines, and are also common in the Holy Week processions of Andalucía and other regions of Spain. Along with their associated devotions, they all express a Franciscan emphasis on the real humanity of Jesus: they invite "an empathic response . . . *compassio,* an identification with the suffering Christ."[8]

The church on the small island of Caguach is home to this image and is also the center of the most important annual religious feast of the whole archipelago: the island itself is referred to as *la isla de la devoción.* The particular circumstances which brought the statue of Nuestro Padre Jesús Nazareno to Caguach form an important part of the complex of meaning associated with the cult, both in its original location and in its modern reiteration in Chilote diaspora. In 1776, the Spanish Franciscan Hilario Martínez brought the inhabitants of five, continually warring islands together to organize a feast in honor of the statue. There being no agreement about which island church would house the statue and host the feast, there was a concomitant risk of breaking the tense and fragile peace. Martínez chose the unusual method of proposing a canoe race to decide the issue, each island fielding a canoe with its crew. The winners were to have the statue in their church, with the agreement that the other communities would share the financial responsibility for holding an annual feast in its honor. Rowers from Caguach were victorious. Since then, at the beginning of the last week of August each year, the race is reenacted, and residents of the five islands begin the historical labor of coming together on Caguach to prepare for the annual feast day.

On the morning of August 30, boats arrive at Caguach bringing thousands of pilgrims from all parts of the archipelago and beyond. They come to fulfill promises or to make prayer requests. August is early spring, and during the sowing season, Chilote farmers pray to Nuestro Padre Jesús Nazareno for propitious weather and healthy livestock: "We come to our

---

7. Stevens-Arroyo, "Marriage Made in America," 54.
8. Morgan, *Visual Piety,* 63.

Divine Jesús of Nazareth because this is something that comes to us from our elders," said one pilgrim. "If we don't, we will get bad harvests."⁹

The social organization of the feast has remained unaltered since colonial times. The *Cabildo* (Chapter), a highly hierarchical lay institution created by the Franciscans, organizes the feast festivities and strictly controls all activities. The feast day proper is the apogee of several days of traditional festivities, including *la preba*, the reenactment of the original canoe race, and a flag-waving ritual that has been variously interpreted as a semaphoric greeting to the saints or a stylized portrayal of the inter-insular skirmishes that were put to an end by the arrival of Jesús Nazareno. Several days before the feast, a small maritime procession brings over to the island other ancient statues, each of which are zealously curated by their own *Cabildos* and accompanied by their devotees.

Following the mass on August 30, the statue is dressed in a new robe. The previous year's robe is cut up and pieces of it are distributed, being highly prized as devotional objects. Accompanied by the statues from the other islands, Jesús Nazareno is taken out of the church after the main mass and processed along the esplanade of the island to the accompaniment of traditional music and songs. A lively market also contributes to the most important social gathering of the year for the inhabitants of the whole of the archipelago.

Devotions and Reform

The existence of the cult of Jesús Nazareno on Caguach is in many ways a result of particular geography, and its unbroken history should not be taken as a historical given. A word concerning devotional images in colonial Latin American Catholicism is useful at this point. Taylor notes the existence of a widely shared and perduring conviction that such images "could come alive with the sacred."[10] This unofficial, popular religious statue engendered a perpetual clerical concern about idolatry. This matter, as we will see, had already been discussed at the Council of Trent, and reforms were implemented in the subsequent centuries. Yet the use of devotional images continued to be a matter of theological inquietude in the new Chilean republic.

The nineteenth-century Chilean Catholic Church undertook a vigorous reform of religious practice, part of the trans-Hispanic *Ilustración Católica*. In Chile, this reform was itself a local, if late, working-out of the

---

9. Mancilla, "El Nazareno de Caguach." (All translations from Spanish, unless otherwise noted, are mine.)

10. Taylor, *Shrines and Miraculous Images*, 57.

Catholic Enlightenment, that broad and centuries-long thrust that sought, inter alia, to "make Christianity . . . more reasonable and useful to society, (which) naturally translated into an opposition to or suppression of the excesses of baroque Catholicism."[11] Enlightenment thought in Catholic circles in Europe had long been calling for "a reduction of the cult of the saints and of pilgrimages and for the discouragement of superstitious religious practices."[12] Generations of Chilean bishops came from patrician families of Spanish descent and were educated in ultramontanist mold at the Collegio Pio-Latino Americano, the Roman seminary for Latin America. By upbringing and training alike, the Chilean reformers were allergic to popular devotions. Sensitive to secular accusations of Catholic primitivism and irrationality in religion, the bishops sought to purge the Church of liturgical immoderation.[13] Familiar, too, with European Catholic doubts about Latin American religious idiosyncrasy and syncretism in cult, they hoped to bring their dioceses into the mainstream of Catholic civilization and, thus, to claim for Chilean Catholicism a rightful and respectable place at the table with its European counterparts.[14]

Bounded as it is on all four borders—by the Atacama Desert of the north, the austral Patagonian icefields, the Andes in the west, and the Pacific of the eastern littoral—Chile is comparatively isolated in terms of its geography. The precolonial territory of today's Chile, in addition, had never developed material culture as rich as some of the Andean cultures, and it had never been home to a large and powerful polity. By the mid-nineteenth century, its sparse population was predominantly European or mestizo, and its indigenous cultures numerically small and undergoing a relentless weakening. All these geographical and social factors made the extirpation from public religiosity of pre-Columbian and many folkloric elements a comparatively easy ecclesiastical endeavor. Some particular devotional practices

---

11. Smidt, "*Luces por la Fe*," 409. In the same volume, Ulrich L. Lehner, in his "Introduction: The Many Faces of the Catholic Enlightenment," explains inter alia the composite and often contradictory nature of the phenomenon in which we find, for example, strands of Jesuit intellectualism coexisting with Jansenism, and earlier Gallicanism in Spain finding its progeny in nineteenth-century Chilean ultramontanism.

12. Lehner, "What is 'Catholic Enlightenment?,'" 169–70.

13. Góngora's "Aspectos de la Ilustración Católica," notes the tension between the Chilean bishops and the religious orders as another factor of their hostility toward popular devotions.

14. Eastman's *Preaching Spanish Nationalism across the Atlantic* notes the complex intertwining of conceptions of Enlightenment patriotism, Catholicism, and liberal nationalism in Mexico. Without wishing to conflate the Chilean and Mexican experiences, it is fair to note that the Chilean prelates' broad program of reform was also influenced by a combination of these three factors.

still flourish in today's Chile, however. *Cuasimodo*—a feast which involves taking Holy Communion to the sick on the second Sunday of Easter, with the Host being carried on decorated horse-drawn carriages, and accompanied by *huasos*, traditionally attired cowboys, and which typically includes enthusiastic feasting and drinking along the way—remains a popular devotion in the Santiago region. However, fruit of the bishops' reform is that although today's Holy Week in Santiago includes some public processions, its public manifestation is noticeably less colorful and effusive than one might find, for example, in other South American cities, being rather generically "European" in style.

Nonetheless, in remote and thinly populated areas, especially where there were stronger mestizo or indigenous populations, an earthier piety survived the liturgical bowdlerization, although not without some opposition. The *Bailes Religiosos* of the Aymara people in the far north of Chile have had a checkered history as regards ecclesiastical approbation. Even following the post-conciliar espousal by the church of conscious inculturation, they have until recently tended to exist as a parallel manifestation of faith, outside—and sometimes opposed by—episcopal supervision. (Their value for the tourism industry has, however, been easily recognized by the Chilean government.) Only in recent years have these paraliturgical religious dances been championed by the hierarchy, as an exemplar of consciously national Chilean Catholicism. In contrast, however, the cult of Jesús Nazareno de Caguach never seems to have encountered significant ecclesiastical opposition. The devotion was always incorporated into the liturgical cycle of the diocese. Lay-led from its very beginnings, the prayers, pilgrimages, and feasts of Caguach were simply an organic and indelible part of the warp and weft of life in the archipelago, so much so that it seemed to merit neither reform nor suppression.

The Diaspora

Today's Chiloé is home to some 150,000 inhabitants. More than double that number, however, are estimated to have settled in Patagonia. In the nineteenth century, the government in Santiago began a project of territorial and economic expansion into the far south of the continent—an urgent need given the increasing interest of France in acquiring the territories—and made use of Chiloé, the then-de facto southern frontier, as a starting point. The warship "Goleta" was built in Chiloé in 1843 to take definitive possession of the strategically important Magellan Straits, which had been only nominally part of the republic since the 1822 declaration of the Chilean constitution. Following the effective acquisition of Patagonia, there was a need to populate and develop the territories. Chilote shepherds, already well versed in dealing with harsh climates, became the mainstay of the immense and highly successful livestock enterprises that were subsequently established in the vast expanses of Magallanes and Tierra del Fuego. They also constituted a large proportion of the skilled workforce of the southern Atlantic fishing industry.

Chilote emigration, both to Patagonia and the copper mines of northern Chile, continued into and throughout the twentieth century. The harshness of a life based on subsistence agriculture and fishing in dangerous waters made leaving the ancestral homeland in search of a better life an almost foregone conclusion for many Chilotes. Periodic failures of the potato crop, the disastrous 1960 earthquake and its devastating tsunami, and the development of the oil industry all led to new waves of settlement in Patagonia in the 1950s and '60s.

Yet in the communities of this internal migration, when it came to the expression of faith, Chilotes faced some challenges. Whereas Jesús Nazareno was central to the faith life of the inhabitants of Chiloé, in Patagonia, the devotion seems to have been largely ignored by the Salesians who had been running the tip of Chile as their mission territory since Don Bosco sent a group of ten Italian priests to the windblown and icy hinterland of Patagonia in 1879. In exile from Caguach, Jesús Nazareno de Caguach dwindled to memory, or was at the most a small domestic devotion that had no communal or public expression.

To what might we ascribe this ecclesiastical ignoring or exclusion of popular piety? I would like to suggest three factors, the first of which is social class and the distance between metropolitan and rural pieties. The first Salesians were Italians, who would certainly have been familiar with the Via Crucis and statues of the bruised and bloodied Jesus in their places of origin. Their Chilean successors, however, were for the most part, alumni from the elite Salesian high schools in Santiago and other cities. Since the Chilotes were a lower class, rural population, their particularistic devotions would not have found a particular welcome amongst the Salesians, who brought their own Italian devotions with them.

It was perhaps the socio-geographical origin of the Caguach cult, rather than any suspicious religious practice, that meant that the Salesians did not adopt or cherish it. Devotionalism was, after all, in fact a hallmark of the piety of nineteenth-century Catholicism. By way of comparison with other Hispanic contexts, Orlando Espín describes how the Catholic Church in nineteenth-century Mexico and Antilles first championed popular religiosity to defend itself against the attacks of secularist intellectual elites, at least until "the rationalist intellectuals and the church establishment [discovered] a sufficiently comfortable dialogue and then turn[ed] their sights and disdain onto popular Catholicism."[15] Yet not all devotions had the same value in the eyes of the hierarchs. Although the nineteenth-century papacy "co-opted" devotions to "bolster an ultramontane Catholicism that sought to equate the universality of the church with a standard discipline that came from Rome,"[16] it promoted such "universal" devotions as Lourdes which had a dogmatic and ultramontane aspect. In such circumstances then, a local devotion, particularly when it was cherished by a small group of uneducated immigrants from a remote and insignificant region, would not likely have merited much attention from the Salesians. Obviously related to these class and metropolitan factors comes also the ongoing mind-set of the Chilean Ilustración Católica, with its distaste for the particularistic, the "primitive," and the potentially superstitious.

A second reason is economic and practical. Catholic immigrants typically carry with us copies of images of their homelands, and reiterate our particular devotions in our new settlements, in the first and then succeeding generations. Chilotes, however, were not sufficiently distinct in terms of ethnicity or language from other Chileans to merit the establishment of something like the "national parishes" that characterized nineteenth- and twentieth-century American Catholicism. The Patagonia mission territory was vast, but thinly populated. The Chilotes were poor, and engaged on the *estancias* and in the fishing fleet: they simply did not have the social or economic wherewithal to gather together in the diaspora. Moreover, Jesús Nazareno de Caguach was still *in* Caguach, there being no copy of that particular statue in Punta Arenas to which they could offer their prayers, kiss, touch, dress, or celebrate in procession.

Behind these factors, however, lies perhaps a third, theological reason, one that is chronologically and geographically more distant but no less potent for that. In response to the Reformers' accusations of Catholic iconolatry, the Council of Trent had taught that images of Christ, Mary, and the saints were to be revered

> not because some divinity of power is believed to lie in them . . . or because anything is to be expected from them; but rather, because the honor showed to them is referred to the originals which they represent; thus, through the images which we kiss

---

15. Espín, *Faith of the People* 135.
16. Francis, "Liturgy and Popular Piety in a Historical Context," 41.

... we give adoration to Christ and veneration to the saints, whose likeness they bear.[17]

According to the Tridentine theology of image, Jesús Nazareno de Caguach would be a channel through which humans make themselves, as it were, present to the divine. The divine, in its turn, would in no way "come alive" in the image, as Taylor puts it. Rather, it would be present only at a psychological and spiritual level, in the mind and heart of devotees.

In practice, however, devotional images often express a more ambiguous theology, one that is charged with a visceral affectivity. The theologians' ratiocinations of distinction between "direct" and "indirect" worship, and between sacraments and sacramentals, do not necessarily apply so neatly when it comes to what people actually do with the images they cherish. Rather, in what is an alternative, practiced theology, potent images can be a locus and channel of salvific presence. In the words of David Morgan, "religious images seem 'real' to believers by virtue of incarnating the spirit of Christ that floats in myriad depictions in the history of Christianity."[18] They are the three-dimensional point of engagement in a relationship between the temporal life of devotees and the realm of the spiritual. The life-sized image of a suffering Jesus communicates a fleshly immediacy: it can be seen from afar, touched, kissed, and embraced. The fact that Nuestro Padre Jesús is taken out of the sanctuary and into the streets expresses a baroque experience of God "in a vastness, freedom and goodness, flowing through a world of diversity, movement, and Order," in which Christ appear[s] in a ... human way ... and God is not distant nor utterly different from creatures."[19] In a society where the complexions of Chilotes have historically marked their lower social status, the dark skin of the Jesus of the image renders appreciating his humanity both more immediate and more poignant.

From the origins of the cult in truce, reconciliation, and fraternity, the statue of the suffering Jesus of Caguach has marked and made community that is present not only in the church buildings, but out in the public, secular domain—in its processions, festivities, and feasts—in its Cabildo, and among its musicians and cooks, canoeists, flag wavers, and seamstresses. Ana María Piñeda tells us that "the devotional piety that precedes any such journey already bears a communal character, which is thereby brought into unity. [The pilgrimages] create a sense of community among those preparing for the pilgrimage ... The activity itself nurtures a communal

---

17. Tanner, *Decrees of the Ecumenical Councils*, 774.
18. Morgan, *Visual Piety*, 50.
19. O'Meara, *Theology of Ministry*, 115–16.

spirituality."[20] Orlando Espín is not alone among US Latino theologians in explaining that *religiosidad popular* is *popular* in the sense that it is "of the people," i.e., a collective expression of a visceral *sensus fidelium*.[21] For the Chilotes, Jesus of Caguach is very much *nuestro*. Rather than a focus of a suburban "me-and-Jesus" spirituality, he is an earthy Padre to his people as a people. He is "ours" for the Chilotes of Magallanes in many ways: by virtue of his complexion, his presence on Caguach, his journeying to Patagonia with his people in their faith, and his suffering humility.

Together with the Angels and Saints

According to the classical theology of image expounded by Basil of Caesarea, John of Damascus, Theodore the Studite, and others, there exists an ontological relationship between heavenly original and earthly image. In other words, in the *scala naturae*, a holy image participates in the being of what it represents.[22] Otto Demus's seminal study of Byzantine aesthetics and iconology explains that an image is not a mere external and extrinsic reproduction of its original. Rather, "the Prototype, in accordance with Neo-Platonic ideas, is thought of as producing its image *of necessity*, as a shadow is cast by a material object . . . This process of *emanation* imparts to the image something of the sanctity of the archetype: the image is *identical* [with its prototype] according to meaning . . . The picture, if created *in the right manner* is a *magical* counterpart of the prototype, and has a *magical identity* with it."[23] Demus's comments, if taken at face value, serve to help understand why the Chilean bishops of the Ilustración might feel nervous about popular devotions to images being perilously close to idolatry. Quite equally, however, his explanation gives metaphysical expression to the religious instinct of devotees that the Jesús Nazareno statue can indeed guarantee good harvests: the image participates in the apotropaic identity and powers of its archetype.

A relationship of participation in being exists, however, not only between a spiritual reality or person and its representation in a physical image such as a statue or a picture. It also exists between original statues, buildings, shrines, portraits, and their copies in other places. Many revered "wonder-working" Orthodox icons, for examples, are copies of a long lost or distant

---

20. Piñeda, "Shrines and Pilgrimages," 161.

21. Espín, *Faith of the People*, 70.

22. For a detailed explanation of iconodule and iconoclastic theologies, see Pelikan, *Imago Dei*, especially chapter 6.

23. Demus, *Byzantine Mosaic Decoration*, 6. Original emphases.

original. Yet the fact that they are reproductions—even mass-produced mechanical ones—does not limit the thaumaturgical power that their devotees ascribe to them, for they too participate in the being and the power of the originals they represent.[24] The Jesús Nazareno of the Santuario of Punta Arenas is also a copy of a venerable original, but it is also, in this sense, a complete re-presentation of the original, one in being with it. Despite the fact that the Punta Arenas statue, although carved on Chiloé by an artisan *santero*, is interestingly not a particularly close reproduction of its original, it is as it were consubstantial with its archetype, at the very least in the esteem in which it is held. Difference in appearance notwithstanding, then, in a process to which we might refer broadly speaking as sacramental, the Jesús Nazareno of Barrio 18 de Septiembre brings along with its presence in Punta Arenas all the manifold history, the affective bonds, and much of the social and religious practices of its prototype in Caguach.

At the same time, and in the same mechanism, a religious image is also an expression of exile and yearning, for there is a necessary distance between the image and the original reality that it represents and re-presents. Morgan perspicaciously points out that in a "metaphysics of presence . . . representation harbors the yearning to overcome the difference between sign and referent and join the other in one's own body."[25] Built into the relationship between sign, referent, and devotee, there is a necessary awareness of exile, a longing for a relationship which is "already-not-yet," *in germene* in this world, but whose consummation can only happen beyond this world. It is, therefore, a presence that is also an expression of distance and absence. The cult of Jesús Nazareno de Caguach on Caguach is a reminder that "our citizenship is in heaven" (Phil 3:20). In the transplanted devotion in Patagonia, the statue and the pilgrimage in Punta Arenas adds to this expression of spiritual exile the poignant secular reminder that their cultural citizenship—or at least their roots as Chilotes—are in Chiloé, and not where they are currently living.

Travelers of all sorts, exiles, and emigrants invariably take with us reminders of our home. Owning copies of renowned religious objects from the homeland in new contexts might hardly seem to merit comment. The same might hold true for religious practices such as communal worship, except for a theology of diasporic devotion; it is worth considering some of

---

24. Famous "wonder-working" icons that are, in fact, copies of long lost miraculous icons are the Mother of God of Kazan and the Kursk Root Icon. A current example of this process of "transferred sanctity" is a commercially produced icon currently reputed to exude holy oil at Holy Theotokos of Iveron Russian Orthodox Church in Honolulu, Hawaii.

25. Morgan, *Visual Piety*, 66.

the potential imports of the tenets of liturgical theology. The praise of God by his people brings participants into the presence of events that happened in distant places and times. As Aleksander Gomola puts it, "Time/space compression stands at the centre of the Christian faith."[26] At one level, the liturgical cycle itself translates events, which were once bounded by place into temporal experience. The eternal "today" and "now" of liturgical texts being the continuation of what were originally experiences of the "there" of the events of the drama of salvation. At the same time, Christian worship is done, in the words of each preface in the Roman Missal, "together with the angels and saints." In this view—a concept perhaps more familiar to Orthodox Christians than to many Catholics—collective worship and religious practice is a proleptic experience of active participation in the eschatological liturgy of the timeless life of heaven, in which all the events of redemption are continually present.[27]

In the broad field of public devotions, this sacramental instinct appears in many Hispanic contexts, both historical and modern, in Spain and in formerly imperial cultures. Morgan describes how the development of Holy Week processions in seventeenth-century Spain fostered a piety, which "effected through visual means, sought a vicarious participation in Christ's suffering, death, and resurrection. If the devout viewer suffered and died with Christ in empathic response to images of the innocent Jesus . . . the believer was likewise resurrected and restored with the vindication of Jesus."[28] Late medieval *compassio* and Baroque spirituality are likewise a part of the American Catholic religious world. At a remove of over three centuries and four thousand miles, Karen Mary Davalos relates how, for Hispanic participants in a live Via Crucis in Chicago, the events of the procession and those of the passion of Jesus are interpenetrated as to be almost indistinguishable.[29]

But ritual also performs, expresses, and encounters relationships that are horizontal as well as vertical, geographical, secular, and social as well as religious, and communal as well as individual. Thomas Tweed's study of Miami's Shrine of Nuestra Señora de la Caridad del Cobre, patroness of Cuba, employs the category of "translocative" piety.[30] The Miami church is more than a location for exilic nostalgia or expressing loss. Rather, the presence

26. Gomola, "Cognitive Mechanisms at Work," 292.

27. Particularly in the matter of sacred places of worship, we connect with a very ancient stratum of ideas that see the earthly temple as a copy of the courts of the god, a theme that runs throughout the work of Mircea Eliade.

28. Morgan, *Visual Piety*, 64–65.

29. Davalos, "'Real Way of Praying,'" 31.

30. Tweed, *Our Lady of Exile*.

in the shrine of a modern image, a faithful copy of the Cuban image, by dint of the very fact that it *is* a copy, renders the homeland present to the exile and vice versa. The small statue is also—particularly for the succeeding generations who must negotiate a new set of identities as hyphenated Cubans—a bulwark against the loss of distinctive cultural identity, an object which makes a place for them in the communal, diasporic narrative.

Shrines, according to the 2001 *Directory on Popular Piety and the Liturgy* issued by the Congregation for Divine Worship and the Discipline of the Sacraments, may fulfill many functions, including issuing a call to conversion, and being centers of social assistance and places of hospitality. The Santuario is a modest building with an adjoining hall, rather than the sort of venerable and hallowed shrine which the *Directory* seems to have in mind. Yet it is well worth noting that all these functions are to be found there. Thoughtful and dedicated pastoral work carried out over three decades by the rector has made the church the hub of a lively community, a flourishing center for revitalization and education in a depressed neighborhood. Part of the diocesan ministry to migrants, the Santuario is technically not a parish, and this administrative status allows for greater pastoral flexibility. At the same time, however, the Shrine does function effectively as a sort of ethnic (and class-based) parish. The presence at the Shrine of the Jesús Nazareno statue is the affective center that makes Punta Arenas' inhabitants of Chilote descent feel particularly at home, where some of the Chilote traditions of shared labor and large, communally prepared meals as well as worship are perpetuated, and recast in the diaspora. On Caguach as it is in Barrio 18 de Septiembre, the spiritual is also social and material.

As a point of reference, then, the devotion is present in many ways, but particularly so in liturgy. When Fr. Velásquez preaches at Sunday masses, he consistently refers to Jesus of the Gospels as "nuestro Padre Jesús," and points to the statue, which stands near the altar. In his work with the young men and women who are the mainstay of the annual procession, he tells them that their work as porters of the image, as singers and musicians, as flag wavers and ushers, is "for Jesus," and assures them that Jesus knows and appreciates the sacrifices and efforts they are making for him. These simple gestures and words of pastoral encouragement make manifest a rich complex of implicit connections: between the life of Jesus and the lives of the inhabitants of the barrio; between the person of Jesus and the statues which represent him; between devotion and sacrament; and between the treasured memories of shared existence in Chiloé and its ongoing realization in the community that has grown up and solidified around the Santuario.

Public Space, Faith Performed

Popular piety, according to Espín, is symbolic and experiential rather than lexical in its predilections and expressions. It "does not *show* the sophistication of the educated elites," but rather "*displays* the medieval predilection for the visual, the oral, and the dramatic."[31] The annual Jesús Nazareno processions that have taken place in Punta Arenas over the last thirty years have inscribed another level of meaning on the theological palimpsest of the devotion in the diaspora.

As we have seen above, the classical theology of image argues that an image is connected with its prototype. Analogically then, as Jesús Nazareno de Caguach along with its devotees traverses the city streets of Punta Arenas, we might argue that by analogy, the collective journey of image and devotees not only recounts but also participates in the journey of Jesus and his disciples through Galilee and into the final path of the Via Crucis. The feast does not take place in Holy Week, but in late August and is therefore a spring festival. The Holy Week of the church's liturgical year is based on the seasons of the northern hemisphere. As such, the feast on Caguach and in the Chilote diaspora express something of the natural seasonal cycles that lie in the remote pastoral and agricultural strata of the Paschal feast. The statue depicts the suffering Christ of the way of the cross, a motif so recognizable in the Christian imaginary that it is able to evoke in the minds and hearts of devotees all the events and personages of the Passion, even though these are not depicted by other statues or explicitly related in words during the procession. The 2007 "Aparecida Document"—the final document of the Fifth General Conference of Bishops of Latin America and the Caribbean (CELAM)—describes how in such practices, "the believer celebrates the joy of feeling surrounded by myriad brothers and sisters, journeying together toward God who awaits them. Christ himself becomes pilgrim, and walks arisen among the poor."[32] Such processions are broadly speaking liturgical pilgrimages, and as such have dimensions which are vertical as well as horizontal, and communal as well as individual.

The *Directory on Popular Piety and the Liturgy* notes the different aspects of the piety of pilgrimage: eschatological, penitential, apostolic, communitarian, and liturgical. Liturgical theology, as we have noted, stresses that collective worship joins the prayers and praises of its participants with the songs of praise of the courts of heaven. Ana María Piñeda relates how the Holy Week processions of Spain (in which family of ritual the image of

---

31. Espín, *Faith of the People*, 70. Emphases added.

32. Fifth General Conference of the Bishops of Latin America and the Caribbean, "Concluding Document: Aparecida," no. 259.

Jesús Nazareno originated and to which the devotion is intimately related), "move in a subliminal time that creates a mystical experience for the participants. Those who take part in the processions seem to be transported into another sacred space and time. The mysteries of the suffering and death of Jesus are communicated."[33] But this communication in Punta Arenas has another dimension: the annual procession in Punta Arenas also mimetically reproduces and participates in the same journey that the original statue is making on Caguach. Synecdochically, therefore, the devotion in Punta Arenas also evokes the whole warp and weft of life in Caguach—both the Caguach of today and of yesterday. Image, devotion and procession, type and prototype, the hardscrabble grittiness of life in Barrio 18 de Septiembre, and the more bucolic life of the *isla de la devoción*, memories of ancestral roots and the experiences of new home, participate in each other's being. In other words, in the generically Chilean Catholicism of Punta Arenas, the Shrine and its pilgrimage earth Chiloé in the diaspora in ways which are a sacrament of community.[34]

In the ritual of this diasporic procession then, differing orders of existence involving different communities, places, and times are brought and welded together: first-century Palestine, eighteenth-century and modern Caguach, today's Patagonia. This compression is more than a juxtaposition; in the ritual act, these times and places become interpenetrated with each other, so that one cannot be understood or experienced without necessarily invoking all the dimensions of the other. The procession makes "there" into "here," "then" into "now," and "them" into "us"—and vice versa. If the experience of the procession is "mystical," as Piñeda would have it, it is also simultaneously material and profoundly embodied in the physical substantiveness of the image, in the collective body of worshipers, and not least in the physical efforts of the porters, musicians, flag wavers, and crowds who accompany the image.[35]

---

33. Piñeda, "Shrines and Pilgrimages," 151.

34. Ibid., 161. Piñeda notes that pilgrimage and shrine are, by their very essence, expressions of a communal devotionalism. Questions of individualistic, European devotions v. communitarian Latino devotions and the relationship of both types to the official liturgy are taken up by Espín, *Faith of the People*, especially chapter 5, and Goizueta, "Making Christ Credible." Where Espín posits a radical difference between post-Tridentine popular religiosity and the clerically controlled liturgy, Goizueta nuances this argument and sees both as necessarily connected expressions of a sacramental imagination.

35. On the bodily aspect of Catholic visual devotion, see Morgan, *Visual Piety*, 60, following Caroline Bynum Walker; he describes how the devotional image of the later medieval period "seized on the body as the medium for identifying oneself with Christ."

Such rituals inevitably make claims on the streets they pass. An image, says David Morgan, "declares by virtue of its . . . iconic presence or its incursion into otherwise profane space that . . . the devout should pay special heed."[36] Images and objects "displace rival images and ideologies."[37] The inhabitants of Barrio 18 de Septiembre turn out in large numbers to accompany their Nuestro Padre Jesús. The statue is taken out from the Santuario, and carried to the accompaniment of the traditional music of Caguach, downhill into downtown, the center of the commercial and civic life, and ends up in the Cathedral, whose bishop—unlike his predecessors—cherishes the importance of the devotion. The procession—complete with its own young flag wavers, accordionists, drummers, and its Cabildo just as in counterpart on Caguach—renders Punta Arenas into liminal space that "dislocates established structures and reverses hierarchies."[38]

The final chorus of T. S. Eliot's *Murder in the Cathedral* includes the much-quoted lines:

> "[W]herever a saint has dwelt, wherever a martyr has
>   given his blood for the blood of Christ,
> There is holy ground, and the sanctity shall not depart
>   from it.
> Though armies trample over it, though sightseers come
>   with guide-books looking over it . . .
> From such ground springs that which forever renews
>   the earth
> Though it is forever denied."[39]

Eliot's insight is that holiness pervades and makes a mark on place. In a process of implicit consecration by contact, the procession "renews" the meaning and associations of the commercial and administrative center of the city Punta Arenas, showing the place to be translucent to sacred history, and in the process changing its meaning.

But this revealed alternative history also has obvious political and class resonances in addition to religious meaning. The established route passes in front of the mansions which were once the luxurious homes of the Patagonian sheep barons who employed the forefathers of today's Chilotes and which are now government buildings or divided up into hotels. As such, the procession is also an *ubi sunt* to wealth and status, and an affirmation of God's "raising up the lowly." I have heard middle class non-Chilote

---

36. Morgan, *Sacred Gaze*, 56.
37. Ibid., 55.
38. Horvath et al., "Introduction," 3.
39. Eliot, *Murder in the Cathedral*, 85.

puntarenses refer to the religious life of the Santuario as *religiosidad popular*, not necessarily pejoratively so, but in a way that strongly suggests a distance from the normative center. In reality, the annual processions are not only "religion" in a narrow sense: they are also an expression of pride in the presence of a Chilote community and its piety, a claim to acknowledgement and a voice in the life and self-image of the diocese, the city, and the region. They perform, perpetuate, and recreate what it is to be Chilote, which is as much about class as place of origin. Unlike the Mapuche people of Chile, Chilotes seem to shelter no particular impulse for social revindication, and there exists to my knowledge no Chilote independence movement. On the whole, Chilote emigrants have been willing to leave homeland in search of employment. At the same time, nevertheless, the devotion seems to flourish in response to a need, a lacuna, a desire to find recognition and meaning in a territory in which Chilotes lived but without feeling totally at home.

Like its Caguach archetype, the Punta Arenas devotion is cross generational, a willing attempt to preserve and cultivate a patrimony that might otherwise disappear. The cultural, pastoral, and religious entrepreneurship that characterize the Punta Arenas version of the cult is clearly open to the suspicion that it is, in the phrase of Hobsbawm and Ranger, an "invented tradition,"[40] a folk revival which is a response to the experience of loss of identity. In two distinct senses, respectively intellectual and experiential, cultural identity in the diaspora cannot be taken for granted. First, questioning the very concept and existence of cultural "identity" (where this is conceived of as an immutable set of defining characteristics that include a collective religious component) is now a long-established academic commonplace, even an intellectual cliché. Secondly, the process of leaving one's homeland and community threatens to dissolve the cultural identity of both individuals and groups, as they are deracinated and replanted in new, exilic surroundings, a process that almost ineluctably brings in its train nostalgia and a sense of diminishment. Certainly, according to Chih-Yun Chang, "the diasporic memory tends to focus on a collective memory of a lost homeland, childhood, [and] cultural identity,"[41] a memory which may well be fossilized in an idealized, romantic past. Romantic nationalism, according to Hobsbawm, is the product of exiled intellectuals, who invent a history that is useful to their current situation.[42] The same accusation might be leveled against many forms of identity politics, which is exiled from a preconscious,

---

40. Hobsbawm and Ranger, *Invention of Tradition*.

41. Chiang, "Diasporic Theorizing Paradigm," 36.

42. Many of his writings, notably *Nations and Nationalism since 1780* and *The Invention of Tradition*, make this case forcefully.

previously invisible cultural milieu. The category of the ethnic, according to David Lloyd, has a "retrospective constitution."[43] It emerges into focus only when it has been isolated as a potentially indigestible trace element in the ineluctable process of assimilation into a new, larger, and more powerful cultural milieu.

The Punta Arenas devotion clearly has elements which could be described as "performative," in the sense that it can be seen as an act which makes diasporic Chilote identity happen, rather than as reflection of a pre-existing state of being. The procession is also, quite simply, a cultural performance as well as a liturgy. Artistic performance involving (or creating) particularistic, national, and regional expressions of *Volksgeist* was certainly amongst the many ways in which the entrepreneurs of century romantic revivalism sought to express the specificity of their own people. (This tendency finds its Catholic offspring today in some of the clumsier attempts at liturgical inculturation.) Certainly, both performativity and performance characterize the life of the Santuario. This need not be a demerit or a cause for intellectual embarrassment. Yet I would like to think nonetheless that these aspects do not circumscribe the cult of Jesús Nazareno in Punta Arenas. Rather, at its heart, this diasporic devotion is no attempt at imitating a static, originary purity, but in fact a creative assimilation and development of tradition.

The Punta Arenas cult continues to accrue new meanings which are based on its Caguach original. Given its different geography and sociology, these meanings are unique to the diasporic setting. Over the last twenty years—and largely inspired by the Punta Arenas Shrine—the *devoción* along with its statue and procession has spread to other Chilote communities in the region of Magallanes and Tierra del Fuego, and links between the different *Cabildos* are strong. But the historical patterns of Chilote emigration mean that communities inhabit both sides of the border between Chile and Argentina in south Patagonia. Given the complex geography of the Beagle Channel and its distance from any major center of population, the exact line of delineation there between the two countries was contested for many decades. During the 1970s and '80s, the two countries were at the brink of war in the so-called "Beagle Conflict," a political standoff solved only through the mediation of Pope John Paul II and the return of democratic government to Chile in 1984. The origin of the Caguach devotion lies in reconciliation between warring parties. Now, in a new and transformed iteration of peacemaking, transnational pilgrimages accompany Jesús Nazareno statues and their devotees from Chilean Patagonia to meet their counterparts across

---

43. Lloyd, "Ethnic Cultures," 222.

the border in Argentinian Patagonia and vice versa. These encounters have become important expressions of international friendship, making real in a new context the first purpose of Hilario Martínez. They express a unity in (as well as a unity *of*) faith, community, and culture that is more life-giving than the lucubrations and posturing of the politicians of far-away Santiago and Buenos Aires.

Considerations and Conclusions

Today's cult of Jesús Nazareno de Caguach might easily be considered as no more than a somewhat interesting historical survival, and it has to be admitted that devotional practices in Punta Arenas are aesthetically less arresting by far than other manifestations of folk piety in other parts of the Hispanic world. The inhabitants of Chiloé are a small and largely unknown community, and the Chilote diaspora at the far southern end of the inhabited world is even more thinly spread out. These indicators suggest that the topic of this chapter, therefore, is of only minor significance to North American Christians, including theologians and specialists in religious studies. I would like to suggest that, to the contrary, the history of the devotion to Nuestro Padre Jesús Nazareno de Caguach and its rebirth on the different soil of Patagonia can teach Christians in North America, including theologians and specialists in religious studies, things that are useful. The phenomenon is significant not only despite our different cultural milieus but also *because* the history and traditions of this continent are different from those of the Chilotes.

Three points come to mind. First, the vitality of the cult of Jesús Nazareno reminds us of *the power of imagery to move hearts in a way that is different from lexical intelligibility*. This is a truth so obvious that it can easily be ignored or downplayed. Educated Catholics in the United States, one might argue, are by virtue of a commonly held American intellectual ancestry that includes Puritan iconophobia as well as Enlightenment rationalism, particularly prone to a cultural preference for language over images, for univocal statement rather than multivalent symbol, and generally for turning flesh back into words. The North American appropriation of the Second Vatican Council saw in many places not only a "stripping of the altars," but also a widespread decline in devotionalism and the demise in the use of religious images, the only holdouts being ethnic and traditionalist sectors.[44] At a distance now of over fifty years, it is, I think, appropriate and intellectually responsible to question the inchoate class and sociocultural

---

44. See the classic study of Orsi, *Between Heaven and Earth*.

assumptions that went into some of the more iconoclastic interpretations of "the spirit of Vatican II." These influences made themselves notably salient in the areas of church reordering and liturgical life—precisely those parts of Catholic life in which the physical senses are most involved. We might also wonder what the insights of the psychology of perception or art history have to say to the comparative downplaying of the traditional visual elements of our religious culture.

During those past fifty years, at the same time, patterns of immigration—especially from Latin America but also from Asia—are causing a rapid sociological change in North American Catholicism. These developments will ineluctably also change its visual culture. And since *lex orandi* ontologically precedes *lex credendi*, its theological emphases will also change, even when the theological establishments of the academy or the church are one or more steps behind what is going on at the coalface. The diaspora on these shores of Catholics from Latin America, Africa, Vietnam, and the Philippines offers a gift of the resurgence of devotions, particularly in connection with images. This gift is also a pastoral challenge that will demand a reordering of aesthetics as well as theological assumptions. The Aparecida document reminds us that "popular piety includes the bodily, the perceptible, the symbolic, and people's most concrete needs. It is a spirituality incarnated in the culture of the lowly."[45] Peruvian theologian Diego Irarrázaval notes that devotees "come to those images asking for health, social and economic progress, personal, familiar, (and) communitarian well-being . . . The images of Christ summon and gather people, groups, crowds. In this reinvigorating context, personal and group faith develop."[46] For the Chilotes, Jesús Nazareno statues produce solidarity between people and are life giving in the social activities which they inspire as well as in the faith they foster. Yet they are hardly unique in this respect: I write this on the day after being present at a Mass for Immigration at the Cathedral of Los Angeles, attended by an estimated five thousand people, largely Latinos, many of whom had come to venerate the statue and relics of Santo Toribio Romo González.[47]

In the context of North American Catholicism, ever prone to an individualistic faith, collectivist devotions are potentially subversive. They propose an organic worldview and an interpersonal solidarity which includes but also transcends the ethical. Goizueta writes that "the greatest threat to true faith is not that of mistaking a wooden statue for the real Christ," but

---

45. Fifth General Conference of the Bishops of Latin America and the Caribbean, "Concluding Document: Aparecida," no. 263.

46. Irarrázaval, "Religious Windows," 20.

47. See Bermudez, "Faithful Flock"; Linthicum, "Unacommpanied Children."

rather "a rationalist... Christianity that preaches... a Christ without a face, without a body, without wounds, a cross without a corpus."[48] The emphases on rationality and the ethical usefulness of faith for society that made the nineteenth-century alumni of the Collegio Pio Latino Americano suspicious of popular devotions has not disappeared. Rather, it might be argued that the potential idolatry of some sectors of US Catholicism is to reduce the practice of faith to a commitment to social justice, and to center faith and theology alike on ethics alone.[49] Latino devotionalism, to that extent, is a concrete and necessary corrective that balances out one good with another.

A second area that the history of the cult of Jesús Nazareno illustrates is *the inseparability of faith and culture*. The final document of the 1992 Fourth General Conference of CELAM refers to popular religion as "a privileged expression of the inculturation of the faith. It involves not only religious expressions but also the values, criteria, behaviors, and attitudes that . . . constitute the wisdom of our people, shaping their cultural matrix."[50] This inseparability is of course true of all manifestations of faith, but it is particularly evident in those faith acts which stand out from the perceived or desired norm, whether that be cultural or religious. To that extent we might argue that there is a difference between the cultural matrix of the *devoción* on Caguach and its reiteration and reimagination in the diaspora. In Chiloé, the cult of Jesús Nazareno is simply an indispensable part of what faith looks like. In Punta Arenas, on the other hand, the devotion cannot help but take on a more self-conscious stance. It involves a preservationist attitude toward ethnic identity, one that "celebrates" and "maintains" its own ancestral particularity by performing it.

It is good to ponder the difference between the two locales. The experience of diaspora reinscribes the manifestations of faith in a new setting. It thereby inevitably changes their meaning, throwing their cultural function into greater relief. It is useful at this point to distinguish between two uses of the terms "culture": (1) a more anthropological use of the word to mean, broadly speaking, the features of everyday existence of a particular group which are so woven into its life that they appear to be connatural to it; and (2) the distinctive, especially artistic, manifestation of the values and identity of a particular group. We might argue that the distinction between the two senses of culture is also one of location: whereas in Caguach, the cult of

---

48. Goizueta, "Making Christ Credible," 176.

49. Ibid., 169, notes that while this moralism was also found among the first generations of liberation theologians, skeptical as they were about the usefulness of popular devotions in the struggle for social justice, a later generation have come to see popular religiosity as a "source of hope and empowerment for the poor."

50. Hennelly, *Santo Domingo and Beyond*, 86.

Jesús Nazareno is an age-old and organic part of Chilote life, the diasporic devotion is more consciously a cultural moment as well as a religious one. This "performed culture" certainly has political implications too, but is not circumscribed to the sphere of the political either.

The distinction between two notions and experiences is particularly important in the context of US Catholicism, which includes in its embrace many diasporic populations, of different generations. Any number of diasporic communities run the risk of having their communal sense of self in their new setting limited to, say, ethnic food festivals and folk dances. This reduced version of identity may be imposed by others, tokenistically. Quite equally, diasporic communities can end up performing their own culture in ways that are self-limiting. Where religious identity is closely tied in with ethno-cultural identity, e.g., among Arab-speaking Christians in the United States, the potential dangers of religious and cultural fusion include the loss of religious allegiance as the memories of the place of origin fade with succeeding generations. Quite equally, it can lead to compartmentalization and confusion.

It is important therefore to distinguish between different generations of diasporic communities, whose varying experiences differ. Chilotes are Chileans and Catholics, and they are also *Chilote* Catholics, with their own particular history and traditions. Despite their shared history and traditions, however, *Caguachano* Chilotes are different from their *Puntarense* cousins. Equally, it is important to honor the specificity of the many different national groups that constitute, say, the Asian populations of the US church. Community leaders, academics, and church leaders alike often fall into an easy essentialization of "Latino culture," as if this were univocal and uniform, or to reduce it to a political trope.

Diasporic culture—particularly in its performative, self-aware aspect—certainly has important and valid political implications. However, we should resist any impulse to conceive of self-conscious and intentional identity in diasporic culture *only* in terms of power dynamics, as projects of social revindication. We would do well, on the other hand, to note the mutually implicating relationship between particular local or national religious devotions and the different levels of ethno-cultural identity. Chilote Catholics are both *Chilote* Catholics and Chilote *Catholics,* and marrying those two emphases is the task of good pastoral labor. In many immigrant communities, pastoral work is done in the tension of what it is to be a disciple of Christ, in whom there is "neither Greek nor Jew," and at the same time a member of a distinctive culture in the diaspora. This pastoral work is a *fides* perennially in search of the reflective *intellectum* of theology. Diaspora, emigration, and exile are categories of deep and rich scriptural resonance.

We have at hand many studies of the religious experience of many different ethno-cultural Catholic groups, both in their places of origin and in the experience of immigration. What is less clear is whether ethno-cultural identity has been developed much as a fully theological category, rather than say a sociological one.[51]

A final point of consideration concerns the intellectual analogue of the theological import of culture, namely *the cultural milieu in which theology itself is done and its relation to theological method*. At a remove of almost fifty years since the publication of Gustavo Gutiérrez's *Teología de la Liberación*, it has become common to note the first generation of liberation theologians' quick dismissal of popular religiosity as irrelevant or obstructive to the work of calling down the fire of God's justice. It remains true that in the US academic context, "popular religion" is too frequently patronized as "piety" or sidelined (and sometimes self-guided) to the corner of particularistic, ethnic theologies. Such attitudes suggest a lamentable disconnect with contemporary pastoral realities. Taking the dictum *lex orandi, lex credendi* seriously will increasingly demand that theologians of all stripes in the United States take into more generous account the reality of popular religiosity, devotional spirituality, and what Wendy Wright and other scholars are calling "lived religion"—that complex of "faith expressions, social structures, cultural horizons, bodily existence, everyday lives, and the local circumstances of practitioners."[52] This matrix includes but is not limited to the *theologia prima* of devotion, prayer, procession, and liturgy exemplified by the religious life of the Chilotes on Caguach and in Punta Arenas, and by the faith of the many diasporic communities who make up what is the demographic mainstream of American Catholicism.

I began this essay referring to the relationship between nature and grace as *primum analogatum* for the relationship between theology and religious studies. If it is indeed true that "theologians have usually stayed away from the study of popular religion, preferring to leave the field to anthropologists and other social scientists,"[53] then theologians of all stripes ignore the investigations and data of sociology and anthropology and other fields of study at our peril when we consider popular religion, particularly in its connection to culture and identity. At the same time, however—and especially given the innate disciplinary predilections of the social sciences—a theology of devotions and popular piety cannot be reduced *merely* to history,

---

51. See Buell, *Why This New Race*; Llywelyn, *Toward a Catholic Theology of Nationality*.

52. Wright, *Lady of the Angels and Her City*, 4.

53. Espín, *Faith of the People*, 63.

anthropology, sociology, or to particular ideological or social agendas. The datum of faith is needed. But I would also argue that the benefits can flow in both directions. In the search for truth, social scientists, psychologists, art historians, and others who study religious imagery and popular religiosity will find their own investigations tempered, questioned, and enriched by a comparative dialogue with a centuries-long intellectual corpus of theological thought.

To return, finally, to the small church that stands on the corner of the Avenida de la Circunvalación and Calle Salvador Allende in Barrio 18 de Septiembre. The image and cult of Jesús Nazareno de Caguach are central to the evolving sense of identity of the Chilotes of Punta Arenas, since they serve to root both their Catholic faith and their cultural identity in the diaspora and across the generations. The devotion of that small community incarnates those tensions and harmonies between the universal and the particular, the sacred and the secular that are the heart of the central mystery of the Incarnation. This incarnational paradox, it seems to me, lies at the heart of all belonging to the church. Materially, the Jesus Nazareno of Caguach in Punta Arenas in its modest home is no more than a piece of carved and painted wood on the physical and social margins of one of the most remote cities in the world. It is a humble, small world. Despite that—and because of that—the image and the devotion of the community gathered there to worship God participates in that Kingdom which is both in and at the same time beyond all the realms of our earth.

11

Negotiations In-Between: Indian Catholics in Diaspora

JAISY JOSEPH

In his seminal work, *A Theology of Liberation: History, Politics, and Salvation,* Gustavo Gutiérrez argues that this theology emerged from a profound consciousness of *kairos*. Understood biblically, *kairos* is "a propitious and demanding time in which the Lord challenges us and we are called on to bear a very specific witness."[1] In the fifty years since the Second Vatican Council, liberation theology has borne specific witness to the *irruption of the poor*. This witness has inspired the global community to recognize the presence of those who were once considered

> "absent" from our society and from the church. By "absent" [he] means: of little or no importance, and without the opportunity to give expression themselves to their sufferings, their camaraderies, their plans, their hopes.[2]

Meditating on the *kairos* of the third millennium, Gioacchino Campese, CS, argues that we are in the midst of a related, but distinct phenomenon: *the irruption of migrants*.[3] This irruption also demands a specific witness to make present those who are often absent from societal and ecclesial consciousness.[4] Migration both characterizes and conditions the global village of the third millennium. As of 2011, estimates of human

---

1. Gutiérrez, *Theology of Liberation*, xx.
2. Ibid.
3. Campese, "Irruption of Migrants," 4.
4. Ibid.

mobility include 214 million migrants worldwide, 27.1 million internally displaced people, and 15.2 million refugees.[5]

Despite the expansive nature of this irruption, systematic theology—and ecclesiology in particular—has often relegated human mobility to a social phenomenon and has not fully engaged the theological potential of this human experience.[6] Nevertheless, Asian American theologies, Campese observes, provide an important theological current that contribute to this emerging consciousness of migration. Because more than sixty percent of Asian Americans are first generation immigrants, the reality of living in-between the culture of their ancestors and the culture of their residence profoundly influences how they understand reality as existing in-between.[7]

In light of this existential experience of living in-between two or more cultures, I will first examine the pan-ethnic Asian American articulation of a hyphenated identity and its attending epistemology. I will then focus on two negotiations made within the current diaspora of SyroMalabar Catholics from Kerala, India. I will conclude by examining the potential ecclesiological contributions of migration for the church of the third millennium.

The Existential In-Between:
Asian American Identity and Epistemology

According to the 2010 US Census, there are 17.3 million Asian Americans in North America. Including those with origins in the Indian subcontinent and Far East and Southeast Asia, this group represents 5.6 percent of the American population and has grown by 43 percent in the past decade. The five largest groups are Chinese (3.3 million), Asian Indians (2.8 million), Filipinos (2.5 million), Vietnamese (1.5 million), and Koreans (1.4 million).[8] Phenotypically and culturally distinct from the European immigrants of the late nineteenth and early twentieth centuries, the Asian Americans of the post-1965 migrations are highly conscious of their immigrant status. In light of this consciousness, Vietnamese American theologian Peter C. Phan argues that "the very existential condition of the immigrant . . . entails a distinct epistemology and hermeneutics, a particular way of perceiving and interpreting reality, that is, oneself, others . . . the cosmos, and ultimately God."[9]

5. Cohen, "On the Move," 14–17.
6. Campese, "Irruption of Migrants," 5.
7. Ibid., 15.
8. Hoeffel et al., "Asian Population: 2010," 3, 15.
9. Phan, "Experience of Migration," 7.

Existing between the culture of their ancestors and the culture of their residence, they belong fully to neither culture, but participate within both. This existential predicament suggests that the individual is neither fully here nor fully there, neither fully Asian nor fully American. Phan describes the multiple dimensions of this condition when he states that

> spatially, it is to dwell at the periphery or at the boundaries. Politically, it means not residing at the centers of power of the two intersecting worlds but occupying the precarious and narrow margins where the two dominant groups meet and clash, and denied the opportunity to wield power in matters of public interest. Socially, to be betwixt and between is to be part of a minority, a member of a marginal(ized) group. Culturally, it means not being fully integrated into and accepted by either cultural system, being a *mestizo*, a person of mixed race. Linguistically, the betwixt-and-between person is bilingual but may not achieve a mastery of both languages and often speaks them with a distinct accent. Psychologically and spiritually, the person does not possess a well-defined and secure self-identity and is often marked with excessive impressionableness, rootlessness, and an inordinate desire for belonging.[10]

Existing at the margins, the concerns and experiences of Asian American migrants and their children are often absent from society and from the church. Yet, their suffering and soul-searching seeks and deserves expression as they come to terms with their hyphenated existence.

Caught in-between two worlds with regards to identity, the Asian American's epistemological framework is naturally multi-perspectival. Korean American theologian Sang Hyun Lee argues for the creative potential of existing between multiple perspectives by using anthropologist Victor Turner's concept of liminality. According to Turner's theory of ritual and social change, liminality is "a transitional time in which persons are freed from social structure, hierarchy, and role playing."[11] Moreover, this theory involves three stages: "(1) the first stage of *separation* or departure from social structure, especially social status and social role; (2) the middle stage of *liminality* in which a person is neither one thing nor another but betwixt and between; and (3) the final stage of *reincorporation* into structure with a new identity or with a new perspective on the existing structure."[12]

---

10. Phan, "Betwixt and Between," 113.
11. Sang Hyun Lee, *From a Liminal Place*, x.
12. Turner, *Ritual Process*, 94–113.

While existing in-between multiple worldviews and perspectives can cause confusion and tension, Sang discovers three creative potentials of this liminal space that can contribute to a new perspective on reality. First, the liminal space leads to an *openness to the new*. According to Turner, a society is revitalized by the dialectic between structure and anti-structure. Because one is between, neither here nor there, one is freed of the normal obligations that belong to a particular status or social identity. Turner describes liminality as society's "subjunctive mood, where suppositions, desires and hypotheses, possibilities and so forth, all become legitimate."[13] While chaotic and frightening because the validation and guidance of the old system has been left behind and the future lays indeterminate, it promises new beginnings.[14]

The second creative potential is the *emergence of communitas*. According to Turner, liminality also contributes to genuine human community. Because individuals must set aside old social roles and statuses when they leave the homeland, they are open to more spontaneous expressions of community with others. Such *communitas*, however, cannot stand alone but must give way to structure to meet organizational and material needs of people.[15] Yet, any structure that is not infused with the values of *communitas* becomes inhospitable.

Finally, the liminal space provides a *creative space for prophetic knowledge and action*. The existential in-between naturally places the individual at a distance from the centers of power. This distance enables the freedom to be critical of these centers and to de-familiarize the familiar. "Novelty," according to Turner, "emerges from the unprecedented combinations of familiar elements."[16] In addition to being critical, this space possesses a transformative capacity.

In light of the epistemological situation that emerges from the existential in-between of the Asian American experience, the next section will specifically examine two recent negotiations made in the SyroMalabar Catholic diaspora of immigrants from Kerala, India.

Borderline Negotiations in the SyroMalabar Catholic Diaspora

When discussing the experience of migration, Phan claims that "each culture contains within itself several significant varieties and is itself an

---

13. Ibid., vii.
14. Bridges, *Transitions*, 199.
15. Turner, *Ritual Process*, 129.
16. Turner, *From Ritual to Theater*, 27.

ever-changing and dynamic reality."[17] This description is no less true of SyroMalabar Catholics. Noted church historian Placid Podipara describes their hyphenated existence even prior to migration when he defines this Eastern Catholic community as "Hindu in culture, Christian in religion, [and] Oriental in worship."[18] Serving as a narrative of origins, he claims that these Christians are Hindu to the extent that they are formed by the same socioeconomic and political milieu that dictates caste and gender relations as a way of life within Indian society. This culture, however, was also Christianized by a faith presumably rooted in the missionary endeavors of the Apostle Thomas, who reached the southwestern coast of India via the Silk Road in 52 AD. Thus, these Christians are also referred to as Thomas Christians. In addition to expressing the faith according to a Malabar worldview, their liturgy is influenced by the East Syrian (Oriental) form of worship adopted from Syrian migrants during the fourth century. SyroMalabar Catholics belong to one of eight ecclesial communities that trace their heritage to the Thomas Christians.

Migration to the West, especially in the past fifty years, interrupts this narrative of origins and creates a liminal space in which old patterns and social statuses are contested within a new context. This situation leads to what postcolonial theorist Homi Bhabha refers to as "borderline negotiations." Resisting "binary representations," these negotiations produce hybrid, hyphenated identities amidst experiences of conflict, questioning, and critical honesty.[19]

The following, therefore, will consider two recent borderline negotiations within the SyroMalabar Catholic community in the United States. The first negotiation is related to how North American views of catholicity challenge caste endogamy practiced by a subset of SyroMalabar Catholics known as Knanaya Catholics. The second negotiation is a product of Portuguese colonization and is related to the use of the Syrian cross or the European crucifix in a Dallas SyroMalabar Catholic parish. While these borderline negotiations present deep tensions within the community, they will be examined in light of Turner's theory of liminality in order to discover any creative potential for resolution and contribution to Catholic ecclesiology.

---

17. Phan, *Experience of Migration*, 11.
18. Podipara, "Hindu in Culture," 107.
19. Bhabha, "Culture's In-Between," 58.

Endogamy and Catholicity

During the third century, persecutions led to a mass migration of Syrian Christians from Persia to areas throughout Asia. Many of them settled in the Malabar, or southwest India, because of previous trade connections with the Thomas Christians. Legend has it that upon leaving, these Knanaya Christians swore to their patriarch that they would maintain their racial purity and remain true to the faith.[20] While introducing the liturgy that the two communities share and establishing stronger ties between the East Syrian patriarchs and the Thomas Christians, the Knanayas remained endogamous throughout the centuries. A papal bull ecclesiastically recognized this separation in 1911 when Pope Pius X established the vicariate of Kottayam exclusively for Knanayas.[21] After migration to the United States, Knanaya Catholics continue to establish separate faith communities.

In the liminal space of migration, however, many question the catholicity of endogamous practices. Leaving behind the social structures influenced by Hindu caste practices, many migrants from mixed marriages challenge the custom of denying church membership to those who marry non-Knanayas. These questions surfaced internally as communities in the United States organically developed in the 1980s. In 2001, however, immediately after the official inauguration of the SyroMalabar Catholic diocese in North America, Roman Catholic Bishop Patrick J. McGrath of San Jose wrote a letter to Bishop Mar Jacob Angadiath, the first SyroMalabar Catholic bishop for the community in the US. In this letter, Bishop McGrath reported a bi-ritual priest who served both the SyroMalabar mission and a Roman Catholic community. While welcoming the SyroMalabar presence in San Jose, McGrath emphasized that the practice of endogamy, allowed by this priest, was unacceptable because it "breeds a sense of 'classism' and racism and is totally out of keeping with ecclesial or civil life in the United States."[22] In addition to being contradictory to North American Catholic practices, McGrath quotes the 1986 instruction from the Congregation for Oriental Churches, which states that

> the special ministry for the Knanaya Community can be faithfully conducted only on the basis that those Knanaya Catholics who married non-Knanaya spouses enjoy equal status in the ministry. This Congregation does not accept that the customary practices followed in Kerala, or excluding from the community

---

20. Katz, *Who Are the Jews of India?*, 18.
21. Pius X, "Papal Bull."
22. McGrath, "Letter to Bishop Jacob Angadiath."

those who marry non-Knanaya spouses, is extensible to the United States of America.[23]

Bishop Jacob responded in 2003 that he upholds the statement of the Congregation for Oriental Churches. He states that "Knanaya Missions are for all Knanaya Catholics. But no Knanaya Mission in this diocese is strictly endogamous. Knanaya Catholics who get married to non-Knanaya spouses will continue in their Knanaya missions along with their spouses and children."[24] This stance was officially promulgated in 2012, when Bishop Jacob sent a letter to all of the Knanaya priests and faithful in the United States. Because "family unity and spiritual well-being are our primary concerns," Knanayas who marry non-Knanayas cannot be discriminated or excluded from the community. Angadiath ended his letter with the proposal that though mixed-families may wish to attend the SyroMalabar parishes, they must have the freedom to also participate in Knanaya communities.

Three months later, hundreds of Knanaya Catholics from all over the United States flew to Chicago to protest the bishop's letter in front of his house. Extolling endogamy as a 1,700-year-old tradition, the protest coordinator further expressed how the Knanayas felt hurt by the Catholic Church's rejection of their right to continue this practice. In a separate interview with NPR, another individual claimed that "endogamy is the essence of the Knanaya community, and that the larger Catholic Church should not ask the Knanaya to sacrifice a defining characteristic of their identity."[25] In contrast, a few Knanayas who have married outside of the community are filing a canonical lawsuit for discriminatory practices against their family. Such discriminatory practices include the refusal of the sacraments of baptism and marriage to mixed-Knanaya families, the rejection of church donations from mixed-Knanaya families, and the lack of admission to parish council meetings.[26]

In the midst of this liminal border space between old practices of endogamy and an American ethos of inclusivity, the SyroMalabar Church is given the task of negotiating its understanding of catholicity. When Podipara claimed that these Thomas Christians were "Hindu in culture," he wanted to emphasize that this Christian tradition belonged to Malabar soil and was not a product of Western colonization or missions. In the context of migration, however, the question arises about the extent to which Hindu social structures influence the identity formation of Knanaya Catholics within

23. Ibid.
24. Angadiath, "Letter to Cyriac Parathara."
25. Yousef, "Local Indian Catholics Allege Discrimination."
26. Ritty, "Letter to Bishop Jacob Angadiath."

the SyroMalabar Catholic church. Second, this community must question the viability of claiming endogamy, rather than the Gospel kerygma, as an essential characteristic of their ancient ecclesial identity. In the midst of this liminal space, it appears as though a deep misunderstanding of catholicity and communion frustrates any creative potential for newness, *communitas*, and prophetic action. Because of this misunderstanding, both sides resort to equal rights language that accuses the other side of discrimination.

A Tale of Two Crosses

In November of 2013, an individual in Dallas recorded a YouTube video of himself burning the Mar Thoma Silva (St. Thomas cross).[27] This liturgical symbol is often displayed throughout the sanctuary during the Holy Qurbana (Mass). He claims that the cross is unscriptural and that only the crucifix, which contains the body of Jesus, should be used in the community. His actions are baffling unless placed within the larger narrative of the SyroMalabar church's colonial history. The conciliar document *Orientalium Ecclesiarum* (Decree on the Catholic Churches of the Eastern Rite) alludes to the complicated colonial relationship between Roman Catholic and Eastern Catholic churches when it states that

> all members of the Eastern Rite should know and be convinced that they can and should always preserve their legitimate liturgical rite and their established way of life, and that these may not be altered except to obtain for themselves an organic improvement. All these, then, must be observed by the members of the Eastern rites themselves. Besides, they should attain to an ever greater knowledge and a more exact use of them, and, if in their regard they have fallen short owing to contingencies of times

---

27. The Mar Thoma Silva (St. Thomas cross) is a dynamic Christian symbol of the life and death of Jesus the Messiah, as received in the Indian context through Syrian Christian missionaries. The empty cross (i.e., without the body of Christ) symbolizes the empty tomb as the first indication of the resurrection. The experience of the resurrection convicted St. Thomas the Apostle to exclaim, "My Lord and My God," and therefore, to preach the Gospel to the ends of the world, presumably including India in 52 AD. The blooming buds on the ends of the cross symbolize the new life received through Christ and the growth of the church. The Holy Spirit is depicted as descending upon the cross, enabling this new life and growth as a community. The cross also resides on a lotus, which represents how Christianity has been embraced in the land of Buddha. Finally, the lotus rests on three steps, which symbolizes Jacob's vision of the stairway to heaven in Genesis 12.

and persons, they should take steps to return to their ancestral traditions.[28]

In the particular case of SyroMalabar Catholics, this reference to preserving the "legitimate liturgical rite and established way of life" and the need "to return to ancestral traditions" refers to the disastrous consequences of the sixteenth-century colonial latinizations imposed on the Thomas Christians.

The Synod of Diamper (1599) was the main means of colonizing the Thomas Christians and imposing greater Latin conformity. One of the latinizations included the European devotion to the suffering Christ of the crucifix. The synod also severed the ecclesial ties between the Thomas Christians and the East Syrian patriarchs and burnt many of their ancient books and records. According to George Nedungatt, SJ, the "changes in the life and mores of the Thomas Christian community" enacted by the presumed knowledge and power of the Portuguese missionaries during the synod "were charged with a latent explosive potential destined to detonate after half a century . . . leaving behind cataclysmal ecclesial debris," the reverberations of which are still experienced today.[29] He is referring not only to the multiple divisions within the Thomas Christian community that resulted from the synod, but also the liturgical debates that still overwhelm the hierarchy in Kerala and the United States.

In light of this colonial devastation, many bishops who attended the Second Vatican Council interpreted the aforementioned section from *Orientalium Ecclesiarum* as a mandate to restore the oriental nature of one of the most highly latinized Eastern Catholic churches. One attempt was to encourage a veneration of the St. Thomas cross. Nevertheless, there has been a strong resistance to these efforts. Disputes over liturgical reform irrupted along the lines of Syrian restoration and Indian inculturation.[30] Eventually, the two sides became institutionalized as the Diocese of Changanacherry became associated with syrianization and the Diocese of Ernakalum became associated with inculturation. Because these two metropolitan dioceses were of equal rank, there was no head to decide the matter.

While aligning liturgical views with major metropolitan dioceses worked as a temporary solution for the generation immediately after Vatican

---

28. Second Vatican Council, *Orientalium Ecclesiarum*.

29. Nedungatt, "Interpreting the Synod of Diamper," 11.

30. Both Syrian restoration and Indian inculturation are reactions against Portuguese latinizations of the Catholic faith. Syrian restoration seeks to return to the patristic sources in order to restore the oriental nature of the church, while Indian inculturation wishes to make the faith more relevant to the dominant Hindu context of contemporary India.

II in Kerala, it proved faulty when individuals migrated to the United States. They found themselves with other SyroMalabar Catholics who were liturgically formed from the other side of the spectrum. In order to help resolve the issue, Pope John Paul II raised the SyroMalabar Church to a major archiepiscopal church and appointed a cardinal from the community to serve as its head in 1992. In 1999, the Liturgical Research Center was established to help bring resolution to this matter. Migration, however, has caused the controversy to spill over the boundaries of the Malabar Coast and take on global dimensions.

This situation became critical in 2010, when both factions in Dallas created internet blogs that anonymously attacked the other. The tensions began with a small controversy over whether the St. Thomas cross or the crucifix should hang in the center of the new worship space above the altar. The insults, however, became increasingly vociferous and threatened to tear apart the community. In September 2010, members of St. Alphonsa SyroMalabar Catholic Church staged a protest outside of their parish when Bishop Jacob insisted on placing the St. Thomas cross above the altar. They accused the bishop of favoring the liturgical traditions of his hometown in Kerala.[31]

Although tensions have cooled and a crucifix now hangs above the altar, this borderline negotiation reveals much more than an isolated controversy over religious symbols. In terms of the creative potential of this liminal situation, it reveals how much the laity, in addition to the clergy, need a deeper catechesis of the symbolic significance of the liturgy. In a post-Vatican II era, active participation of the entire community is expected. Without proper mystagogical formation, misinterpretations will continue to abound. A proper understanding would be that the fullest articulation of the faith necessitates both Christ's resurrection, as represented by the empty cross, and His crucifixion. Because this liminal space frees the community to question the hierarchy in a way that was unknown in previous generations, the clergy must be ready to engage the questions with answers that guide the entire flock toward greater understanding. Finally, the community in the United States can serve as a prophetic voice to the Indian hierarchy in two ways. First, these immigrant communities reveal the necessity of finding a resolution to the liturgical debates. This diaspora community also reveals how the hierarchy must take the faithful, who now belong to a global phenomenon, more seriously. With migrants not only in the United States, but also in Europe, the Middle East, Southeast and Far East Asia, and

---

31. McCartan, "Crucifix, Cross at Center of Battle."

Australia, the SyroMalabar hierarchy can no longer confine itself to the local Kerala context.

Ecclesiological Implications of the Existential In-Between

Reflecting on the global dimensions of human mobility, the Catholic Church, as a universal whole, cannot remain unaware of what this irruption of migrants means for the church. In an attempt to contribute to greater visibility, we have explored the contemporary experience of the SyroMalabar Catholic faithful. Resisting romantic idealizations, I have strived to present an honest portrayal of both the strengths and weaknesses of this community.[32] Indeed, endogamy and liturgical confusions reveal the necessity of a more robust understanding of what it means to be Catholic. Given this necessity, the following will explore the potential contributions of the existential in-between to Catholic ecclesiology.

The experience of migration and the existential in-between naturally lends itself to a reflection on catholicity. Catholicity does not imply a global uniformity according to a particular standard, such as the aforementioned Latin conformity of colonialism. Catholicity is the mark of the church that is radically open to God's work in the midst of and through the expressions of various cultures and ideologies. Campese reminds us that immigrants, "with their rich diversity and urgent need of inclusion, continue to remind the whole church of the fundamental importance of catholicity that is at the same time a gift, a mission, and a hope."[33] Because the foundational experience of any ecclesial community is God's love, all persons are potential members, regardless of their ethnicity or the ethnicity of their spouse.

Moreover, while many Asian Americans view the ecclesial space as a refuge within a foreign culture, it becomes harmful when they regard the space as a bastion of cultural preservation. Catholicity calls the church to welcome the stranger to experience the healing, forgiveness, and reconciliation that Christ offers. Rather than escape from the larger society, migrants and their children are called to develop an empathic sensitivity to the liminal and marginal experiences of others.

Another way of engaging Catholicity is to retrieve the conciliar image of the church as a pilgrim people of God in light of migratory experiences. Indonesian American theologian A. Bagus Laksana notes the particular fecundity of the pilgrimage metaphor for the ecclesiological and existential in-between. The migrant experience illuminates the significance of being a

32. Phan, *Experience of Migration*, 17.
33. Campese, "Irruption of Migrants," 25.

Christian pilgrim. It reveals a journey not only inward, but also vertically in ascent to God and horizontally in relation to neighbor. A crucial element in this journey, he argues, is that despite the distance between the present moment and the eternal destination, the pilgrim is committed to never losing sight of the goal.[34] The existential in-between, therefore, becomes a lifelong committed journey to the other, both God and neighbor.

From the perspective of pilgrimage, the entire ecclesial experience is defined by a faith that "has the courage to refuse the temptation to absolutize any one of the finite factors . . . and thereby to set up a false source of security."[35] To embrace this experience of liminality is to experience what Japanese American theologian Fumitaka Matsuoka calls "holy insecurity." It is to place one's unresolved and ambiguous narrative into the hands of the divine writer and to live with a sense of integrity in the in-between.[36] The church of the third millennium, therefore, must acknowledge the irruption of migrants as a time of *kairos*, in which the church is not just a church *for* migrants, but a church *of* migrants—on pilgrimage together toward the Heavenly Jerusalem.

---

34. Laksana, "Comparative Theology," 9.
35. Sang Hyun Lee, *From a Liminal Place*, 117.
36. Matsuoka, *Out of Silence*, 62.

12

Vietnamese Catholics and Diaspora: Re-imaging Mary as Vietnamese

LINH HOANG, OFM

Introduction

The study of diaspora is "trending" in Asian American studies. More accurately, Asian American studies is actually re-examining diaspora and reappropriating it, as David Palumbo-Liu (Asian American scholar) argues, that "the discourse of diaspora is often used as a litmus test for conservative and conserving predilections for establishing what it means to be authentically Chinese, Indian, and so on."[1] This argument stresses the fact that for Asian Americans, the turn to diaspora continues to uphold the idea of the "foreignness" and "strangeness" of the Asian "race," which has effectively excluded Asians from the traditional race debates in the United States, pitting the majority whites against the minority blacks. Furthermore, within this discussion, for Vietnamese American Catholics, their religious identity plays a central role in who they are as Vietnamese and as American.

My reflection on the Vietnamese diaspora is part of this broader Asian American consideration that holds in tension diaspora and race as necessary points of departure. This tension provides a tool to understand Vietnamese Catholics who, through fashioning a concrete image of the Virgin Mary Mother of God as Vietnamese, have asserted race as important in the diaspora experience. From Catholic mission history, already many of the images of Mary, Jesus, and some saints resemble white Europeans rather than possessing the distinctive cultural features of the Middle East or, for

---

1. Palumbo-Liu, *Asian/American*, 335.

that matter, any indigenous culture that was colonized. This would only occur in a postcolonial period. The production of statues in colonial Vietnam features dramatically white Europeans rather than any local characteristics. These remain in many areas of Vietnam today. Similarly, church buildings mirroring the European Gothic façade dot the landscape, consciously maintaining the "foreignness" of Christianity all the while trying to be relevant in Vietnam. Nevertheless, the difference maintains a conscious divide that is religious, cultural, and racial.

At the end of the war in Vietnam in 1975, many refugees fled to the United States and other parts of the world, and diaspora communities began to rebuild their lives. There were five waves of refugee flight out of Vietnam starting in 1975 and tapering off by 1990. The first wave included over 170,000 Vietnamese refugees who were transported to the United States. After a resettlement strategy of dispersing the Vietnamese refugees throughout the fifty states, there was a conscious second migration effort by the Vietnamese themselves to be closer to family, friends, and, for some, warmer climes. Through this second migration, Vietnamese communities forged new enclaves and created new identities. Building up enclaves aligns Vietnamese refugees with other immigrants who built communities to better adjust to the United States. It is interesting to note that "enclaves" is applied to Asian immigrants while "ghetto," the term often used to describe poor black communities, has a more derogatory connotation. Within these enclaves, Vietnamese Catholic communities were very visible through their construction of churches, parish centers, and other outreach centers.

The Vietnamese Catholics, similar to many traditional Catholic communities, possess a strong devotion to the Blessed Virgin Mary in order to fashion not just a Catholic identity but a particular Catholic identity grounded in their racial/ethnic experience. This presentation discusses the Blessed Mother's importance for Vietnamese Catholics in the diaspora as they transform a European-looking Mary to a Vietnamese-looking Mary through a contested history of her apparition to persecuted Vietnamese. First, I will discuss the apparition of the Virgin Mary at La Vang in central Vietnam and set it in a historical context of the church. Second, I will examine the image chosen to represent Mary at La Vang and how the local religious practices influenced the popularity of her apparitions. Third, I will trace the production of the statue of Our Lady of La Vang in Orange County, California, for the two hundredth anniversary of her apparition in Vietnam. The statue molded out of a diasporic imagination now situates race as an important aspect of religious practice. The conclusion will be a call for further reflection on diaspora and race as important examinations for Asian and Asian American Catholic studies.

Apparition in Historical Context

The prominent Yale historian Jaroslav Pelikan wrote, "The Virgin Mary has been more of an inspiration to more people than any other woman who ever lived."[2] Stories of Mary offer hope and comfort to individuals. She is seen as a supernatural healer and guide. Of course, the oldest stories about Mary are found in the New Testament; early Christians further maintained and further emphasized the importance of the Virgin Mary. This is evidenced by the patristic writings of Irenaeus of Lyons (140–202 CE), Tertullian (155–240 CE), Athanasius, and Augustine. Belief about Mary was concretized at the Ecumenical Council of Ephesus (431 CE). The council's statement identified Mary as *Theotokos*—the one who gave birth to the One who is God.[3] From these writings, as well as from visual art found in the third- and fourth-century Roman catacombs, there is ample evidence that Mary was highly esteemed and viewed as a maternal intercessor.

Over the centuries, more regional stories of the Virgin May appeared. It is from these regional stories collected from various corners of the world that stories of her apparition to downtrodden people, young children, and those fleeing persecutions began to influence a new and different turn in Marian devotion. These apparitional stories now have been passed down from local faith communities to the universal church, and they continue to inspire and to interest millions of believers and nonbelievers as well.

In December 1997, Pope John Paul II wrote to the archbishop of Hue exclaiming that "on this happy occasion of the second centenary of the apparitions of the Blessed Virgin, I send you, Your Eminence, my affectionate Apostolic Blessing which I willingly extend to the Bishops, to the priests, and to those preparing for the priesthood, to the religious and to all the faithful of Việt Nam and the diaspora."[4]

The pope's reference to the apparitions is most interesting because there were two places in Vietnam of Marian apparitions, one in La Vang (more popularly known) and the other, lesser known and actually disputed, at Tra Kieu. The account of Mary at La Vang was passed orally and thus, no written documents exist. The last survivors in the nineteenth century are not even named by the priest who took their statements. The oral transmission continues to be the only authority to Mary's apparition at La Vang.

The meaning of La Vang is significant to consider. There are actually two meanings depending on the diacritical marks: La Vang can mean

---

2. Pelikan, *Mary through the Centuries*, 2.
3. Ibid., 55.
4. John Paul II, "Letter to Cardinal Paul Joseph Pham Dinh Tung."

"leaves of the trees" in the forest, and it can also mean "crying out." So, when the story was passed down, some people said it was the lady in the forest and others emphasized the crying of those seeking refuge. The context is this: in 1798, the Tay Son rebellion (a grassroots uprising against the ruling class, especially the emperors) drew to its conclusion when a strong Nguyen empire regained power. King Canh Thinh (crowned in 1792) perceived the Catholic Church as a foreign enemy and began a cruel persecution of Catholics that lasted beyond his death until 1886 when the French ceased full control.

The first apparition of Mary at La Vang occurred in August of 1798, when refugees from the town of Quang Tri hid in the forest. She appeared as a beautiful lady wearing a dress and long cape, holding a baby and accompanied by two angels. She heard their cry for help, and her message was that she would always help them in time of need. The Virgin Mother gave the people solace and instructed them to boil the la' vang leaves for use as a medicine. She also said that from that day on, all who come to this place would have their prayers heard and answered. A tiny altar was built at the site, which became a refuge for thousands fleeing persecution. There were accounts that she appeared several more times during that period. The apparition did not immediately draw believers to La Vang, because the harsh terrain and continual persecution made the journey quite treacherous. Nonetheless, small pilgrimages to La Vang began in 1882. After the persecution ended in 1886, an official church was built there. In 1901, with the dedication of a new church to Our Lady of La Vang, more pilgrims flocked there. It was destroyed in 1972 during the war. In 1985, the people began to restore the buildings around the place of the apparition, especially since pilgrims were interested in coming. Today, pilgrims numbering in the hundreds of thousands come from Vietnam and around the world.

The Vatican has had an ambivalent history in terms of its veneration of Mary and its official position on Marian apparitions. This attitude has created openings for apparitional claims and complicated the church's ability to contain those claims. Official church policies offer clerical leaders a range of options in responding to apparitional claims. Diocesan bishops may determine whether or not to initiate an investigation, depending on how significant the event appears to be. The Vatican may launch an investigation on its own initiative or at the request of laity or bishops. With respect to any particular claim, the church may ultimately accept the apparition as representing supernatural activity, issue no decision on the apparition, state that there is no evidence of supernatural activity, or state that there is evidence that supernatural activity did not occur. Assessments of apparitional claims often have spanned many decades, and full acceptances have been extremely rare.

Even though the apparition of Mary at La Vang was never fully accepted or denied, John Paul II still recognized it and congratulated the Vietnamese Catholics on their faithful devotion to Mary. He went further to support the rebuilding of the La Vang Basilica for this commemoration. Subsequently, an article in *L'Osservatore Romano* on August 12, 1998, confirmed that the apparition had no written documentation.[5]

The church has faced several problems in dealing with apparitional events, including the sheer number of such events, their implications for official doctrine, and choosing an appropriate response. The church has therefore been selective in dealing with these events and has elected to study only a few hundred of them. The basic premise upon which the church has responded is that revelations (public) that add to the body of faith ended during the era of the Apostles. Apparitions have been accepted as breakthroughs of transcendent power, which demonstrated Mary's continuing care and protection of humankind, but have been understood as emphasizing some existing aspect of Roman Catholic doctrine rather than adding to the body of that doctrine. Individual revelations, therefore, are private events that may confirm but do not modify church doctrine, and Catholics may, but have not been required, to accept such events.

There are a few points of distinction about the La Vang apparitions that are unlike the apparitions in Europe, especially at Lourdes and Fatima, which were institutionally approved (and where Mary's message was of apocalyptic divine punishment). In Vietnam, her message was of protection and well-being. Mary's liberation of the persecuted believers creates the image of a divine mercy that speaks so powerfully to Vietnamese Catholics who have been persecuted since missionary times. Hence the date of Mary's appearance in Vietnam, preceding that of both Lourdes and Fatima, creates a significant milestone for the faithful.

Images of Mary, Images of Goodness

Mary did not appear to colonizers but to those who were persecuted; since there were no written documents, one can only speculate what the people saw. Was the Mary they saw a Vietnamese woman? Did she look like them? Or did she appear European because of the missionaries' influences? Was she Our Lady of Victory? In other places where Mary had appeared, such as the more famous Guadalupe and Medjugorje, the artistic renderings

5. *L'Osservatore Romano*, "Catholics of Viet Nam."

portray regional characteristics of the people looking adoringly at Mary and express the local people's experience with the sacred. Before I directly discuss the image that was the official Our Lady of La Vang, I turn to the traditional culture of Vietnam that had a reverence for goddesses and matriarchal prowess.

Some skeptics of the La Vang apparitions have stated that the woman the people actually saw was Kwan Yin, which would make her a Bodhisattva rather than Mary. This is intriguing because it affirms that the local people would have seen her as one of them, making her a local person rather than a foreign colonizer.[6]

In "The La Vang Event: The Martyrs' History," Nguyen Văn Thông stated that in 1820, at the beginning of the reign of Minh Mang, three local villages—Thach Han, Be Tru, and Co Thanh—built a *mieu* (a kowtowing platform, joss house, or incense burning place). In reality, it was a raised platform with a fence surrounding it. The villagers who had used it then learned that decades before Catholics had described a woman's appearance at that very site. Thus, the villagers yielded the site to the Catholics. Văn Thông really did not mention the traditional tension between the Buddhist and Catholic faithful. The vicar of the local parish modified the platform into a thatch-roofed building. This was the first church built in La Vang.[7] The conflation of Catholicism with Buddhism was not only caused by external factors of persecution and the need for camouflage but was also strongly affected by an internal theological element common to both religions.

This speculation supports the natural acceptance of Mary not only by Vietnamese Catholics but also the larger population. Added to this layer is the fact that many villagers in Vietnam practiced a native spiritual tradition. The association with the Goddess of Vietnam, also known as the Lady of the Realm, can also be applied to the rather easy acceptance of Mary. Traditionally, the cult of Mother Goddess in Vietnam is a symbol of freedom from the oppressive Confucian structure.[8] Because so little is known about the Mother Goddess, stories that exist survive through oral transmission and the collective consciousness of the people.[9] Nevertheless, there was not a statue made of Mary at this particular time (1820–1886); only an altar existed with a cross to indicate a Catholic place.

6. See http://lexuannhuan.tripod.com/LaVangE.html. Also, Philip Taylor in *Goddess on the Rise: Pilgrimage and Popular Religion in Vietnam,* describes the warm receptivity of Vietnamese to female deities.

7. Nguyen, "Su-Kien La Vang," 46–48.

8. Historically, Vietnam shuttered all Confucian schools by 1901 which would diminish the Confucian influence in later years.

9. Taylor, *Goddess on the Rise,* 251.

Furthermore, goddess worship endured and survived from what is claimed to be Vietnam's matriarchal and hence primitive period of history.[10] Urban intellectuals in Vietnam believe prejudicially that people living in rural and remote areas, with a "low level" of education, are more prone to misapprehend the forces of nature or redress their failings in the face of a potent nature through a religious lens. However, rather than disparage goddess worship as an example of "low" knowledge or cultural "levels" (*trinh do thap*) or "superstition" (*me tin di doan*), national folklorists and ethnologists accord this practice integrity by glossing it as a "folk belief" (*tin nguong dan gian*). This more nuanced designation makes it more palpable and also commercially appealing to a global world that has now descended on Vietnam as a tourist hotspot destination.

The goddess worship has also uncovered the culturally hybrid Lady of the Realm (Ba Chua Xu) as typical of the multiethnic, heterodox, constantly mutating cultural landscape of Vietnam herself (here more particular to the southern region)[11] and as an "original" cultural accomplishment, which has enriched the "storehouse" of Vietnamese national culture.[12] This enrichment of the Vietnamese national cultural identity has been grasped by the government to reimagine itself on a global scale, in order to improve the country financially and politically.

This backdrop is important to remember as we move back to how Mary is then represented. In 1900, under French colonization, on the occasion of the first Our Lady of La Vang Convention, Bishop Louis Casper placed a French-modeled statue of Our Lady of Victory (Notre-Dame des Victoires) in the new church built to honor Our Lady of La Vang. The Holy Mother wears a cloak. Her head is adorned by a golden crown, and she is standing on top of a cluster of clouds. She looks at a group of faithful with a gentle and majestic face. Her two hands support the Baby Jesus on her right side as if she wants to introduce Him to us. From 1900 on, every three years, on the third day of the Vietnamese Lunar New Year, a procession carries this statue from Co Vuu village to La Vang village. This event recalls the seventeenth- and eighteenth-century history of religious persecution and the flight to safety on the ground where Mary appeared.

On December 8, 1954, the statue of Our Lady of La Vang was brought from Tri Bun back to the holy shrine. The Vietnamese Bishops' Conference chose the Church of Our Lady of La Vang as the national shrine in honor of

---

10. Nguyen, *Nhung Thanh Nu Danh Tieng*.

11. Huynh, "Tong Quan ve Van Hoa Nam Bo [An Overview of Southern Culture]," 59–70.

12. Nguyen, *Tiep con tin Nguong Dan da Viet Nam*.

the Immaculate Conception. La Vang became the National Marian Center of Vietnam on April 13, 1961. Pope John XXIII elevated the Church of Our Lady of La Vang to the rank of a minor basilica on August 22, 1961.

The original statue was destroyed during the bombings of 1972. In 1975, another statue was constructed to represent Our Lady of La Vang. Like the first one, it was modeled after the image of Our Lady of Victory. This statue represented Our Lady of La Vang until 1998, when it was replaced on the occasion of the apparition's 200th anniversary.

Reappropriation: Making Mary "Vietnamese"

Vietnam is not unique now in possessing a native-looking Mary; other Asian countries have an Asian-looking Mary such as Taiwan, Cambodia, Macau, and Japan. The first attempt to indigenize or "Vietnamize" Our Lady of La Vang was through the efforts of Vietnamese Catholics living in Southern California.

During the 1980s, Vietnamese Catholics in the United States began organizing outside the ecclesiastical structure in order to mobilize their representation within the Catholic Church. In 1983, Vietnamese Catholics of Orange County, California, created a Vietnamese Catholic Cultural Center, and Vietnamese Catholics were required to make an annual monetary contribution to the diocese. Masses were not held at the center, but it became a place for Vietnamese Catholics to share faith and socialize. The center was built in more of an Asian style with sweeping roofs and geometrically placed doors and windows. The attention to the architecture would be important as a geomancer would be consulted to guarantee the best placement of the new center.

It is within this context of structural marginalization that Vietnamese Catholics in the United States turned toward Our Lady of La Vang as a unique cultural representation of their identity within the Catholic Church. Our Lady of La Vang was not commonly known outside of Vietnam, and some speculate that the lack of recognition from the Vatican has limited her popularity to a larger Vietnamese Catholic population. Perhaps it was precisely because of its particular associations with Vietnam and Vietnamese identity within the Catholic Church that Our Lady of La Vang became a symbolic ethnic and racial marker with which Vietnamese Catholics distinguished themselves from other Catholics in the United States.

In 1985, Vietnamese Catholics in the United States began to concentrate their efforts to elevate the symbol of Our Lady of La Vang as an ethnic marker to a global scale. In this year, Catholics in Vietnam petitioned the

Vatican to canonize its 117 martyrs. Vietnamese American Catholics joined the request, marking a reconnection with their compatriots after more than a decade. The Vatican approved the canonization; in 1988, Pope John Paul II elevated Andrew Dung-Lac and his companions as saints. Their feast day is November 24 in the church calendar. During this canonization process, Vietnamese Catholics campaigned for recognition from the Vatican of the apparition of Our Lady of La Vang. The pope held a meeting with Vietnamese representatives to that effect. The pope also established a Center of Pastoral Apostolate for Overseas Vietnamese to serve the Vietnamese Catholic diaspora during the same year.

In 1994, Vietnamese American Catholics in Orange County, California, constructed their version of Mary, initially named Our Lady of Vietnam. A Vietnamese artist and sculptor named Van Nhan created the statue. Visiting priests from the Diocese of Hue, Vietnam, invited Van Nhan to create a new statue of Our Lady of La Vang modeled on Our Lady of Vietnam that he had previously sculpted. Our Lady of Vietnam for Viet Kieu now became Our Lady of La Vang. This change for the Vietnamese in the diaspora is significant as Mary is shifted from a national symbol to a very Catholic one, placing her in a unique historical position. This change would be officially recognized when Pope John Paul II blessed the newly created statue of Our Lady of La Vang as the patroness of the Catholic Church of Vietnam during the anniversary of her apparition.

The 200th anniversary of La Vang was in 1998, and while it brought official recognition of the apparition, it did not bring Vatican approval. Monsignor Philippe Tran Van Hoai was appointed the first director of the newly established organization. Born and raised in La Vang, he had close ties to and was invested in the cause. The devotion to Our Lady of La Vang—now reimaged as a Vietnamese Mary—reveals the ways in which the diasporic community has used her to reflect upon and renegotiate their ethnic identity within a multicultural society. Also, her image now breaks through boundaries of those who can identify as Catholic. There are now fifteen parishes across the United States that are named for Our Lady of La Vang with a sixteenth to open in 2018 in San Jose, California.

The aesthetics of function from works of art and images can be used for healing and empowerment. In this case of Our Lady of La Vang, this image has begun to heal the pain of those in the diaspora (those who fled persecution) and has empowered Vietnamese Catholics in Vietnam to assert their place. They are no longer foreigners in their own land for having embraced and practiced a foreign religion. Now, their religion is *theirs*, captured in the image of Mary. They are casting off colonial power and embracing a new image of self. The Viet Catholics can see that Mary is now one of them, that she is not just an external protector but one who truly walks with the oppressed and persecuted. Suffering of the oppressed is never legitimate. It is never legitimate and always resisted. The power of common symbols and narratives as well as the negative use of collective identities such as diaspora can transform a tragic history.

Conclusion

Mary's importance as a figure and a symbol has varied through Roman Catholic history. She has been depicted as a queen in heaven and as a peasant girl, but her spiritual status has continued to rise amid fluctuating papal encouragement and discouragement of Marian devotionalism. Her place in Vietnamese Catholic history is quite important as we trace her through the nation's tumultuous history to its diaspora community. For the Vietnamese Catholics around the world, this reinforced identity of the apparition of Mary at La Vang has created a stronger connection to their homeland, especially with Pope John Paul II's recognition of Our Lady of La Vang as the patroness of Vietnam.

The speed at which the country of Vietnam embraced modernity and globalization during the 1990s grossly exaggerated the paradoxes inherent to these two transformative processes. A real energy to develop, to move forward, and to modernize was partnered with an intense desire to look back, to reclaim, and to retrieve what was lost. We can say that the lost identity of the Goddess of Vietnam was then resurrected with the apparition of Mary. Both are now recognized and revered in Vietnam and the diaspora. Further investigation and study is needed, but one can only say that the recent interest in goddess study in Vietnam takes into consideration all matriarchs of Vietnamese history.

Finally, the image in Christianity bears all the intensity of the need and desire to access the inaccessible divine. Conceptions of Mary as human and, in some respect, divine become touchstones of identity, cultural reference points, and beacons of moral constancy that speak to, and are shaped by, the very similar dilemmas people face in these different national and diaspora contexts. For the same reasons that certain readings of these images of Mary are shared across Vietnam's borders, one finds a considerable variety of uses for them within the country. Views of Mary as patroness, business partner, underwriter of smuggling and escape from the country or, alternatively, as shameful marks of backwardness and ignorance, sit side by side with those expressed by folklorists and ethnologists who tie her to the expression or sustenance of the national collectivity. Such diversity of opinions reflects the complexity of the society in which Our Lady of La Vang is now located, just as it suggests the inability of the state to constrain a unified reading of this religious and cultural practice. Mary's role as marker of a range of status, race, ethnic, gender, occupational, and class distinctions also reminds us that there are subtler borders than those of state/non-state membership or of national territory to which Mary gives expression. Such plurality of interpretations points to the multiplicity of social concerns that animate religious practice and underlines the need to attend carefully to the time and the place in which interpretations of Mary are situated. This Mary is a Vietnamese woman who stands in a long line of strong female leaders who have contributed to the formulation and creation of a peoples' identity—an identity which, in the diaspora, is made distinctive and real.

13

From America, with Hate: Bond and the "Black Shirley Temple"

DANIEL MCNEIL

Almost four score and seven years ago, Philippa Schuyler was conceived under a cloud of romantic fancy and racist paranoia. Her mother was Josephine Cogdell Schuyler, a white artist from a wealthy background in Texas, who believed that the "white race" was spiritually depleted and that her daughter and other racially mixed children were needed to save America's soul.[1] Her father was George Schuyler, one of the most prominent African American journalists and authors of the early twentieth century, who thought that his daughter's genius would confound Nazis in Europe as well as right-wing anthropologists in America who invested in pseudoscientific ideas about black intellectual inferiority.[2] Yet many Americans did not share the hopes and dreams of the Schuylers and their friends in a New York avant-garde. During a time in which the Schuylers were unable to marry in Texas and many other states of the union, mainstream journalists expressed their shock and concern for a blue-blooded "blonde Texan" who fell in love with a "coal black Negro." They also filed the prodigious talents of Philippa Schuyler under newspaper reports about a "strange curiosity" or a "Black Shirley Temple."[3]

After being marketed as a child prodigy in America, and then touring the globe as a peripatetic concert pianist sponsored by the US State Department, Schuyler lamented the lack of cultural opportunities available for her in America.[4] She expressed hatred for her home and native land, and drew

1 Talalay, *Composition in Black and White*, 36, 208.
2. G. Schuyler, "Letter to Josephine Schuyler"; Rogers, *Sex and Race*, 408–9.
3. Barnett, "Negro Girl"; Alsop, "Harlem's Youngest Philosopher."
4. P. Schuyler, Diary Entry, April 15, 1960.

on a wide range of cultural materials in order to create a new identity for herself as a woman of Iberian origin who could find gainful employment as a writer of Catholic hagiographies and "sexy novels." Yet whether she wrote under the name Philippa Schuyler or Felipa Monterro, she attacked blackness as an alien Other tied to racial violence, economic underdevelopment, and brute strength. Whether she followed her father into the ultra rightwing John Birch Society or sent letters to her mother praising the beauty of Aryan men, she sought to defend the authority of strong white rule in multiracial environment. Whether composing plays, novels, diaries, letters, or a new identity, she was inspired by a love of "blacks with white skins"—tough whites from working-class or southern European backgrounds who could not be caricatured as prudish Nordics or be legally classified as black. As a result, Schuyler generated excessive power to attack forms of blackness and threatened the authority of whiteness that she sought to defend. Her story is a not only a tale of black and white; it is a special blend of irony, tragedy, and farce.

"I Hate My Country"

When she traveled around the world as a concert pianist, Schuyler described her father as a man of color from Madagascar with no ancestral links to Africa. She also demanded the removal of her name from his encyclopedia of *The Negro in America*,[5] and it is difficult to find a starker, more literal depiction of Philippa Schuyler's flight from blackness than the white piece of paper that George Schuyler pasted over his daughter's entry in his unpublished manuscript of African American life.[6] Yet, rather than explore the psychological dimensions of this family romance, historians and biographers have tended to rely on stereotypes about a "tragic mulatto" trapped between black and white in America, speculated about the "mixed personality disorder" of "Harlem's biracial prodigy,"[7] and indulged in armchair psychiatry about Schuyler's "national, racial, and personal identity confusions."[8] Such comments say more about the influence of assertively nationalistic commentators who talk about the rootlessness of African Americans who try to escape racial shame,[9] and rather less about the routes plotted by

5. P. Schuyler, "Une Métisse a la Reserche de son ame"; "Letter to J. Schuyler," September 22, 1954; "Letter to Josephine Schuyler," June 9, 1963.
6. G. Schuyler, *Negro in America*.
7. Talalay, *Composition in Black and White*, 294.
8. Ferguson, *Sage of Sugar Hill*, 152.
9. Asante, "Book Review," 847–51.

Schuyler as a precursor of "that contemporary quest of individuals who resist the one-drop rule and navigate the uncharted waters of multiracial identity."[10] Rather than dismiss Schuyler's self-fashioning as a cautionary tale about "little yellow dream children,"[11] or develop a revisionist history that celebrates her struggle to resist the impositions of a one-drop rule, this paper provides some further context for us to analyze Schuyler's pursuit of love and security in the 1950s and '60s. I am interested in her attempts to unite with something or someone larger than herself in a Cold War context riddled with racism, sexism, and homophobia; her self-conscious adoption of national stereotypes in the hopes of becoming a creative artist who would be popular with European audiences; and the voracious and wide-ranging reading that informed her contribution to perennial debates about art and commerce, truth and popularity, revolution and reaction.

Schuyler's transformation into the exotic femme fatale Felipa Monterro was informed by her reading of iconoclastic writers such as Simone de Beauvoir and Sidonie-Gabrielle Colette. Yet Anaïs Nin, a writer with French, Spanish, and Cuban roots, is perhaps the most intriguing female influence on the motifs of race, sexuality, freedom, and marriage that would play such a major role in Schuyler's self-fashioning. To give one revealing example, Nin's diary described a trip to Harlem in which she sought to repay the wisdom of her psychologist, the Austrian-born Otto Rank, with a night that was filled with the "natural rhythm" and "wild dancing" of blacks.[12] Such depictions of rational European masculinity were further indulged by Rank's social psychology about birth trauma (the violent separation from the mother) and the so-called "masculine ideology" of art and myth. In Nin's diaries, Rank tells his most famous American patient, "When the neurotic woman gets cured [from the pain of birth trauma], she becomes woman [or a mother]. When the neurotic man gets cured, he becomes an artist."[13] In his own, unfiltered work, he proffers the following maxims: "the woman's strength lies in her sex, the man's in his creative will"; "she needs the man as a rational guide through this man-made world"; "whereas man develops his psychology to protect himself by control (will), woman takes on his psychology from an opposite motive, that is, to lose herself, to give herself to him."[14]

10. Daniel, *More than Black*, 96.
11. Washington, *Invented Lives*, 160.
12. Nin, *Diary of Anaïs Nin*, vol. 2, 6.
13. Nin, *Diary of Anaïs Nin*, vol. 1, 291.
14. Rank, *Beyond Psychology*, 256–58, 265, 284.

If Nin found the masculinist views of Rank reinforced by personal contact, Schuyler's feminist readings were combined with trips to the movies. She could lose herself—and fashion a self—while watching epic tales of exotic adventure such as *Lawrence of Arabia* (directed by David Lean, 1962), which won the best picture and best director Oscars at the 35th Academy Awards and explored the double consciousness of an Englishman and an Arab; *The Leopard* (directed by Luchino Visconti, 1963), a film based on the novel about Don Fabrizio Corbera, Prince of Salina, and the changes in Sicilian life and society during the *Risorgimento*, which won the 1963 Palm d'Or from the Cannes film festival; and the James Bond series of films, which adapted the novels and short stories created by a white Englishman in the neocolonial settings of Jamaica. In other venues, I have considered Schuyler's relationship to *The Leopard* and *Lawrence of Arabia*.[15] In this chapter, I will primarily use Schuyler's engagement with Bond to connect her ideas about black primitiveness to her hopes of becoming a femme fatale who would honor and obey powerful white men.

The Woman of Color and the White Man

Ian Fleming's stories about James Bond were first published at a time of profound anxiety in British life. In 1953, various foreign policy crises displayed the continuing decline of British military power, and Winston Churchill, the nation's eloquent and imperialist leader during World War II, suffered a major stroke. The Bond series provided readers with an anti-hero who led the United States and the English-speaking nations of the Commonwealth with his wit, bravery, and bravado. Put more bluntly, Bond was vital to the Anglosphere that Churchill championed in his "Sinews of Peace Address" at Westminster College in Fulton, Missouri, on March 5, 1946. Lest we forget, this notion of an Anglosphere often served as a euphemism for white leadership or "white blood" protecting nonwhites from barbarity and irrelevance. One thinks, for example, of Sir Hugh Trevor-Roper, Regius Professor of History at Oxford University, who asserted that African history was the study of "unrewarding gyrations of barbarous tribes in picturesque but irrelevant parts of the globe"; Sir Christopher Masterman, the first British Deputy Commissioner for South India, who promoted the idea that blacks had "no culture, no architecture, no written language" and were desperately in need of Aristotelian "natural rulers"; and Austin Ferraz, editor of *The Sunday Mail* of Salisbury, Rhodesia, who thought it was common sense

15. McNeil, *Sex and Race in the Black Atlantic*; and McNeil, "Black Devils, White Saints & Mixed-Race Femme Fatales," 360–76.

to believe that "out of the 20 million negroes in the US almost none have achieved anything and those who are claimed to have done so—like Ralph Bunche and Thurgood Marshall—are whiter than they are black."[16]

Drawing on his experiences as a student in European universities, an intelligence officer in the British armed forces and journalist with Reuters, Fleming also conveyed in his novels a concern about the ability of Africans to govern themselves. Black Jamaicans were depicted as kind and lazy "with the virtues and vices of a child" in *Dr. No*. In *Quantum of Solace*, Bond describes the "simple, kindly natures" of black Nigerians who know nothing about birth control. And, when an evil black genius threatens Bond in *Live and Let Die*, readers are reminded that he has a "healthy dose" of European blood. Yet the racist ideologies that informed Fleming's ideas about race and racial mixing were not only linked to political intelligence; they were also tied to a beauty mystique in which Bond dispatched grotesque villains (such as Le Chiffre, a "Portuguese with a dash of Chinaman") and aligned himself with Solitaire and other racially mixed individuals whom he deemed friendly and beautiful.[17]

Schuyler adapted the racism and beauty mystique of the Bond novels when she hoped to become a Catholic writer and an exotic femme fatale. She chose to pass as an Iberian woman because she considered Portugal to be "the world's only major nation, having a large nonwhite populace, to accord half-castes absolute equality with whites" and reminded the readers of *Jungle Saints* that leading figures in Portugal's parliament were married to women of Chinese descent.[18] Yet while Schuyler praised Portuguese men in Angola who were willing to acknowledge their attraction to nonwhite women and grant the children of interracial relationships absolute equality with whites, she also expressed her belief that blacks were "simple children of nature." Drawing on the pseudoscientific racism of eugenicists who contrasted the forceful personalities of Mediterranean "races" with the "sexually conservative" Anglo-Saxons or Nordics,[19] Schuyler praised Portuguese conservatives who were free of that "strained attempt to prove one is a liberal [by asserting the equality of blacks], so often to be seen in Anglo-Saxon countries."[20] In addition, her missives for the far-right John Birch Society condemned the

---

16. Trevor-Roper, "Rise of Christian Europe," 871; Masterman, "You Do Not Invite Children"; Ferraz, "Letter to Sir Patrick Wall."
17. Synott, "Beauty Mystique," 407–26.
18. P. Schuyler, *Jungle Saints*, 166, 168.
19. Freyre, *Masters and the Slaves*.
20. P. Schuyler, *Virgin and the Cross*.

"awful" characters and "primitive savagery" of "pure blacks,"[21] and warned readers about the supposed threat of "deviant" homosexuality to Western civilization.[22] She not only argued that "[f]airies, weaklings, opportunists, climbers, avaricious money-grabbers, socialists and Reds lost the Congo for the West,"[23] but offered the following reflections on her failure to find a real-life Commander Bond while staying near a British military base:

> In Nicosia, [I] went and sat in a bar. Seven Englishmen were seated at the bar stools. I sat next to them for *one hour* and not one of them cast *one glance* at me! God, the difference between Englishmen and Italians! No Italian would leave me unlooked-at for one hour! I went to bed, woefully convinced of my decline and failure as a femme fatale. At dawn, I was awakened by some wild whooping out in the corridor. One of the Englishmen, who had the room on my left, was running around the hall, shouting in purest Anglo-Saxon, to the two Englishmen who had the room on the right. The language (!**%**) he used, and their replies, made it quite clear they were, all seven of them, homosexuals! No wonder the British have lost their empire! They were all RAF officers too.[24]

Bond and BDSM

Fleming created Commander Bond as he contemplated his upcoming marriage on a neocolonial estate in Jamaica that overlooked a private beach. The antics of his hero—perhaps the most famous bachelor in the West—allowed Fleming one way to extend his own bachelorhood and appeal to different classes of readers concerned about Britain's declining role in the world. He wanted the Bond novels to appeal to an "A" readership, but he was also aware that the republication of his books for the mass paperback market, and their serialization in newspapers like *The Daily Express* and magazines such as *Playboy*, would attract different types of readers.

Based in Katanga for a musical recital when the region sued for independence and precipitated a civil war in Congo that led to the death of Patrice Lumumba (the country's first democratically elected leader), Schuyler was also enlisted by conservative newspapers who hoped to provide their readers with Bondian tales of adventure, intrigue, and sex. Her creation of

21. P. Schuyler, Notebook, 1964; Notebook, 1965; "Letter to J. Schuyler," n.d., 1966.
22. P. Schuyler, *White Leopard of Katanga*.
23. P. Schuyler, *Who Killed the Congo?*
24. P. Schuyler, "Letter to J. Schuyler," April 27, 1960.

a Bondian hero for southern Africa in plays and novels such as *Evil Eville*, *The Demons of the Jungle*, and *The White Leopard of Katanga* provide a vivid portrait of an artist anxious about marriage and her position in the wider world. In what she considered her best work, Schuyler drew on her experiences in the Congo in the hopes of appealing to readers who were tired of "thought books" without alienating readers who could appreciate the sophistication and the background of her stories.[25]

Schuyler initially assumed that she would need to adapt her plays for an American audience and depicted the Congolese city of Elizabethville as "Evil Eville," a frontier "much like the [American] Wild West." She constructed white male heroes who believed that indigenous blacks interpreted "the white man's Christian principles, and accordance of excessive liberty to his women" as weakness rather than strength.[26] This meant that she defined Jack, the rugged hero from a working-class background in northern Europe, against middle-class Nordics (who were thought to be excessively prudish and effeminate) and indigenous blacks (who were depicted as "animals," "primitive savages," and "rapists"). In later drafts, Schuyler described her female characters' "rejoicing" when Jack ordered them out of a car in order to engage in sadomasochistic sexual encounters that left them bloodied and bruised, much like Commander Bond's sexual conquests were said to enjoy his "sweet brutality" and "semi-rape."[27] If the blackness of indigenous Africans meant that they were criminalized as rapists, the whiteness of Jack and Bond granted them a license to inflict bodily harm without punishment. They could even be claimed as potentially progressive figures who offered readers an alternative to mainstream novels and films in which sex outside of marriage was deemed shameful.[28]

With that said, Schuyler could not entirely ignore the shaming practices of male friends such as the sensitive British intellectual who was unwilling to carry contraceptives in his car so that he could have sex in public, or the married Dutchman who disapproved of her interest in sex outside of marriage. Her plays and novels set in Congo often end with Suzanne—the female protagonist who shares more in common than a name with Suzanne May, an infamous sex worker who travelled across the British Empire—expressing shame and guilt about extramarital sex, the possibility of having a child outside of wedlock, and her desire to carve out an independent

25. P. Schuyler, "Letter to Josephine Schuyler," July 12, 1963.

26. P. Schuyler, *Evil Eville*, ix; *Congo*, i.

27. P. Schuyler, *Demons of the Jungle*, 62–63; Johnson, "Sex, Snobbery, and Sadism"; Fleming, *Spy Who Loved Me*, 15.

28. P. Schuyler, "Letter to Josephine Schuyler," August 15, 1953; Bennett and Woollacott, *Bond and Beyond*; Halliwell, *American Culture*.

existence as a creative artist.²⁹ As much as Suzanne might dream of a "glorious and golden" life as a female courtesan in Europe in earlier drafts of her adventures in Congo,³⁰ she ends later drafts of the book longing to marry a South African mercenary who demands that she seeks happiness "by obedience, by lack of ambition, by abandoning one's plans, by bowing to another's will—the will of 'White Africa.'"³¹ Such attempts to explore the limits of white female agency in an African context were also crucial to Schuyler's demands for a suitable husband and an "Aryan child"—demands that reveal her failure to uphold the ideals of her parent's "mulatto-minded" milieu in New York in the 1930s.

Looking for Mr. Right

In 1958, Philippa Schuyler penned an article for *Ebony* in which she talked about her life as a young artist who travelled the world but was unable to find her ideal man. Tired of overbearing men who were unwilling to accept her constant travelling as a concert pianist and wanted to keep her in a box as a "slave," Schuyler hoped to meet a man who would support her career. Modelled on Albert Schweitzer, Schuyler's ideal man would be

> temperate, charming, intellectual, sweet, affectionate, humanitarian, well-read, never cruel or unjust, never shrewd or conniving, never dissipated or brutal, with high moral standards of honesty, purity and unselfishness, never gambling or improvident, not neurotically insecure or super-critical, but he must be kind and sincerely religious, always looking to God as the true guide and arbiter of human affairs . . . [I'd] like him to be a doctor, writer, poet, scientist, social worker, archaeologist, or missionary, someone who brings good to society, not working merely for selfish gain for himself.³²

Five years later, Schuyler wrote a letter to her mother in which she replaced her desire for a doctor and missionary (à la Schweitzer) for a European aristocrat (à la Bond):

---

29. Talalay, *Composition in Black and White*, 156, 247–48; P. Schuyler, "Letter to Josephine Schuyler," April 27, 1960; "Letter to Josephine Schuyler," October 29, 1964; "Letter to Josephine Schuyler," December 26, 1965.

30. P. Schuyler, *Evil Eville*, 63.

31. P. Schuyler, *The White Leopard of Katanga*, 182, 194.

32. P. Schuyler, "Why I Don't Marry."

> What counts is not . . . whether all people are free and prosperous everywhere. What counts is whether I can be successful . . . What do I care whether women are nuclear physicists or ambassadors in a country. I'm an artist!
>
> And I like men to pay for things . . . I don't want to pay for things (I can't anyhow) . . .
>
> What I want is to spend my life in fine hotels, being courted by noblemen and the rich, being successful in my art, and having everything paid for by people other than myself.[33]

Last but not least, Schuyler drew up a checklist for her prospective husband in her notebook in 1964:

> I. He must be white.
> II. He must be European.
> III. He must be able to confer on me a nationality I like.[34]

Maurice Raymond, a "cosmopolitan" man from France, fulfilled Schuyler's romantic fantasy because she thought that he combined northern European "cultural superiority" with the "vital force" of "earthy" southern European folks who were closer to Africa. Even when Schuyler worried about Raymond's intellectual abilities because he came from a working-class background in Lyon, she found solace in his "Aryan looks."

> He is the most Aryan man I have ever known—his mother came from near the German border—so perhaps she had some German ancestry . . . Imagine—if we had a child it could be perfect—because it could have: His green eyes . . . his Aryan appearance. My talent. No negritude.[35]

Such desire for an "Aryan man" like Raymond suggests Schuyler's failure to uphold the "mulatto-minded" culture of her parents in 1930s New York, as does her unwillingness to raise a child that might have "Negritude" or be classified as a "Negro child prodigy."[36] Following an affair with George Apedo-Amah—a Ghanaian who upheld the honor of European culture as a member of the French delegation to the United Nations and the European Economic Community—Schuyler could only admit that she loved Apedo-Amah's "personality." She could not tolerate his "nationality" (a euphemism for his "blackness") and, after their relationship led to an unplanned pregnancy, Schuyler travelled around the world searching for a doctor who

---

33. P. Schuyler, "Letter to Josephine Schuyler," 1963.
34. P. Schuyler, Notebook, 1964.
35. P. Schuyler, "Letter to Josephine Schuyler," June 9, 1963.
36. P. Schuyler, "Letter to Josephine Schuyler," February 21, 1966.

would perform a late-term abortion.[37] In a letter to her mother, Schuyler once again turned to a literary form of self-fashioning in order to explain her decision by evoking Nella Larsen's *Quicksand*, one of the most famous novels of the Harlem Renaissance. In the words of Schuyler:

> Why bring more Negroes into the world? They have their nice side but somehow Negritude just seems to go round and round in circles—and one can't deny that it's better for a child to start life in the white world. I wouldn't even mind having an illegitimate child if I could be sure it would be good looking. All civilizations are brutal—but some are also artistic . . . I will not marry a colored man or an African . . . [I will marry] a white man of European stock, but not a resident European . . . [who has] a virile male force vitale.[38]

In the words of Helga Crane, the mixed-race protagonist of Nella Larsen's 1928 novel, who finds herself to be always a little different and always a little dissatisfied on her travels around the United States and Denmark,

> Why add more suffering to the world? Why add more unwanted, tortured Negroes to America? Why do Negroes have children? Surely it must be sinful. Think of the awfulness of being responsible for the giving of life to creatures doomed to endure such wounds to the flesh, such wounds to the spirit, as Negroes have to endure?[39]

Schuyler and Fanon: An Unlikely Duet

Good Men Die, an account of Schuyler's time as a war correspondent in Vietnam, was published posthumously after her death in a helicopter mission intended to help Catholic nuns evacuate a number of Vietnamese children from a combat zone. In the book, Schuyler took aim at a specific form of American racism that "place[d] obstacles in place of a soldier marrying a Vietnamese girl," remained focused on what might happen to "strong and sensitive . . . half-castes . . . [who] when unattached to or unassimilated by [a Western] society . . . can become violently vocal leaders," and, once again, idealized the French.

---

37. P. Schuyler, "Letter to Josephine Schuyler," December 26, 1965.
38. P. Schuyler, "Letter to Josephine Schuyler," n.d., 1966.
39. Larsen *Quicksand and Passing*, 103.

> The French tackled this problem with Gallic rationality; they did not avoid it with a narrow refusal to tackle the facts. They granted French citizenship to a half-caste child whose French father admitted paternity, even if the man did not marry the girl. This is more just and certainly more humane. Why should a child's life be ruined? Why should his only heritage be one of misery and shame?[40]

Such investment in the honor of European culture and a "light skin tone" is radically different to the sickness of European racism developed by Frantz Fanon. Whereas Schuyler longed to help the Vietnamese "bar-girls" and the children of their relationships with American men by asserting the honor of a Western identity, Fanon identified with the Indo-Chinese who went into battle against European colonizers they blamed for the explosion in "cut-rate boys and women."[41] Whereas Schuyler wrote stories that were based on the James Bond novels and films, Fanon expressed his support for women in Algeria who could dress up as Western women without the "sensation of playing a role she has read about ever so many times in novels, or seen in motion pictures."[42]

Although Fanon is one of the few names from the decolonizing period of the 1950s and '60s whose work remains essential for scholars of postcolonial studies,[43] many discussions of shame and pride in America have followed the lead of contemporary psychologists who marginalize the work of the French war hero, Martinican exile, and Algerian freedom fighter. Some have dismissed Fanon's work as a "dung heap of Freudian analysis" that fails to appreciate American exceptionalism.[44] Others have followed Barack Obama and portrayed Fanon as an outdated remnant of 1960s protests who is only of interest to contemporary radicals on the fringes of college towns.[45] Even when they provide a corrective to studies of Southern honor that ignore the links between Southern pride, whiteness and the shaming of black bodies,[46] sweeping histories of honor and shame in the Western world can omit to mention Fanon's warnings about Western business and its taste for light-skinned, "half-breed girls," and "cut-price boys."[47] For

---

40. P. Schuyler, *Good Men Die*, 196–97.
41. Ibid., 196; Fanon, *Black Skin, White Masks*, 227.
42. Fanon, *Dying Colonialism*, 50.
43. Lazarus, *Postcolonial Unconscious*, 161.
44. Wayde Gayles, *Rooted Against the Wind*, 109.
45. Obama, *Dreams from My Father*, xv, 100.
46. Cohen et al., "Sacred and the Social."
47. Fanon, *Black Skin, White Masks*, 169–78.

example, David Leverenz's recent study of race and shame in American history draws on Huntington's *The Clash of Civilizations?* and suggests that Barack Obama and other prominent African Americans are evidence of a paradigm shift (from pride in a "light skin color" and "white civilization" to a defense of Western civilization as multicultural and tolerant in contrast to the "rest of the world" and "radical Islam"[48]). It does not note the radical spirit of Fanon and other activist-intellectuals who had little time for liberal celebrations of non-racialism that guiltily paraded the incorporation of some (light-skinned) blacks into a privileged caste of American politics.

Fanon's writings, his engagement with the Bandung Conference of 1955, and his participation in the Congress of Negro Writers in Paris in 1956, reveal attempts to excuse the racism of women and men in the 1950s and '60s as clear, simple, and wrong. Schuyler's personal and professional decisions to align her selves with the forces of white supremacy were not simply a product of her time. Yet, Fanon's work is not only of interest to historians wishing to achieve a fuller, richer depiction of the past. His insistent questions and provocative prose continues to inspire activists and intellectuals who are unwilling to assume that the increasing visibility of nonwhite faces in the political-media-entertainment complex means that we have achieved a "post-racial" present. If Schuyler's rugged individualism in colonial contexts is not out of keeping with forms of neoliberalism and neocolonialism in the early twenty-first century, Fanon is read as a contemporary by radical egalitarians who wish to shame the contradictions and confusions of neoliberal universalism and neocolonial governance.[49] Neither seems anachronistic in our post–Cold War context when James Bond enjoys the company of beautiful nonwhite colleagues on our screens, or conservatives express anxiety about the possibility of Idris Elba becoming the first "Black Bond." In our digital age, the past is not dead. It is not even covered up with a white piece of paper.

---

48. Leverenz, *Honor Bound*, 6–7.
49. Gilroy, *Against Race*, 78; *Darker than Blue*, 155; Gibson, *Living Fanon*.

14

Rootedness and Openness: Experiences, Practices, and Theologies of Zimbabwean Catholics in Britain

Dominic Pasura

Introduction

The fundamental question this chapter addresses is how possible it is for Catholic immigrants and refugees to hold on to both particularistic (ethnic/national) modes of collective belonging and Catholicism's global and transnational dimension. The chapter, drawing from debates and discussions on diaspora and transnational studies as well as on cosmopolitan literature, explores what happens to Catholicism when it is swept up into larger patterns of migration and displacement in the contemporary world.

The chapter is based on the Economic and Social Research Council-funded study of Zimbabwean Catholics in Britain from July 2009 to June 2010, and it also builds on the author's multi-cited ethnographic study of the Zimbabwean diaspora in Britain. In examining the experiences, practices, and theologies of Zimbabwean Catholics in Britain, this chapter pays particular attention to how the group emerged; the challenges, tensions, and opportunities which arose within the British context; and how this case study informs us about global Catholicism. The chapter illustrates the way in which embracing a global and transnational Catholic identity is linked to, rather than separated from, its expression in particular cultural contexts. It is the relationality, linkages, and connectivity among the multiple, differentiated, and local expressions of Catholicism that cement the church's transnational character.

Displacement and Migration in the Age of Transnational Diasporas

Although displacement and migration are as old as humanity itself, Castles and Miller identify five general trends of contemporary migration as globalization, acceleration, differentiation, feminization, and politicization.[1] The International Organization for Migration (IOM) estimates that there are approximately 214 million international migrants worldwide, an estimated 3.1 percent of the world's population.[2] In terms of the major migration corridors, the report shows that we are witnessing new pathways and routes from the traditional (South to North and East to West), to newer forms of South to South (e.g., Indonesia to Malaysia; migrants from Lesotho, Mozambique, and Zimbabwe to South Africa), North to South (e.g., Portugal to Brazil and Italy to Argentina) and North to North (e.g., Germany to the United States and the United Kingdom to Australia and Canada).

It has been suggested that we have passed, or are passing, from the epoch of nation-states to the age of migration, border crossings, and transnational diasporas.[3] Although originally used to refer to Jewish, Greek, and Armenian dispersion, the term "diaspora" has been stretched to accommodate "variegated phenomena"[4] such as the white diaspora, the liberal diaspora, the gay diaspora, the deaf diaspora, and the queer diaspora. For classical diaspora theorists,[5] there are three major building blocks or core features of the term "diaspora" which differentiate it from similar phenomena: history of dispersal; connections with the homeland (in terms of myths, memories, desire for the eventual return); and a collective identity or boundary-maintenance.[6]

Are global religious communities—for example, Catholic, Hindu, Sikh, Buddhist, and Muslim—examples of diasporas? There is some reluctance among classical diaspora scholars in applying this concept to world

1. Castles and Miller, *Age of Migration*.
2. International Organization for Migration, *World Migration Report 2013*.
3. See Bhatia and Ram, "Locating the Dialogical Self," and Bauman, "Education in the World of Diasporas."
4. Vertovec, "Conceiving and Researching Transnationalism," 450.
5. See Cohen, *Global Diasporas*; Safran, "Diasporas in Modern Societies"; and Sheffer, *Diaspora Politics*.
6. See Brubaker, "The 'Diaspora' Diaspora."

religions.[7] Sheffer argues that the appropriation of the term diaspora to non-ethnic transnational entities such as "global religions," "trans-national linguistic communities," and "the global youth culture"[8] is a misnomer. For Cohen, however, religion provides "additional cement"[9] to ethnic/national diasporic consciousness. The designation "religious diaspora" is contentious because "whereas members of ethnic diasporas regard certain territories as their actual homelands, most members of the global religions, with the notable exception of Judaism, are attached to a spiritual center that is not the actual historical birthplace of forebears of the group."[10]

In contrast to the classical notion of diaspora, which emphasizes a bounded community which experienced some collective trauma,[11] diaspora has come to be associated with unbounded transnational movements of people, goods, and ideas. The new notion of diaspora makes no specific reference to ethnicity, a "homeland," or to a particular place of settlement but emphasizes hybridity and de-territorialized identities and multiple belonging. As Al-Ali explains:

> In the context of postmodern and postcolonial approaches and the increasingly appeal of cultural studies, the terms "diaspora" and "diasporic communities" have gained new meanings and dimensions . . . More and more, it has been used in a metaphorical sense, referring to hybrid identity formations, arguing against reifications of ethnicity and culture and explaining cultural shifts in general.[12]

Examples of these "de-territorialized diasporas" are Roma (Gypsies), Caribbean peoples, and religious diasporas. Using the term "pan-diasporic tendencies" to describe these non-ethnic transnational entities, Ben-Rafael cites the examples of Latin American immigrants in the United States who are described as "Hispanics" and immigrants from Arab countries in Europe who see themselves as part of the Muslim diaspora.[13] If, as Brubaker suggests,[14] we see diaspora as a process, stance, or category of practice rather than as a bounded entity, then there is a sense in which we can talk of Catholic diasporas. In fact, Gorman described the early and persecuted

---

7. See Cohen, *Global Diasporas*, 2nd ed.; and Sheffer, *Diaspora Politics*.
8. Sheffer, *Diaspora Politics*, 10–11, 65, 68–69.
9. Cohen, *Global Diasporas*, 189.
10. Sheffer, *Diaspora Politics*, 66.
11. See Cohen, *Global Diasporas*, 2nd ed.; and Sheffer, *Diaspora Politics*.
12. Al-Ali, "Gender, Diaspora, and Post-Cold War Conflict," 40–41.
13. Ben-Rafael, "Diaspora," 844.
14. Brubaker "The 'Diaspora' Diaspora," 5–13.

Christian Church as a "classical diaspora of the third kind," which offers "an integrative understanding of the human good rather than a separatist one overemphasizing one's ethnic culture."[15]

A second body of scholarship that I draw upon for this chapter is the literature on cosmopolitanism, particularly the concept of cosmopolitan sociability. Schiller et al. define cosmopolitan sociability as the "ability to find aspects of the shared human experience including aspirations for a better world within or despite what would seem to be divides of culture and belief."[16] Until recently, the cosmopolitan literature focused on the elite travelers, intellectuals, and exiles. Addressing this gap, scholars have explored how ordinary people and migrants contribute to the making of a new cosmopolitan order—for example, Werbner's "working class cosmopolitans"[17] and Bhabha's notion of "vernacular cosmopolitanism," which refers to those who "occupy marginal or minority positions within cultures and societies."[18] As Schiller et al. argue,

> If cosmopolitanism is viewed as arising from social relationships that do not negate cultural, religious, or gendered differences but see people as capable of relationships of experiential commonalities despite differences, then we have another lens through which to view and theorize social experiences. This perspective moves researchers beyond the binaries of inclusion vs. exclusion, sameness vs. difference.[19]

Hence, a cosmopolitan approach acknowledges "individuals are able to hold multiple ethnic, national, or religious belongings simultaneously."[20] Drawing on the concept of cosmopolitan sociability, I want to illustrate the way in which embracing a global and transnational Catholic identity is linked to, rather than separated from, its expression in specific cultural contexts. It is perhaps instructive to provide a brief overview of the migration of Zimbabweans to Britain to contextualize the chapter.

---

15. Gorman, "Classical Diaspora of the Third Kind," 635.
16. Schiller et al., "Defining Cosmopolitan Sociability," 403.
17. Werbner, "Global Pathways," 17–35.
18. Bhabha, "Vernacular Cosmpolitan," 139.
19. Schiller et al., "Defining Cosmopolitan Sociability," 403.
20. Amelina and Faist, "De-naturalizing the Nationals," 1713.

Zimbabwean Migration to Britain

From the late 1990s onwards, Zimbabwe's surge toward social, political, and economic crisis was unprecedented, and the consequences were severe for its citizens. As Crush and Tevera explain, "An economy in free-fall, soaring inflation and unemployment, the collapse of public services, political oppression and deepening poverty proved to be powerful, virtually irresistible, push factors for many Zimbabweans."[21] Under these conditions, a large-scale movement of Zimbabwean migrants who include professionals such as doctors, nurses, teachers, refugees, and asylum seekers reached cities in the UK, South Africa, Botswana, the US, and Australia. In a country of 13 million, it is estimated that between two to three million Zimbabweans live in the diaspora. Estimates suggest that there are more than 200,000 Zimbabweans in Britain, and the majority of them entered the country as asylum seekers, refugees, labor migrants, students, and visitors.

The Formation of the Zimbabwean Catholic Community

Providing an overview of the nature of British Catholicism, Archer points out that "in the period after Vatican II, the internal culture of the church shifted from being predominantly Irish, working class, and northern to being more acculturated, bourgeois, and southern."[22] The recent migration of Catholic migrants from Eastern Europe, Africa, Latin America, and Asia to Britain is further altering the profile and social composition of the church. Davis et al., using a survey of one thousand migrants in London's Roman Catholic community, shows that the church "is undergoing a shift in its ethnic makeup and social diversity, as many Catholics migrate to the UK"; such changes are described as the church's "greatest opportunity" and "its greatest threat."[23]

Fr. Munyongani, now the new bishop of Gweru, was a Zimbabwean-born priest sent over by the Zimbabwe Catholic Bishops' Conference to work as a chaplain for Zimbabwean Catholics in Britain. Prior to his appointment in 2007, Fr. Dzadagu, a Zimbabwean priest, was working as an acting chaplain since 2002. I asked Fr. Dzadagu to describe how the community started. He explains:

---

21. Crush and Tevera, "Exiting Zimbabwe," 1.
22. Cited by Egan, "Lonergan, Evangelization, and the British Context," 796.
23. Davis et al., *Ground of Justice*, 5.

> We started in London and as time goes on, people in Slough started congregating together, then Birmingham followed by Leicester, and then Bolton, Luton. Now there are new congregations in Leeds, Sheffield, Northampton, Bristol, Huntingdon, and Southend. As we speak, I am hearing that people in Manchester and Liverpool are also planning to start their own congregations as well.

The Zimbabwean Catholic community does not have its own ethnic parishes, but it is embedded within local Catholic parishes. Most of the time, the community attends local English mass and occasionally holds Zimbabwean mass once a month. There are currently thirteen Zimbabwean Catholic community centers across England and Wales. The Zimbabwean community has a constitution and an elected National Executive Committee, which facilitates and coordinates the community's activities and programs. It publishes a monthly newsletter and conducts yearly music courses.

Experiences of Zimbabwean Catholics in Britain

Displacement and migration are universal themes in the Bible which signify not only a spiritual search for God or Truth but also "an ethic of hospitality and a call to comfort the stranger."[24] Although Zimbabwean Catholics give several meanings to their conditions and experiences in the diaspora, the majority of them depict it as their Babylon and Egypt.

Zimbabweans' "mode of incorporation into Britain was mediated by a hostile reception from authorities, considerable prejudice and hostility from the host society, and a weak preexisting co-ethnic community."[25] Zimbabweans, particularly pastors and priests, preach an exilic message and depict the diaspora as a place of suffering and hardship, the biblical equivalent of Babylon and Egypt.[26] As Taona, one of the respondents, explains,

> You might want to say the Zimbabweans are in Babylon. The way the Israelites were being treated in Babylon is similar to the way Zimbabweans are being treated here. This is again similar to the treatment Israelites received in Egypt, as asylum seekers and slaves. From a Christian perspective, we are experiencing our Egypt . . . The racism we face everyday resembles the troubles the Israelites faced in Babylon and Egypt.[27]

24. Admirand, "Ethics of Displacement and Migration," 1.
25. Pasura, "Modes of Incorporation," 199.
26. Pasura, "Competing Meanings of the Diaspora," 1445.
27. Ibid., 1452.

This quotation highlights one of the characteristic features of a diaspora—a sense of being marginalized in the country of settlement, being the eternal outsider. Almost all respondents, without exception, narrate stories of racism and discrimination in their daily lives.[28] Starting in the early 1990s, Western countries including Britain tightened migration laws, institutional structures, and border control procedures as part of the broader efforts to control the mass influx of asylum seekers, refugees, and immigrants (and, more recently, to combat terrorism). Hence, the mobility of ordinary people is seen as dangerous and threatening, something which needs to be curtailed. In the process, immobility is normalized. As Glick Schiller and Salazar argue, "There are several different intersecting regimes of mobility that normalize the movements of some travelers while criminalizing and entrapping the ventures of others."[29] Within the European context, debates and discourses on diversity, social cohesion, and the failure of multiculturalism are more pronounced,[30] and immigrants and refugees are often racialized and portrayed as the "other." Hence, the growth of Zimbabwean diaspora congregations in Britain must, among other things, be located within the context of hostility toward asylum seekers, refugees, and migrants. Zimbabwean Christians see Britain as their Babylon and Egypt; they have decided to settle in it but remain insulated from its secular values and norms.

Congregations as Spaces for Belonging and Sociality

Hostile conditions in Britain reinforce migrants' transnational religious ties to the homeland. Hence, the Zimbabwean Catholic congregations in Britain are a kind of modern-day transnational extended family—spaces for belonging and sociality.[31] The absence of proximate extended family and friends in the diaspora means that diaspora congregations are not only sources of spiritual solace, but provide social, material, and financial assistance to its members in times of need. For Zimbabwean Catholics, as Tatenda explains, "people were not satisfied in just attending a Sunday mass—they wanted more from it, spiritually and socially." Zimbabwean Catholic congregations are spaces where feelings of solidarity are exemplified in pragmatic ways such as helping undocumented migrants to participate in the labor market, finding accommodation and engaging in civic campaigns to regularize their

---

28. Ibid.
29. Glick Schiller and Salazar, "Regimes of Mobility," 189.
30. Vertovec and Wessendorf, *Multiculturalism Backlash*, 1–31.
31. Pasura, "Religious Transnationalism," 26.

immigration status as well as providing members with a way of coping with bereavement in the diaspora.

The community also plays an important role in the upbringing of children. As are most of the respondents, Dandaro is concerned about the dangers of bringing up children in Britain. He explains, "It is good that we are going to church as migrants; it's good for our children that they are removed from dangers which are inherent with the young of this society, the drug life, knife crime. The church is a sanctuary for them." The community has started the vibrant guild of St. Agnes and Alois for the youth, conducting weekly meetings and holding their own congress, an occasion where they learn as much or more about "African values" than they learn about their Catholic faith. Fortified by migrants' collective narratives of the Catholic faith and homeland connections, the Zimbabwean community is an example of an institution created and sustained by a desire to belong as well as a response to challenges in the host land.

Spiritual Dryness

The majority of Zimbabwean Catholics in England and Wales refer to the spiritual dryness they experience when attending English mass in local parishes. Chigariro explains, "You go there; it's rather flat, not much activity; finish, mass out! That's the end. Come next week, again the same thing, thirty or forty-five minutes, that's it, out! To me, I missed what I was used to, which makes my prayer more meaningful and even exciting as we go through the service and so on."[32] Hence, forming the Zimbabwean Catholic community was one way to fulfill their spiritual needs which they felt were not adequately addressed. In her study of Ghanaian Pentecostals in the Netherlands, Ter Haar uses the biblical metaphor of the valley of dry bones to depict not only the spiritual condition of Europe, but also the hostile reception African migrants encounter in their everyday lives in the country.[33]

Practices and Theologies: The Shifting Sacred

Zimbabwean Catholics, as do other African Christians, see Britain as a secular society, a non-sacred space, which needs to be re-sacralized and re-evangelized.[34] The majority in the diaspora use African Catholicism as

---

32. Pasura, *African Transnational Diasporas*, 132.
33. Ter Haar, "African Christians in Europe," 246.
34. Pasura, "Religious Transnationalism," 26–53.

a frame of reference—the new center and/or source of authentic Catholic practices. Hence, migrants bring with them sacred associations, practices, and theologies to evaluate not only their behaviors, experiences, and outcomes in the country of settlement, but also non-migrants as well. The appointment of Fr. Munyongani as chaplain strengthened the transnational religious ties between Zimbabwean Catholics in Britain and those in the homeland. As one of the respondents puts it:

> We are under Westminster, which is England and Wales, but because of our special needs which relate to diaspora migrant communities, we still have roots in Zimbabwe. When I talk of "we" I refer to elders; we still buy properties in Zimbabwe; we still bury ourselves in Zimbabwe, until such a time we stop going to bury ourselves there, we can say we might just ignore the Zimbabwean directives. So we remain an extension, under the auspices of Westminster.[35]

As I will illustrate below, Zimbabwean Catholics in the diaspora maintain a transnational relationship with the church in the homeland in a number of ways—for instance, the periodic financial contributions to the training of priests, learning new songs, and the establishment of men's and women's guilds.

New Hymns

Catholic members in the diaspora yearning to compose new hymns are required to submit their hymns for approval to the bishops in Zimbabwe. As Rutendo explains, "You cannot compose a hymn here in England and Wales and learn it; I can't do that. It's not allowed because every piece of music sung in the church must go through the Music Composers Association in Zimbabwe and be approved. If you compose a song here, you must put it on a tape recorder and send it to Zimbabwe for approval."[36] Fr. Dzadagu concurs:

> There are aspirations that members of the community have, especially the composing of new hymns. And because the structures for Zimbabwean composition are based in Zimbabwe what it means is the people from here if they are to compose new hymns they have to submit to the association at home and

---

35. Ibid., 47.
36. Pasura, "Modes of Incorporation," 210.

you will be assessed impersonally where it's just a tape recording and which is different from a live audition.[37]

This example of the hymn is "another illustration of the willingness within the community to maintain sustained connection to the church's authority, beliefs, and practices in the homeland."[38]

Women's Guilds: Enacting and Contesting Identities

One striking feature of Zimbabwean Catholics in Britain is the extent to which women are embracing guilds, donning their distinctive uniforms on British streets. So far, six different guilds have been formed in the diaspora: St. Anne, Mary Queen of Heaven, Sacred Heart of Jesus, Our Lady of Mount Carmel, and the Sodality of our Lady. Catholic women's guilds are the foundations upon which diasporic congregations are built; equally, they are the engines of Catholicism in Africa.[39] The religious uniforms worn by Zimbabwean women belonging to different guilds in the UK show how embracing a global and transnational Catholic identity is linked to, rather than separated from, its expression in particular cultural contexts. As Ntokozo explains, "These uniforms are imported from Zimbabwe, and this shows your commitment and love of God. This is a voluntary organization; you are not forced to join the guild."[40]

One of the major challenges of initiating Zimbabwean Catholic guilds in Britain relates to question of whether or not to keep old boundaries. The boundaries, based on the idea of traditional family, are becoming increasingly difficult to implement. As Tawanda explains,

> A married woman may come to this country and her husband may be denied a visa, so what would you do, you can't deny her the chance to join an association. The woman may just say "I am married and my husband is in Zimbabwe," and you can't say "we have to see the husband first," because he hasn't got the visa. Or it could be that the husband is taking care of children in Zimbabwe so he can't come to Britain.[41]

37. Ibid.
38. Ibid.
39. See, for example, Martin, *Catholic Women of Congo-Brazzaville*, and Hinfelaar, *Respectable and Responsible Women*.
40. Pasura, *African Transnational Diasporas*, 125
41. Pasura, "Modes of Incorporation," 211.

Many women find themselves without husbands, partly a consequence of the host land's restrictive immigration policies, and this makes the relationship with monogamist parent guilds difficult. However, some Catholic members like Mhlawuli are keen to keep the original rules and guidelines. Mhlawuli describes the gradual erosion of original guild guidelines thus:

> It's a very, very serious problem happening within the guilds as most of them are no longer following their guidelines. If you look at those wearing uniforms, it should be a certain length. When wearing a hat, no hair should be visible. They wear the uniforms going to local parishes where the priest is not aware of the rules. They have thrown quite a few things out through the window. They are not following what they should do.[42]

As can be seen from the above quotations, women are constructed as the guardians and repositories of African Catholicism and respectable behavior, evident through wearing of uniforms of "a certain length" and emphasis on traditional marriage.[43]

Guild members in the diaspora are expected to keep abreast of developments within parent guilds at home, and those failing to adhere to the strict rules and guidelines are asked to be stripped of their uniforms. Ruramisai, one of the members of the Chita ChaMaria, explains the significance of the uniform:

> The uniform which we put on symbolizes the way we live; we must live a Christian life, being witnesses in our everyday lives. There is the question that comes, what happens when your life does not mirror the uniform you have. As you know, the guidelines for putting on uniforms are clear. You are not given uniforms just like a football team; there are procedures and rules that have to be followed. One of them is to give authority to the priest to take the uniform back without paying the cost incurred in buying the uniform. So, when some women are not living a life worthy of the guild to which they belong, some Christians would be saying we want to see her stripped of the uniform. This is not an easy decision.[44]

Among Zimbabwean Catholics in the diaspora, there are constant conversations about this or that guild woman who must be stripped of her uniform because her lifestyle does not conform to the parent guild's values

---

42. Ibid., 212.
43. Ibid.
44. Pasura, *African Transnational Diasporas*, 130.

and guidelines. It is no coincidence that, in 2010, a new guild called Non-Aligned Ladies was formed in the diaspora but later renamed Gracious Catholic Women (GCW). In contrast to other guilds, the GCW organization has no uniform to mark its identity and does not insist on marriage as a condition for membership. It can be argued that the GCW guild was influenced by a desire to break away from constraints imposed by elite guilds and by the incentives for women to gain control over their bodies, what they wear, and how many partners they should have.

In contrast to the enthusiasm shown by women in forming guilds, men established the Men's Forum, which is not affiliated with any guild but is a space for men to discuss issues pertaining to their faith and the challenges of living in Britain. Recently, some men formed the guild of St. Joseph, and other men are affiliated to Chita cheMwoyo Musande.[45]

Reverse Mission

I must emphasize that Zimbabwean Catholic congregations in Britain emerged as public spaces to construct transnational identities and provide alternative forms of belonging, and have reinvented themselves as agents of re-evangelization in the host society. Just as the London Missionary Society seized the opportunities provided by European imperial expansion to spread Christianity to Africa, Asia, and Latin America, for many African Christians, "migration to Europe is not just an economic necessity, but also seen as a God-given opportunity to evangelize among those whom they believe to have gone astray."[46]

For Zimbabwean Christians, Britain is a country they have decided to settle in but in which they want to remain different, insulating themselves from its secular norms and values. "In most cases, gay marriages provide a reference point, and this comes out clearly in sermons about how the British society has deviated from God's plan."[47] The majority of respondents explicitly made parallels between their role in postcolonial Britain and early missionaries in Africa. Batsirai explains the parallel:

> People in this country are godless people. Look at how the British people live their lives, their culture, gay marriages, divorces, the collapse of the family. There are no Christian values in this

---

45. Pasura, *African Transnational Diasporas*, 128.
46. Ter Haar, "African Christians in Europe," 245.
47. Pasura, "Modes of Incorporation," 207.

country; they are now dead. It's now a pagan society that needs to be preached to again for it to regain its Christian past.[48]

What is significant from the above quotation is the view that this is a godless society; it gives migrants the moral and divine imperative to re-evangelize it. Fr. Munyongani describes how the religious uniforms worn by Zimbabwean women and men who belong to different guilds has transformed local Catholic parishes, with the women becoming the face of reverse evangelization:

> On an ordinary Sunday, a religious man who belongs to the guild of St. Joseph would wear his religious uniform and at the same time go and mix. So, people would ask, "What does this mean?" and this gives him an opportunity to explain what he stands for. Similarly, a religious woman who belongs to the guild of St. Anne, the guild of Mary Queen of Heaven . . . would also be asked, "What does this religious uniform you are wearing stand for?" In that way she will also defend her faith and explain what it stands for. In that way, it will be like a pulpit where they are preaching what they believe in.[49]

Zimbabwean Catholics conceptualize reverse evangelization in terms of being Christ's witnesses, typified in the wearing of (African) religious garbs, enthusiastic singing accompanied by African drums, and being embedded in local parishes. Yes, immigrants need the church to stand up for their rights and provide a "safety net" in their new places of settlement, but the church also needs immigrants to change the religious landscape in host societies. Wan describes the "diaspora mission strategy"[50] as ministering to, through, and beyond the diaspora communities.

> We are to recognize the golden opportunity to evangelize (*minister to*) the diaspora who are transient and receptive to the gospel. We should also maximize the immense potential of the diaspora groups by motivating and mobilizing them (*ministering through and beyond*) for the fulfillment of the Great Commission.[51]

Exploring African migration and the transformations in global Christianity, Hanciles suggests that "migrant movement (in this case from the 'global South' to the industrial North) will play an increasingly decisive role

---

48. Pasura, "Religious Transnationalism," 41.
49. Ibid., 43.
50. Wan, "Diaspora Mission Strategy," 3.
51. Ibid., 6–7. Emphasis original.

in reshaping the Western religious landscape."[52] As I explain in paragraphs below, these practices are perceived and framed differently by migrants and non-migrants.

Rootedness and Openness

The examples I have given on new hymns and women's guilds illustrate the shift in the center of gravity of Catholicism from Europe to Africa. However, what is at stake here particularly for Catholic immigrant communities, as Schiller et al., describe it, is how to maintain simultaneously bounded forms of belonging—ethnic/national ties or religious commitments—as well as openness to the world. Using another example of what I refer to as a choice between the piano and African drums, I want to illustrate some of these tensions and opportunities affecting Catholicism when it is swept up into larger patterns of migration and displacement.

The different practices of liturgy and prayer in cosmopolitan congregations are common sources of anxiety. Fungisai explains the tensions:

> On the part of (Zimbabwean) migrants, the conduct of the mass is different; we would prefer our own drums and our own songs, and this brings us closer to God, whereas the others (non-migrants) service they do their piano thing and sing . . . So, the dynamics we are operating from is different, we are from different wave lengths but we are praying to the same God.[53]

As part of the church's integration strategy, the Zimbabwean congregation participated in pilgrimage trips to Harvington[54] and the Intercultural Mass, introducing the group to the wider British society and bringing some level of attachment to the host land. Most of the congregants recounted to me the welcome reception they received in Harvington, Kidderminster. As Zvipani explains:

> When we went to Harvington, it was the first time for the [Birmingham] Archbishop to see us although he had already approved us holding a Shona mass. We were given a hymn during the readings. After communion, he sent an alter server asking us to sing another song. When the mass was ending, he again sent someone instructing us to sing again. When we were singing, many people loved our songs clapping hands. He said he didn't

---

52. Hanciles, "Beyond Christendom," 96.
53. Pasura, *African Transnational Diasporas*, 133.
54. A site for pilgrimage where priests used to hide in caves during the war.

> know that in Birmingham there were African people doing such a wonderful work. At the end of the mass, he came to us and said "I must bless them [drums]."[55]

Yet it is not surprising that not everyone liked the singing and drumming by Zimbabwean Catholics; as Yevedzo noted, "When we sing by nature we are loud and vibrant and the drums, and you could see that some people, especially some old white ladies, would try to close their ears to indicate that you are making noise."[56]

The tensions and conflicts within the mixed congregation are often embedded within assumptions of racial and cultural superiority. Fr. Cownley, the parish priest, narrated a story that illustrates this point.

> I am not being negative to you but I have been here for a bit; somebody said to me, "Lots of dark faces in the church, father" and I just said, "Yes, and they are all Catholics" (laugh). We are not having it; in the parish next door, this sounds bad, two families came to the priest and said, "We are not coming to the church because there are too many dark faces, and we are going to so-and-so because they don't have any dark faces there." And the priest said, and I wouldn't have said that, "Don't ever come here again," which is bad. He was rejecting them because they were rejecting others. You should never reject people like that; you should always encourage them, whatever community of race or wherever people come from.[57]

Emphasizing the universality of the Catholic Church, Fr. Cownley explains, "We are not an Irish Catholic Church; we are not an Italian Catholic Church; we are not a Shona Catholic Church; we are a Catholic Church. Polish, [the] same thing, [and] all these national groups . . . Moreover, it's a long struggle to teach people to pray together, you know."[58] Members of the Zimbabwean Catholic community see themselves as having transformed, to a larger extent, Britain's religious landscape by going on pilgrimage trips, wearing [African] religious garb, singing enthusiastically with the accompaniment of African drums, and being embedded in local Catholic parishes. Within these congregations, it can be argued that Catholicism shuttles between what both migrants and non-migrants might perceive as the sacred and the profane. As Eade tells us,

---

55. Pasura, *African Transnational Diasporas*, 136.
56. Pasura, "Religious Transnationalism," 45.
57. Ibid., 46.
58. Pasura, *African Transnational Diasporas*, 135.

Global migration has provided the Anglican, Methodist, and Catholic communities with both an opportunity and a challenge. Local congregations could be revived by welcoming the newcomers from other countries through the kinds of adaptive dexterity evident in other rapidly globalizing cities, which included material changes especially inside the churches to make them more homely and attractive. At the same time, those bringing different religious and ethnic customs could test the extent to which religious leaders were prepared to adapt, thereby exposing the power embedded in the structure of religious institutions.[59]

Conclusion

The examples of Zimbabwean Catholics in England illustrate how Catholics in diaspora can simultaneously keep bounded forms of attachments while they remain nested within the global Catholic community. What is striking about Zimbabwean Catholics in Britain is the manner in which they use their distinct African practices and theologies to build relationships and identities of both closure and openness. By emphasizing their African Catholicism—embodied in liturgical practices such as the use of African drums, singing, and dancing as well as women and men's guilds—Zimbabwean Catholics in Britain concurrently maintain their rooted forms of belonging and religious commitments, as well as an openness to global Catholicism. For instance, Zimbabwean Catholics consider themselves as tasked with a divine mission to re-evangelize the host society. It is this awareness and ability to influence and shape the face of Christianity in Britain that gives African Christian migrants the agency to participate in other aspects of British society. It represents one way in which migrants "give back Christianity" to "secular" culture in contrast to discourses of taking away jobs, overcrowding schools, and depending on state benefits.[60] However, maintaining and balancing the duality of preserving group identity and integrating into local parishes is problematic. Marta Trzebiatowska examines the consequences of the encounter between Catholic Poles living in Britain and indigenous Catholics. She argues:

> The conflict between the newcomers and the locals is shown to be caused by a mismatch between Polish Catholic habitus and British religious context. While for British Catholics their

59. Eade, "Religion, Home-Making, and Migration," 481.
60. Pasura, "Religious Transnationalism," 44.

religion is "universal," for Polish migrants Catholicism symbolizes their national culture, which makes them resistant to religious integration.[61]

The danger of affirming ethnic labels is that this can reproduce and reinforce stigma, exclusion, and inequalities. As the example of the working-class Catholics and Protestants in Northern Ireland illustrates, religion in some cases can reproduce ethnic differentiations. However, religion can also supersede other attributes of ethnicity as a primary means of identification, belonging, or exclusion. My work among the Zimbabwean diaspora in Britain clearly demonstrates how immigrants embraced transnational religious identities, Catholicism in particular, as one way of bridging pre-migration ethnic, political, and gendered divides as well as depoliticizing the diaspora by moving away from the divisive party politics to new and explicitly non-partisan frameworks.[62]

The chapter has illustrated the ways in which embracing a global and transnational Catholic identity is linked to, rather than separated from, its expression in particular cultural contexts. The example of Zimbabwean Catholics in England demonstrates how Catholics in diaspora can simultaneously maintain bounded forms of attachment while they remain nested within the global Catholic community. As Schiller et al. argue, "rootedness and openness cannot be seen in oppositional terms but constitute aspects of the creativity through which migrants build homes and sacred spaces in a new environment and within transnational networks."[63] Zimbabwean Catholics in Britain underpin their transnational religious flows by their desire to consume homeland products, expressed differently by celebrating mass in vernacular languages, embracing women's guilds, and playing African drums as well as by their desire to transform existing religious practices and communities. Although Zimbabwean Catholics in England enact diasporic identities that mainly utilize the homeland as a frame of reference, the religious practices and theologies they foster are Catholic and global. Therefore, it is imperative to see Zimbabwean Catholics in Britain as floating and bounded within the global and transnational Catholic community. It is the relationality, linkages, and connectivity among the multiple, differentiated, and local expressions of Catholicism that cement the church's transnational character. Thus, as my example of Zimbabwean Catholics in Britain has demonstrated, migration and displacement provide spaces for

61. Trzebiatowska, "Advent of the 'EasyJet Priest,'" 1055.

62. McGregor and Pasura, "Diasporic Repositioning," and Pasura, *African Transnational Diasporas*.

63. Schiller et al., "Defining Cosmopolitan Sociability," 400.

immigrant and refugee Catholics and communities to create new identities, possibilities, and opportunities. In a globalized world, we need to see the scattered immigrant and refugee Catholic communities as a new frontier in missionary work.

Bibliography

Abu-Laban, Baha. *An Olive Branch on the Family Tree: The Arabs in Canada.* 1st ed. Toronto: McClelland & Stewart, 1980.

Admirand, Peter. "The Ethics of Displacement and Migration in the Abrahamic Faiths: Enlightening Believers and Aiding Public Policy." *Journal of Ethnic and Migration Studies* 40 (2014) 671–87.

Ahmed, Sara. *The Cultural Politics of Emotion.* New York: Routledge, 2004.

Ahn, Ilsup, Agnes Chiu, and William O'Neill. "'And You Welcomed Me?' A Theological Response to the Militarization of the U.S.–Mexico Borders and the Criminalization of Undocumented Migrants." *Cross Currents* 63 (2013) 303–22.

Al-Ali, Nadje S. "Gender, Diasporas and Post–Cold War Conflict." In *Diasporas in Conflict: Peace-Makers or Peace-Wreckers?*, edited by Hazel Smith and Paul B. Stares, 39–61. New York: United Nations University Press, 2007.

Alsop, Joseph, Jr. "Harlem's Youngest Philosopher Parades Talent on Third Birthday." *New York Herald Tribune*, August 3, 1934.

Amelina, Anna, and Thomas Faist. "De-naturalizing the National in Research Methodologies: Key Concepts of Transnational Studies in Migration." *Ethnic and Racial Studies* 35 (2012) 1707–24.

Anderson, Benedict. *Imagined Communities: Reflections on the Origins and Spread of Nationalism.* London: Verso, 1983.

Andraos, Michel Elias. "Christian Communities and Islam in the Middle East: A Shift in the Self-Definition of Eastern Catholic Churches." *The Ecumenist* 48 (Summer 2011) 1–4.

Angadiath, Jacob, Bishop. "Letter to Cyriac Parathara, Bishop Patrick J. McGrath, and Fr. Dominic Joseph." December 19, 2003.

Archdiocese of Miami. *Historia de la Arquidiócesis de Miami, 1958–2008: Walking in the Light of Christ.* Strasbourg: Signe, 2007.

Asante, Molefi Kete. "Book Review: *Against Race: Imagining Political Culture Beyond the Color Line.*" *Journal of Black Studies* 31 (2001) 847–51.

Augustine, Saint. *Confessions.* Translated by F. J. Sheed. New York: Sheed & Ward, 1943.

Baduel, Alessandra. "Quei Bimbi in Bianco e Nero in Fuga dal Dramma Siria: Così Dico No alla Guerra." *Repubblica*, March 10, 2014. http://ricerca.repubblica.it/repubblica/archivio/repubblica/2014/03/10/quei-bimbi-in-bianco-nero-in-fuga.html?ref=search.

Bailey, Betty Jane, and J. Martin Bailey. *Who Are the Christians in the Middle East?* 2nd ed. Grand Rapids: Eerdmans, 2010.

Barber, Daniel. *On Diaspora: Christianity, Religion, and Secularity.* Eugene, OR: Cascade Books, 2011.

Barnett, Lincoln. "Negro Girl, 2 1/2, Recites Omar and Spells 5-Syllable Words." *New York Herald Tribune*, February 8, 1934.

Bauböck, Rainer, and Thomas Faist. *Diaspora and Transnationalism Concepts, Theories, and Methods.* Amsterdam: Amsterdam University Press, 2010.

Bauman, Zygmunt. "Education in the World of Diasporas." In *Diasporic Philosophy and Counter-Education*, edited by Ilan Gur-Ze'ev, 193–206. Rotterdam: Sense, 2011.

Beauvoir, Simone de. *The Second Sex.* London: Cape, 1953.

Benedict XVI, Pope. *Deus Caritas Est.* Washington, DC: US Conference of Catholic Bishops. http://www.vatican.va/holy_father/benedict_xvi/encyclicals/documents/hf_ben-xvi_enc_20051225_deus-caritas-est_en.html.

Benhabib, Seyla. *The Claims of Culture: Equality and Diversity in the Global Era.* Princeton: Princeton University Press, 2002.

Bennett, Tony, and Janet Woollacott. *Bond and Beyond: The Political Career of a Popular Hero.* New York: Metheun, 1987.

Ben-Rafael, Eliezer. "Diaspora." *Current Sociology* 61 (2013) 842–61.

Bermudez, Esmeralda. "Faithful Flock to See Statue of Santo Toribio, the Immigrants' Saint." *Los Angeles Times*, July 12, 2014. http://www.latimes.com/local/la-me-immigrants-saint-20140713-story.html.

Bevans, Stephen B. *Models of Contextual Theology.* Rev. ed. Maryknoll, NY: Orbis, 2002.

Bhabha, Homi K. "Culture's In-Between." In *Questions of Cultural Identity*, edited by Stuart Hall and Paul Du Gay, 53–60. London: Sage, 1996.

———. "The Vernacular Cosmopolitan." In *Voices of the Crossing: The Impact of Britain on Writers from Asia, the Caribbean, and Africa*, edited by Ferdinand Dennis and Naseen Khan, 133–42. London: Serpent's Tail, 2000.

Bhatia, Sunil, and Anjali Ram. "Locating the Dialogical Self in the Age of Transnational Migrations, Border Crossings, and Diasporas." *Culture and Psychology* 7 (2001) 297–309.

Block Lewis, Helen. *Shame and Guilt in Neurosis.* New York: International Universities Press, 1971.

Breen, John. "The Danger is Ever Present: Catholic Critiques of the Yasukuni Shrine in Postwar Japan." *Japan Mission Journal* 63 (2009) 111–22.

———. "Popes, Bishops, and War Criminals: Reflections on Catholics and Yasukuni in Postwar Japan." *Asia-Pacific Journal* 8 (March 1, 2010). http://www.japanfocus.org/-John-Breen/3312.

———. "Shinto and Christianity: A History of Conflict and Compromise." In *Handbook of Christianity in Japan*, edited by Mark R. Mullins, 249–76. Leiden: Brill, 2003.

Bridges, William. *Transitions: Making Sense of Life's Changes.* Reading, MA: Andover-Wesley, 1980.

Brown, Robert McAfee. *Unexpected News: Reading the Bible with Third World Eyes.* Philadelphia: Westminster, 1984.

Brubaker, Rogers. "The 'Diaspora' Diaspora." *Ethnic and Racial Studies* 28 (2005) 1–19.

Bruneau, Michel. "Diasporas, Transnational Spaces, and Communities." In *Diaspora and Transnationalism: Concepts, Theories, and Methods*, edited by Rainer Bauböck and Thomas Faist, 35–50. Amsterdam: Amsterdam University Press, 2010.

Budde, Michael. *The Borders of Baptism: Identities, Allegiances, and the Church.* Eugene, OR: Cascade Books, 2011.

Buell, Denise K. *Why This New Race: Ethnic Reasoning in Early Christianity.* New York: Columbia University Press, 2005.

Bulliet, Richard W. *The Case for Islamo-Christian Civilization*. New York: Columbia University Press, 2006.
Buswell, Robert. *Religions of Korea in Practice*. Princeton: Princeton University Press, 2007.
Campese, Gioacchino. "'But I See that Somebody Is Missing': Ecclesiology and Exclusion in the Context of Migration." In *Ecclesiology and Exclusion: Boundaries of Being and Belonging in Postmodern Times*, edited by Dennis M. Doyle et al., 71-91. Maryknoll, NY: Orbis, 2012.
———. "¿Cuántos Más? The Crucified Peoples at the U.S.-Mexico Border." In *A Promised Land, a Perilous Journey: Theological Perspectives on Migration*, edited by Daniel G. Groody and Gioacchino Campese, 271-98. Notre Dame: University of Notre Dame Press, 2008.
———. "The Irruption of Migrants: Theology of Migration in the Twenty-First Century." *Theological Studies* 73 (2012) 3-32.
———. "Mission and Migration." In *A Century of Catholic Mission: Roman Catholic Missiology 1910 to the Present*, edited by Stephen B. Bevans, 247-60. Oxford: Regnum, 2013.
———. "Theologies of Migration: Present and Future Perspectives." In *Migration als Ort der Theologie*, edited by Tobias Kessler, 167-88. Regensburg: Pustet, 2014.
Capécia, Mayotte. *Je suis Martiniquaise*. Paris: Corréa, 1948.
Castles, Stephen, and Mark Miller. *The Age of Migration: International Population Movements in the Modern World*. 3rd ed. Basingstoke, UK: Palgrave Macmillan, 2009.
Catholic Bishops' Conference of Japan. *Katorikku kyōkai no shakai mondai ni kansuru kōteki hatsugen shū* [A Compendium of Official Statements of the Catholic Church on Social Problems]. Tokyo: Catholic Bishops' Conference of Japan, 2002.
———. *Nihon Katorikku Shikyō Kyōgikai Yearbook 2008* [Catholic Bishops' Conference of Japan Yearbook 2008]. Tokyo: Catholic Bishops' Conference of Japan, 2008.
———. *Shinkyō no jiyū to seikyō bunri* [Freedom of Belief and the Separation of Church and State]. Tokyo: Catholic Bishops' Conference of Japan, 2007.
———. "Statement of Protest Against the Cabinet Decision that Allows the Exercise of a Right to Collective Self-Defense." Catholic Bishops' Coference of Japan, July 3, 2014. https://www.cbcj.catholic.jp/2014/07/03/5034/.
———. *Statistics of the Catholic Church in Japan 2012*. Tokyo: Catholic Bishops' Conference of Japan, 2013. https://www.cbcj.catholic.jp/wp-content/uploads/2016/05/statistics2012.pdf.
"The Catholics of Viet Nam Pay Homage to Our Lady of La Vang." *L'Osservatore Romano* 32/33 (August 12, 1998). https://www.catholicculture.org/culture/library/view.cfm?recnum=481.
Chiang, Chih-Yun. "Diasporic Theorizing Paradigm on Cultural Identity." *Intercultural Communication Studies* 19 (2010) 29-46.
Choi, Jai-Keun. *The Origin of Roman Catholic Church in Korea: An Examination of Popular and Governmental Responses to Catholic Missions in the Late Choson Dynasty*. Seoul: Hermit Kingdom, 2006.
Clark, John. *Religious Repression in Cuba*. Miami: University of Miami Press, 1985.
Clifford, James. "Diasporas." *Cultural Anthropology* 9 (1994) 302-38.

Coday, Dennis. "US Bishops to Celebrate Mass on US–Mexico Border." *National Catholic Reporter*, March 7, 2014. https://www.ncronline.org/blogs/immigration-and-church/us-bishops-celebrate-mass-us-mexico-border.

Cohen, Dov, et al. "The Sacred and the Social: Cultures of Honor and Violence." In *Shame: Interpersonal Behavior, Psychopathology, and Culture*, edited by Paul Gilbert and Bernice Andrews, 261–82. New York: Oxford University Press, 1998.

Cohen, Robin. *Global Diasporas: An Introduction*. London: University College London Press, 1997.

———. *Global Diasporas: An Introduction*. 2nd ed. London: Routledge, 2008.

———. "On the Move: The Migration Imperative." *Global: The International Briefing* 5 (January 2011) 14–17. https://www.imi.ox.ac.uk/news/new-piece-by-robin-cohen-on-the-migration-imperative/global5_insight_migrationzzzz.pdf.

Colette, Sidonie-Gabrielle. *Gigi*. London: Penguin, 1953.

Colzani, Gianni. *Missiologia Contemporanea: Il Cammino Evangelico delle Chiese: 1945–2007*. Cinisello Balsamo, Italy: São Paolo, 2010.

Comunidades de Reflexión Eclesial Cubana en la Diáspora (CRECED). *CRECED Final Document*. Miami: Graphic Ideas Corporation, 1996.

Congregation for Divine Worship and the Discipline of the Sacraments. *Directory on Popular Piety and the Liturgy: Principles and Guidelines*. Boston: Pauline, 2002. http://www.vatican.va/roman_curia/congregations/ccdds/documents/rc_con_ccdds_doc_20020513_vers-direttorio_en.html.

Connolly, William E. *The Ethos of Pluralization*. Minneapolis: University of Minnesota Press, 1995.

Cousins, Ewart H. *Bonaventure and the Coincidence of Opposites*. Chicago: Franciscan Herald, 1978.

Crahan, Margaret E. "Cuba." In *Religious Freedom and Evangelization in Latin America: The Challenge of Religious Pluralism*, edited by Paul E. Sigmund, 87–112. Maryknoll, NY: Orbis, 1999.

Cripps, Denise. "Flags and Fanfares: The Hinomaru Flag and Kimigayo Anthem." In *Case Studies on Human Rights in Japan*, edited by Roger Goodman and Ian Neary, 76–108. Richmond: Curzon/Japan Library, 1996.

Crosby, Michael. "Justice." In *The New Dictionary of Catholic Spirituality*, edited by Michael Downey, 579. Collegeville, MN: Liturgical, 1993.

Crush, Jonathan, and Daniel S. Tevera. "Exiting Zimbabwe." In *Zimbabwe's Exodus, Crisis, Migration, Survival*, edited by Jonathan Crush and Daniel S. Tevera, 1–51. Kingston: SAMP, 2010.

Cruz, Gemma T. "A New Way of Being Christian: The Contribution of Migrants to the Church." In *Contemporary Issues of Migration and Theology*, edited by Elaine Padilla and Peter C. Phan, 95–120. New York: Palgrave Macmillan, 2013.

Cruz, Oscar V. "Pastoral Letter on Filipino Spirituality." Manila: Catholic Bishops' Conference of the Philippines, July 10, 1999. http://www.cbcponline.net/documents/1990s/1999-filipino_spirituality.html.

Daniel, G. Reginald. *More than Black? Multiracial Identity and the New Racial Order*. Philadelphia: Temple University Press, 2001.

Darwin, Charles. *The Voyage of the Beagle*. Garden City, NY: Doubleday, 1906.

Davalos, Karen Mary. "'The Real Way of Praying': The Via Crucis, *Mexicano* Sacred Space, and the Architecture of Domination." In *Horizons of the Sacred: Mexican*

Traditions in U.S. Catholicism, edited by Timothy Matovina and Gary Riebe-Estrella, 41–68. Ithaca: Cornell University Press, 2002.

Davis, Francis et al. *The Ground of Justice: The Report of a Pastoral Research Enquiry into the Needs of Migrants in London's Catholic Community*. Cambridge: Von Hugel Institute, 2007. http://www.vhi.st-edmunds.cam.ac.uk/resources-folder/ground-justice.

Davis, Leo. *The First Ecumenical Councils (325–787): Their History and Theology*. Wilmington, NC: Glazier, 1983.

Del Grande, Gabriele. "Un Cimitero Chiamato Mediterraneo." Fortress Europe (blog), February 16, 2016. http://fortresseurope.blogspot.it/2012/04/ragazzi-di-tunisi-dispersi-al-largo-di.html.

Delio, Ilia. *Simply Bonaventure: An Introduction to His Life, Thought, and Writings*. New York: New City, 2001.

Demus, Otto. *Byzantine Mosaic Decoration: Aspects of Monumental Art in Byzantium*. London: Routledge, 1948.

Dianich, Severino. *La Chiesa Cattolica verso la sua Riforma*. Brescia: Queriniana, 2014.

Díaz, Maria Elena. *The Virgin, the King, and the Royal Slaves of El Cobre: Negotiating Freedom in Colonial Cuba, 1670–1780*. Stanford: Stanford University Press, 2000.

Dykstra, Laurel A. *Set Them Free: The Other Side of Exodus*. Maryknoll, NY: Orbis, 2002.

Eade, John. "Religion, Home-Making, and Migration across a Globalizing City: Responding to Mobility in London." *Culture and Religion* 13 (2012) 469–83.

Eastman, Scott. *Preaching Spanish Nationalism across the Atlantic: 1759–1823*. Baton Rouge: Louisiana State University Press, 2012.

Ebaugh, Helen Rose, and Janet Saltzman Chafetz, eds. *Religion across Borders: Transnational Immigrant Networks*. Walnut Grove, CA: AltaMira, 2002.

Egan, Philip. "Lonergan, Evangelization, and the British Context." *Heythrop Journal* 49 (2008) 794–821.

Eliot, T. S. *Murder in the Cathedral*. New York: Harcourt Brace, 1935.

Elizondo, Virgilio. *Guadalupe, Mother of the New Creation*. Maryknoll, NY: Orbis, 1997.

Espín, Orlando. *The Faith of the People: Theological Reflections on Popular Catholicism*. New York: Orbis, 1997.

Fanon, Frantz. *Black Skin, White Masks*. translated by Charles Lam Markmann. New York: Grove, 1967.

———. *A Dying Colonialism*. Translated by Haakon Chevalier. New York: Grove, 1965.

———. *The Wretched of the Earth*. Translated by Constance Farrington. New York: Grove, 1968.

Federazione delle Chiese Evangeliche in Italia [Federation of Evangelical Churches in Italy]. "Being One Church Together." http://www.fedevangelica.it/en/comm/ecio1.php.

Ferguson, Jeffrey B. *The Sage of Sugar Hill: George S. Schuyler and the Harlem Renaissance*. New Haven: Yale University Press, 2005.

Fernández, Damián J. *Cuba Transnational*. Gainesville: University Press of Florida, 2005.

Fernandez, Eleazar S. *Burning Center, Porous Borders: The Church in a Globalized World*. Eugene, OR: Wipf & Stock, 2011.

Ferraz, Austin. "Letter to Sir Patrick Wall." September 6, 1966. University of Hull Archives, DPW/48/492.

Fifth General Conference of the Bishops of Latin America and the Caribbean. "Concluding Document: Aparecida." Bogota, Colombia, May 13–31, 2007. http://www.aecrc.org/documents/Aparecida-Concluding%20Document.pdf.

Fish, Stanley. *The Trouble with Principle*. Cambridge: Harvard University Press, 1999.

Fleming, Ian. *Dr. No*. London: Cape, 1958.

———. *Live and Let Die*. London: Cape, 1954.

———. "Quantum of Solace." In *For Your Eyes Only*. London: Cape, 1960.

———. *The Spy Who Loved Me*. London: Cape, 1962.

Forfar, David. "Individuals against the State? The Politics of Opposition to the Reemergence of State Shintō." In *Case Studies on Human Rights in Japan*, edited by Roger Goodman and Ian Neary, 245–76. Richmond: Curzon /Japan Library, 1996.

Fox, Thomas C. *Pentecost in Asia: A New Way of Being Church*. Maryknoll, NY: Orbis, 2002.

Francis, Mark R. "Liturgy and Popular Piety in a Historical Context." In *Directory on Popular Piety and the Liturgy: Principles and Guidelines*, edited by Peter C. Phan, 19–44. Collegeville, MN: Liturgical, 2005.

Francis, Pope. "Address to the Ecclesial Convention of the Diocese of Rome." Delivered at the Paul VI Audience Hall, Vatican City, June 17, 2013. http://w2.vatican.va/content/francesco/en/speeches/2013/june/documents/papa-francesco_20130617_convegno-diocesano-roma.html.

———. "Homily for the Beginning of the Petrine Ministry." Homily delivered in St. Peter's Square, Vatican City, March 19, 2013. http://w2.vatican.va/content/francesco/en/homilies/2013/documents/papa-francesco_20130319_omelia-inizio-pontificato.html.

———. "Homily in Lampedusa." Delivered at Salina Quarter, Lampedusa, Italy, July 8, 2013. http://www.vatican.va/holy_father/francesco/homilies/2013/documents/papa-francesco_20130708_omelia-lampedusa_en.html.

———. *The Joy of the Gospel (Evangelii gaudium): Apostolic Exhortation*. Rome: Libreria Editrice Vaticana, 2013. http://w2.vatican.va/content/francesco/en/apost_exhortations/documents/papa-francesco_esortazione-ap_20131124_evangelii-gaudium.html.

Frederiks, Martha T., and Nienke Pruiksma. "Journeying toward Multiculturalism? The Relationship between Immigrant Christians and Dutch Indigenous Churches." *Journal of Religion in Europe* 3 (2010) 125–54.

Freyre, Gilberto. *The Masters and the Slaves (Casa-grande & Senzala)*. Translated by Samuel Putnam. New York: Knopf, 1946.

Fuss, Diana. "Interior Colonies: Frantz Fanon and the Politics of Identification." *Diacretics* 24 (1994) 20–42.

Gandolfi, Maria Elisabetta. "C'è un'indifferenza cattolica? La pastorale dopo Lampedusa: intervista a Maurizio Ambrosini." *Regno Attualità* 18 (2013) 557–59.

García, María Cristina. *Havana USA: Cuban Exiles and Cuban Americans in South Florida, 1959–1994*. Berkeley: University of California Press, 1996.

Gibson, Nigel, ed. *Living Fanon: Global Perspectives*. London: Palgrave Macmillan, 2011.

Gilroy, Paul. *Against Race: Imagining Political Culture Beyond the Color Line*. Cambridge: Harvard University Press, 2000.

———. *The Black Atlantic: Modernity and Double Consciousness*. Cambridge: Harvard University Press, 1993.

———. *Darker than Blue: On the Moral Economies of Black Atlantic Culture.* Cambridge: Harvard University Press, 2010.

———. *Postcolonial Melancholia.* New York: Columbia University Press, 2005.

———. "Shameful History: The Social Life of Races and the Postcolonial Archive." *Moving Worlds: A Journal of Transcultural Writings* 11 (2011) 19–34.

———. "Shooting Crabs in a Barrel." *Screen* 48 (2007) 233–35.

Glick Schiller, Nina, and Noel B. Salazar. "Regimes of Mobility across the Globe." *Journal of Ethnic and Migration Studies* 39 (2013) 183–200.

Goizueta, Roberto S. "Making Christ Credible: US Latino/a Popular Catholicism and the Liberating Nearness of God." In *Practicing Catholic: Ritual, Body, and Contestation in Catholic Faith,* edited by Bruce T. Morrill et al., 169–78. New York: Palgrave Macmillan, 2006.

Goldberg, David Theo. *The Threat of Race: Reflections on Racial Neoliberalism.* Oxford: Wiley-Blackwell, 2009.

Gomola, Aleksander. "Cognitive Mechanisms at Work and their Perlocutionary Effect in Catholic Preaching: A Case Study." In *Texts and Minds: Papers in Cognitive Poetics and Rhetoric,* edited by Alina Kwiatkowska, 287–99. New York: Peter Lang, 2012.

Góngora, Mario. "Aspectos de la Ilustración Católica en el Pensamiento y la Vida Eclesiástica Chilena." *Historia* 8 (1969) 43–73.

Gordon, Jane Anna, and Lewis Gordon. *Of Divine Warning: Reading Disaster in the Modern Age.* Boulder, CO: Paradigm, 2010.

Gordon, Lewis. *Bad Faith and Anti-Black Racism.* Atlantic Highlands, NJ: Humanities Press International, 1995.

Gorman, Robert F. "Classical Diasporas of the Third Kind: The Hidden History of Christian Dispersion." *Journal of Refugee Studies* 24 (2011) 635–54.

Gray, Mark M. "Cultural Diversity in the Catholic Church in the United States." Center for Applied Research in the Apostolate, November 2013.

Grayson, James Huntley. *Korea: A Religious History.* London: Routledge Curzon, 2002.

Greeley, Andrew. *The Catholic Imagination.* Berkeley: University of California Press, 2000.

Gregory, Brad S. *The Unintended Reformation: How a Religious Revolution Secularized Society.* Cambridge: Harvard University Press, 2012.

Grenier, Guillermo J., and Alex Stepick. *Miami Now! Immigration, Ethnicity, and Social Change.* Gainesville: University Press of Florida, 1992.

Groody, Daniel G. *Border of Death, Valley of Life: An Immigrant Journey of Heart and Spirit.* Lantham, MD: Rowman and Littlefield, 2002.

———. "Crossing the Divide: Foundations of a Theology of Migration and Refugees." *Theological Studies* 70 (2009) 638–67.

———. *Globalization, Spirituality, and Justice: Navigating the Path to Peace.* Maryknoll, NY: Orbis, 2007.

———. "The Spirituality of Migrants: Mapping an Inner Geography." In *Contemporary Issues of Migration and Theology,* edited by Elaine Padilla and Peter C. Phan, 139–56. New York: Palgrave Macmillan, 2013.

"Guide: Christians in the Middle East." *BBC News,* October 11, 2011. http://www.bbc.com/news/world-middle-east-15239529.

Gutiérrez, Gustavo. *A Theology of Liberation: History, Politics, and Salvation.* Maryknoll, NY: Orbis, 1988.

Haddad, Robert M. "Conversion and Continuity: Indigenous Christian Communities in Islamic Lands, Eighth to Eighteenth Centuries." In *Conversion and Continuity: Indigenous Christian Communities in Islamic Lands, Eighth to Eighteenth Centuries*, edited by Michael Gervers and Ramzi Jibran Bikhazi, 449–59. Toronto: Pontifical Institute of Mediaeval Studies, 1990.

Hage, Ghassan. *White Nation: Fantasies of White Supremacy in a Multicultural Society*. New York: Routledge, 1998.

Halliwell, Martin. *American Culture in the 1950s*. Edinburgh: Edinburgh University Press, 2007.

Hanciles, Jehu J. "Beyond Christendom: African Migration and Transformations in Global Christianity." *Studies in World Christianity* 10 (2004) 93–113.

Harry-Perry, Melissa V. *Sister Citizen: Shame, Stereotypes and Black Women in America*. New Haven: Yale University Press, 2011.

Hennelly, Alfred T., ed. *Santo Domingo and Beyond: Documents and Commentaries from the Historic Meeting of the Latin American Bishops' Conference*. Maryknoll, NY: Orbis, 1993.

Heyer, Kristin E. *Kinship across Borders. A Christian Ethic of Immigration*. Washington, DC: Georgetown University Press, 2012.

Hinfelaar, Marja. *Respectable and Responsible Women: Methodist and Roman Catholic Women's Organizations in Harare, Zimbabwe, 1919–1985*. Utrecht, Netherlands: Bookcentrum, 2003.

Hing, Bill Ong. *Deporting Our Souls: Values, Morality, and Immigration Policy*. New York: Cambridge University Press, 2006.

Hobsbawm, Eric, and Terence Ranger. *The Invention of Tradition*. New York: Cambridge University Press, 1992.

Hoeffel, Elizabeth M., et al. "The Asian Population: 2010." Washington, DC: US Department of Commerce, Economics and Statistics Administration, US Census Bureau, 2012. https://www.census.gov/prod/cen2010/briefs/c2010br-11.pdf.

Hollenbach, David. *Claims in Conflict: Retrieving and Renewing the Catholic Human Rights Tradition*. Woodstock Studies 4. New York: Paulist, 1979.

Honig, Bonnie. *Political Theory and the Displacement of Politics*. Contestations: Cornell Studies in Political Theory. Ithaca: Cornell University Press, 1993.

Horvath, Agnes, et al. "Introduction: Liminality and Cultures of Change." *International Political Anthropology* 2 (2009) 3–4.

Huynh Ngoc Trang. "Tong Quan ve Van Hoa Nam Bo" [An Overview of Southern Culture]. *Tap Chi Koha Hoc Xa Hoi* [Social Sciences Review] 11 (1992) 59–70.

International Organization for Migration (IOM). *Country Migration Report: The Philippines 2013*. Makati City, Philippines: IOM, 2013. http://www.iom.int/files/live/sites/iom/files/Country/docs/CMReport-Philipines-2013.pdf.

———. *Glossary on Migration: International Migration Law*. Geneva: IOM, 2004.

———. *World Migration Report 2010: The Future of Migration: Building Capacities for Change*. Geneva: IOM, 2010. http://www.iom.int/files/live/sites/iom/files/Newsrelease/docs/WM2010_FINAL_23_11_2010.pdf.

———. *World Migration Report 2011: Communicating Effectively about Migration*. Geneva: IOM, 2011.

———. *World Migration Report 2013: Migrant Well-Being and Development*. Geneva: IOM, 2013.

Irarrázaval, Diego. "Religious Windows in the Latin American Christology." *Ciberteología: Journal of Theology and Culture* 12 (July-August 2007) 11–23. http://ciberteologia.paulinas.org.br/ciberteologiaen/wp-content/uploads/2009/0 8/03Religiouswindows.pdf.

Isasi-Díaz, Ada María. "'By the Rivers of Babylon': Exile as a Way of Life." In *Reading from this Place*. Vol. 1, *Social Location and Biblical Interpretation in the United States*, edited by Fernando Segovia and Mary Ann Tolbert, 149–64. Minneapolis: Fortress, 1995.

John Paul II, Pope. "Letter to Cardinal Paul Joseph Pham Dình Tung, Archbishop of Hà Nôi, President of the Episcopal Conference of Viêt Nam for Bicentenary of the Virgin Mary's Apparitions in La Vang." December 16, 1997. https://w2.vatican.va/content/john-paul-ii/en/letters/1997/documents/hf_jp-ii_let_19971216_hanoi.html.

———. *Sollicitudo Rei Socialis*. Vatican City: Libreria Editrice Vaticana, 1987. http://www.vatican.va/holy_father/john_paul_ii/encyclicals/documents/hf_jp-ii_enc_30121987_sollicitudo-rei-socialis_en.html.

Johnson, Elizabeth A. *Quest for the Living God: Mapping Frontiers in the Theology of God*. New York: Continuum, 2007.

Johnson, Kristen Deede. *Theology, Political Theory, and Pluralism: Beyond Tolerance and Difference*. Cambridge: Cambridge University Press, 2007.

Johnson, Paul. "Sex, Snobbery, and Sadism." *New Statesman*, April 5, 1958.

Katz, Nathan. *Who Are the Jews of India?* Berkeley: University of California Press, 2000.

Kawaguchi, Kaoru. "Interview Record 2: Activities of the Catholic Tokyo International Center (CTIC)." Interview conducted by Takefumi Terada and Yumi Takemura, Sophia University, April 11, 2006. In *Jōchi Ajia Gaku* [Journal of Sophia Asian Studies] 26 (2008) 113–34.

Kelly, Joseph. *The Ecumenical Councils of the Catholic Church: A History*. Collegeville, MN: Liturgical, 2009.

Kerwin, Donald, and Doris Meissner. *DHS and Immigration: Taking Stock and Correcting Course*. Washington, DC: Migration Policy Institute, 2009. http://www.migrationpolicy.org/pubs/DHS_Feb09.pdf.

Khalaf, Samir. *Protestant Missionaries in the Levant: Ungodly Puritans, 1820–1860*. New York: Routledge, 2012.

Kim, Joseph Chang-mun, and John Jae-sun Chung. *Catholic Korea: Yesterday and Today*. Seoul: Catholic Korea, 1964.

Kim, Simon C. *Memory and Honor: Cultural and Generational Ministries with Korean American Communities*. Collegeville, MN: Liturgical, 2013.

Krindatch, Alexei D. "Orthodox (Eastern Christian) Churches in the United States at the Beginning of a New Millennium: Questions of Nature, Identity, and Mission." *Journal for the Scientific Study of Religion* 41 (September 2002) 533–63.

LaCugna, Catherine M. *God for Us. Trinity and Christian Life*. New York: Harper Collins, 1991.

Laksana, A. Bagus. "Comparative Theology: Between Identity and Alterity." In *The New Comparative Theology: Interreligious Insights from the Next Generation*, edited by Francis X. Clooney, 1–20. London: T & T Clark, 2010.

Larrúa-Guedes, Salvador. *Historia de Nuestra Señora la Virgen de la Caridad del Cobre: Reina, Madre y Patrona de la Isla de Cuba*. Vol. 1, *1612–1950*. Miami: Ediciones Universal, 2011.

Larsen, Nella. *Quicksand and Passing*. New Brunswick: Rutgers University Press, 1928.
Lazarus, Neil. *The Postcolonial Unconscious*. Cambridge: Cambridge University Press, 2011.
Leddy, Mary Jo. *The Other Face of God. When the Stranger Calls Us Home*. Maryknoll, NY: Orbis, 2011.
Lefebvre, Henri. *La production de l'espace*. Paris: Anthropos, 1974.
———. *The Production of Space*. Malden, MA: Blackwell, 1991.
Lehner, Ulrich L. "What is 'Catholic Enlightenment?'" *History Compass* 8 (2010) 166–78.
LeMay, Alec. *Inculturating Inculturation: Considering Multiculturalism within the Roman Catholic Church of Japan amongst Japanese, Filipinos, and Filipino-Japanese*. Monograph Series 12. Tokyo: Institute of Asian Cultures, 2013.
Leverenz, David. *Honor Bound: Race and Shame in America*. New Brunswick, NJ: Rutgers University Press, 2012.
Linthicum, Katie. "Unaccompanied Children Are the Focus of L.A. Annual Immigrant's Mass." *Los Angeles Times*, July 20, 2014. http://www.latimes.com/local/la-me-immigrants-mass-20140721-story.html.
Lloyd, David. "Ethnic Cultures, Minority Discourses and the State." In *Colonial Discourse/Postcolonial Theory*, edited by Francis Barker et al., 221–38. Manchester: Manchester University Press, 1994.
Llywelyn, Dorian. *Toward a Catholic Theology of Nationality*. Lanham, MD: Lexington, 2010.
Lonergan, Bernard. *The Way to Nicea: The Dialectical Development of Trinitarian Theology*. Philadelphia: Westminster, 1976.
de Lubac, Henri. *Catholicism: Christ and the Common Destiny of Man*. London: Burns, Oates and Washbourne, 1950.
Mahony, Roger M., Cardinal. "The Challenge of 'We the People' in a Post-9/11 World: Immigration, the American Economy, and the Constitution." The Fifth Annual John M. Templeton Jr. Lecture on the Constitution and Economic Liberty, Philadelphia, May 8, 2007.
Maïla, Joseph. "The Arab Christians: From the Eastern Question to the Recent Political Situation of the Minorities." In *Christian Communities in the Arab Middle East: The Challenge of the Future*, edited by Andrea Pacini, 23–47. Oxford: Clarendon, 1998.
Makdisi, Ussama. *Artillery of Heaven: American Missionaries and the Failed Conversion of the Middle East*. Ithaca: Cornell University Press, 2009.
———. *The Culture of Sectarianism: Community, History, and Violence in Nineteenth-Century Ottoman Lebanon*. Berkeley: University of California Press, 2000.
———. "Reconstructing the Nation-State: The Modernity of Sectarianism in Lebanon." *Middle East Report* 200 (July 1, 1996) 23–30.
Mancilla, Luis. "El Nazareno de Caguach." Patagonia Insular (blog), February 23, 2008. http://patagoniainsular.blogspot.com/2008/02/el-nazareno-de-caguach.html.
Martin, Phyllis M. *Catholic Women of Congo-Brazzaville: Mothers and Sisters in Troubled Times*. Bloomington: Indiana University Press, 2009.
Martos, Joseph. *Doors to the Sacred: A Historical Introduction to Sacraments in the Catholic Church*. Liguori: Liguori/Triumph, 2001.
Masterman, Christopher. "You Do Not Invite Children to a Cocktail Party." *Time and Tide* 46 (May 20–26, 1965).

Masters, Bruce. *Christians and Jews in the Ottoman Arab World: The Roots of Sectarianism.* Cambridge: Cambridge University Press, 2004.

Mathewes, Charles T. "Faith, Hope, and Agony: Christian Political Participation Beyond Liberalism." *Annual of the Society of Christian Ethics* 21 (2001) 125–50.

Matovina, Timothy. *Latino Catholicism: Transformation in America's Largest Church.* New Jersey: Princeton University Press, 2012.

———. "Latino Contribution to Vatican II Renewal." *Origins* 42 (December 20, 2012) 465–71.

Matsuoka, Fumitaka. *Out of Silence: Emerging Themes in Asian American Churches.* Cleveland: United Church, 1995.

McAlister, Elizabeth. "The Madonna of 115th Street Revisited: Vodou and Haitian Catholicism in an Age of Transnationalism." In *Gatherings in Diaspora: Religious Communities and the New Immigration*, edited by R. Stephen Warner and Judith Wittner, 123–60. Philadelphia: Temple University Press, 1998.

McCartan, Kieran. "Crucifix, Cross at Center of Battle between Bishop, Parish." *Clerical Whispers* (blog), May 26, 2010. http://clericalwhispers.blogspot.com/2010/05/crucifix-cross-at-center-of-battle.html.

McGrath, Patrick J. "Letter to Bishop Jacob Angadaith." December 10, 2001.

McGregor, JoAnn, and Dominic Pasura. "Diasporic Repositioning and the Politics of Re-engagement: Developmentalizing Zimbabwe's Diaspora?" *The Round Table* 99 (2010) 687–703.

McLoughlin, Seàn. "Religion, Religions, and Diaspora." In *A Companion to Diaspora and Transnationalism*, edited by Ato Quayson and Girish Daswani, 125–38. Malden, MA: Wiley Blackwell, 2013.

McNeil, Daniel. "Black Devils, White Saints, and Mixed-Race Femme Fatales: Philippa Schuyler and the Winds of Change." *Critical Arts: A Journal of South-North Cultural Studies* 25 (2011) 360–76.

———. *Sex and Race in the Black Atlantic: Mulatto Devils and Multiracial Messiahs.* New York: Routledge, 2009.

Merleau-Ponty, Maurice. "Eye and Mind." In *The Primacy of Perception.* Chicago: Northwestern University Press, 1964.

Min, Anselm Kyongsuk. "The Pastoral Challenges of Asian/Pacific American Catholic Communities: History, Theology, and Recommendations." Paper presented at the US Conference of Catholic Bishops' Committee on Migration's Symposium on Asian American Catholicism, Atlanta, GA, June 12, 2001.

———. *The Solidarity of Others in a Divided World: A Postmodern Theology after Postmodernism.* New York: T & T Clark, 2004.

Min, Pyong Gap. *Koreans in North America: Their Experiences in the Twenty-First Century.* Lanham, MD: Lexington, 2013.

Morgan, David. *The Sacred Gaze: Religious Visual Culture in Theory and Practice.* Berkeley: University of California Press, 2005.

———. *Visual Piety: A History and Theory of Popular Religious Images.* Berkeley: University of California Press, 1998.

Morrison, Andrew P. *Shame: The Underside of Narcissism.* Hillside, NJ: Analytic, 1989.

Mouffe, Chantal. *The Return of the Political.* London: Verso, 2000.

Mullins, Mark R. "Between Inculturation and Globalization: The Situation of Roman Catholicism in Contemporary Japanese Society." In *Xavier's Legacies: Catholicism in Modern Japanese Culture*, edited by Kevin Doak, 171–77. Vancouver: University of British Columbia Press, 2011.

———. "How Yasukuni Shrine Survived the Occupation: A Critical Examination of Popular Claims." *Monumenta Nipponica* 65 (2010) 89–136.

———. "Japanese Responses to Imperialist Secularization: The Postwar Movement to Restore Shinto in the Public Sphere." In *Multiple Secularities Beyond the West: Religion and Modernity in the Global Age*, edited by Marian Burchardt et al., 139–65. Berlin: De Gruyter, 2015.

———. "The Neo-nationalist Response to the Aum Crisis: A Return of Civil Religion and Coercion in the Public Sphere?" *Japanese Journal of Religious Studies* 39 (2012) 99–125.

———. "Sacred Sites and Social Conflict: Yasukuni Shrine and Religious Pluralism in Japanese Society." In *Religious Pluralism, State and Society in Asia*, edited by Chiara Formichi, 35–50. New York: Routledge, 2014.

National Christian Council in Japan. "Position Statement." *Japan Christian Activity News: The Newsletter of the National Christian Council in Japan* 736 (Spring/Summer 2004) 15–16. http://ncc-j.org/english/jcan/2004%20Summer.pdf.

Nausner, Michael. "Alla Luce di Lampedusa: Una Riflessione Teologica sulle Frontiere Europee." *Protestantesimo* 66 (2011) 341–56.

Nedungatt, George, ed. "Interpreting the Synod of Diamper and the Lessons of History." In *The Synod of Diamper Revisited*, edited by George Nedungatt, 11–36. Rome: Pontificio Istituto Orientale, 2001.

"New Joso Church to be Evangelization Center for Multi-Cultural Communities." *Catholic Weekly*, February 15, 2009.

Nguyen, Minh San. *Nhung Thanh Nu Danh Tieng Trong Van Hoa Tin Nguong Viet Nam* [Famous Goddesses in Vietnamese Cultural Belief]. Ha Noi: Nha Xuat Ban Phu Nu, 1996.

———. *Tiep con tin Nguong Dan da Viet Nam* [The Contiguous Beliefs of the Vietnamese People]. Ha Noi: Nha Xuat ban Van Hoa Dan Toc, 1994.

Nguyen, Van Thong. "Su-Kien La Vang: Trang Su Tu-Dao" [The La Vang Event: The Martyrs' History]. *Thang Mo* 852 (August 15, 1998) 46–48.

Nin, Anaïs. *The Diary of Anaïs Nin*. Vol. 1, *1931–1934*. New York: Harcourt, 1966.

———. *The Diary of Anaïs Nin*. Vol. 2, *1934–1939*. New York: Harcourt, 1967.

Noort, Gerrit. "Emerging Migrant Churches in the Netherlands: Missiological Challenges and Mission Frontiers." *International Review of Mission* 100 (2011) 4–16.

Obama, Barack. *Dreams from My Father: A Story of Race and Inheritance*. New York: Random House, 2004.

Ogsimer, Restituto, and Agnes V. Gatpatan. "Filipino Women in Cross-Cultural Marriage: Their Emerging Roles in the Catholic Church in Japan." *Jōchi Aji Gaku* [The Journal of Sophia Asian Studies] 26 (2008) 41–56.

O'Meara, Thomas F. *Theology of Ministry*. New York: Paulist, 1999.

Orsi, Robert Anthony. *Between Heaven and Earth: The Religious Worlds People Make and the Scholars Who Study Them*. Princeton: Princeton University Press, 2006.

———. *The Madonna of 115th Street: Faith and Community in Italian Harlem, 1880–1950*. New Haven: Yale University Press, 1988.

Osborne, Catherine R. "Migrant Domestic Careworkers: Between the Private and the Public in Catholic Social Teaching." *Journal of Religious Ethics* 40 (2012) 1–25.

Pacini, Andrea. *Christian Communities in the Arab Middle East: The Challenge of the Future*. New York: Oxford University Press, 1999.
Palumbo-Liu, David. *Asian/American: Historical Crossings of a Racial Frontier*. Stanford: Stanford University Press, 1999.
Pasura, Dominic. *African Transnational Diasporas: Fractured Communities and Plural Identities of Zimbabweans in Britain*. Basingstoke, UK: Palgrave Macmillan, 2014.
———."Competing Meanings of the Diaspora: The Case of Zimbabweans in Britain." *Journal of Ethnic and Migration Studies* 36 (2010) 1445–61.
———. "Modes of Incorporation and Transnational Zimbabwean Migration to Britain." *Ethnic and Racial Studies* 36 (2013) 199–218.
———. "Religious Transnationalism: The Case of Zimbabwean Catholics in Britain." *Journal of Religion in Africa* 42 (2012) 26–53.
Paul VI, Pope. *Dogmatic Constitution on the Church: Lumen Gentium*. Boston: Pauline, 1990. http://www.vatican.va/archive/hist_councils/ii_vatican_council/documents/vat-ii_const_19641121_lumen-gentium_en.html.
Pedraza, Silvia. *Political Disaffection in Cuba's Revolution and Exodus*. Cambridge: Cambridge University Press, 2007.
Pelikan, Jaroslav. *Imago Dei: The Byzantine Apologia for Icons*. Princeton: Princeton University Press, 1990.
———. *Mary through the Centuries: Her Place in the History of Culture*. New Haven: Yale University Press, 1996.
Pérez, Lisandro. "Cuban Miami." In *Miami Now! Immigration, Ethnicity, and Social Change*, edited by Guillermo J. Grenier and Alex Stepick III, 83–108. Gainesville: University Press of Florida, 1986.
———. "Cubans in the United States." *Annals of the American Academy, AAPSS* 487 (1986) 127–37.
Peridans, Dominique. *What Are They Thinking? A Look at Roman Catholic 'Doctrine' on Immigration*. Washington, DC: Center for Immigration Studies, 2012. http://cis.org/sites/cis.org/files/peridans-10-12.pdf.
Pew Research Center. "Cubans in the United States: Fact Sheet," August 25, 2006. http://www.pewhispanic.org/2006/08/25/cubans-in-the-united-states/.
———. "The Global Catholic Population," February 13, 2013. http://www.pewforum.org/2013/02/13/the-global-catholic-population.
———. "Global Christianity: A Report on the Size and Distribution of the World's Christian Population," December 19, 2011. http://www.pewforum.org/2011/12/19/global-christianity-exec.
Pfister, Paul. "The Church and Shinto Rites: A Historical Note." *Missionary Bulletin* 9 (1955) 264–65.
Phan, Peter C. "Asian Catholics: Challenges and Opportunities for the Catholic Church in the United States." Archbishop Gerety Lecture, Immaculate Conception Seminary School of Theology at Seton Hall University, South Orange, NJ, June 2000.
———. "Betwixt and Between: Doing Theology with Memory and Imagination." In *Journeys at the Margin: Toward an Autobiographical Theology in American-Asian Perspective*, edited by Peter C. Phan and Jung Young Lee, 113–33. Collegeville, MN: Liturgical, 1999.

———. "The Experience of Migration as Source of Intercultural Theology." In *Christianity with an Asian Face: Asian American Theology in the Making*, edited by Peter C. Phan, 3–25. Maryknoll, NY: Orbis, 2003.

———. "Introduction: An Asian-American Theology: Believing and Thinking at the Boundaries." In *Journeys at the Margin: Toward an Autobiographical Theology in American-Asian Perspective*, edited by Peter C. Phan and Jung Young Lee, xi–xxvii. Collegeville, MN: Liturgical, 1999.

Phillips, Earl H., and Eui-Young Yu. *Religions in Korea: Beliefs and Cultural Values*. Los Angeles: Center for Korean-American and Korean Studies, 1982.

Piñeda, Ana María. "Shrines and Pilgrimages." In *Directory on Popular Piety and the Liturgy: Principles and Guidelines*, edited by Peter C. Phan, 151–62. Collegeville, MN: Liturgical, 2005.

Pius V, Pope. *Gaudium et Spes: Pastoral Constitution on the Church in the Modern World*. Washington, DC: National Catholic Welfare Conference, 1965. http://www.vatican.va/archive/hist_councils/ii_vatican_council/documents/vat-ii_const_19651207_gaudium-et-spes_en.html.

Pius X, Pope. "The Papal Bull Instituting the Vicariate Apostolic of Kottayam for the Knanaya Community." *In Universi Christiani*, August 29, 1911. http://kottayamad.org/the-papal-bull-by-st-pius-x-instituting-the-vicariate-apostolic-of-kottayam-for-the-knanaya-community/.

Podipara, Placid. "Hindu in Culture, Christian in Religion, Oriental in Worship." In *Thomapedia*, edited by George Menacherry, 107–112. Ollur, India: St. Joseph's, 2000.

Pohl, Christine D. "Biblical Issues in Mission and Migration." *Missiology* 31 (2003) 3–15.

———. *Living into Community: Cultivating Practices that Sustain Us*. Grand Rapids: Eerdmans, 2012.

———. *Making Room: Recovering Hospitality as a Christian Tradition*. Grand Rapids: Eerdmans, 1999.

Portes, Alejandro, and Alex Stepick. *City on the Edge: The Transformation of Miami*. Berkeley: University of California Press, 1994.

Portuondo Zúñiga, Olga. *La Virgen de la Caridad del Cobre: Símbolo de la Cubanía*. Madrid: Agualarga, 2002.

Poyo, Gerald Eugene. *Cuban Catholics in the United States, 1960–1980: Exile and Integration*. Notre Dame: University of Notre Dame Press, 2007.

Quayson, Ato, and Girish Daswani. *A Companion to Diaspora and Transnationalism*. Malden, MA: Wiley Blackwell, 2013.

Quero, Hugo Córdova, and Rafael Shoji, eds. *Transnational Faiths: Latin-American Immigrants and their Religions in Japan*. Surrey: Ashgate, 2014.

Quero, Martín Hugo Córdova. "Worshiping in (Un) Familiar Land: Brazilian *Nikkeijin* Migrants with the Roman Catholic Church in Japan." *Encontros Lusófonos* 9 (2007) 25–37.

Rank, Otto. *Beyond Psychology*. New York: Dover, 1958.

"Rape in the Fields." *PBS Frontline*, June 25, 2013. http://www.pbs.org/wgbh/pages/frontline/rape-in-the-fields/.

Rawls, John. *Political Liberalism*. New York: Columbia University Press, 1993.

———. *A Theory of Justice*. Cambridge: Harvard University Press, 1972.

Read, Alan, ed. *The Fact of Blackness: Frantz Fanon and Visual Representation*. London: Institute of Contemporary Arts, 1996.
Repeta, Lawrence. "Politicians, Teachers, and the Japanese Constitution: Flag, Freedom, and the State." *The Asia-Pacific Journal: Japan Focus* 5 (February 14, 2007) 1–7. http://www.japanfocus.org/-Lawrence-Repeta/2355.
Ritty, J. Michael. "Letter to Bishop Jacob Angadiath." May 24, 2013.
Robert, Dana L. "Cross-Cultural Friendship in the Creation of Twentieth-Century World Christianity." *International Bulletin of Missionary Research* 35 (2011) 100–107.
Robson, Laura. *Colonialism and Christianity in Mandate Palestine*. Austin: University of Texas Press, 2011.
Rogers, J. A. *Sex and Race: A History of White, Negro, and Indian Miscegenation in the Two Americas*. Vol. 2. New York: H. M. Rogers, 1942.
Rohter, Larry. "For Some on Island, a Planned Project Is a Bridge Too Near." *New York Times*, August 3, 2006. http://www.nytimes.com/2006/08/03/world/americas/03chile.html?_r=0.
Ruiz, Lester Edwin. "Diaspora, Empire, Solidarity: Hope and the Marginalized Subaltern as Rupture(s) and Repetition(s)." *CTC Bulletin* 23 (2007) 39–59.
Sacred Congregation for Bishops. *Instruction on the Pastoral Care of People Who Migrate*. Washington, DC: US Catholic Conference, 1969.
Safran, William. "Diasporas in Modern Societies: Myths of Homeland and Return." *Diaspora: A Journal of Transnational Studies* 1 (1991) 83–99.
———. "The Jewish Diaspora in a Comparative and Theoretical Perspective." *Israel Studies* 10 (2005) 36–60.
Sang Hyun Lee. *From a Liminal Place: An Asian American Theology*. Minneapolis: Fortress, 2010.
Scheff, Thomas J. "Shame in Social Theory." In *The Widening Scope of Shame*, edited by Melvin R. Lansky and Andrew P. Morrison, 205–30. Mahwah, NJ: Analytic, 1997.
Scheff, Thomas J., and Suzanne M. Retzinger. "Helen Block Lewis on Shame: Appreciation and Critique." In *The Widening Scope of Shame*, edited by Melvin R. Lansky and Andrew P. Morrison, 139–54. Hillsdale, NJ: Analytic, 1989.
Schiller, Nina Glick, et al. "Defining Cosmopolitan Sociability in a Transnational Age: An Introduction." *Ethnic and Racial Studies* 34 (2011) 399–418.
Schreiter, Robert. *Constructing Local Theologies*. Maryknoll, NY: Orbis, 1993.
Schuyler, George. "Letter to Josephine Schuyler," October 20, 1935. Josephine Cogdell Schuyler Papers (JCSP), Schomburg Center for Research in Black Culture (SCRBC).
———. "The Negro in America." October 20, 1954. George Samuel Schuyler Papers (GSSP), SCRBC.
Schuyler, Philippa. *Congo*. 1962. Philippa Duke Schuyler Papers (PDSP), SCRBC.
———. *The Demons of the Jungle*. 1963. PDSP, SCRBC.
———. Diary Entry. April 15, 1960. PDSP, SCRBC.
———. *Evil Eville*. 1962. PDSP, SCRBC.
———. *Good Men Die*. 1967. PDSP, SCRBC.
———. *Jungle Saints*. 1963. PDSP, SCRBC.
———. Letter to Josephine Schuyler. August 15, 1953.
———. Letter to Josephine Schuyler. September 22, 1954. PDSP, SCRBC.
———. Letter to Josephine Schuyler. April 27, 1960. PDSP, SCRBC.

———. Letter to Josephine Schuyler. N.d., 1963. PDSP, SCRBC.
———. Letter to Josephine Schuyler. June 9, 1963. PDSP, SCRBC.
———. Letter to Josephine Schuyler. July 12, 1963. PDSP, SCRBC.
———. Letter to Josephine Schuyler. October 9, 1964. PDSP, SCRBC.
———. Letter to Josephine Schuyler. December 26, 1965. PDSP, SCRBC.
———. Letter to Josephine Schuyler. N.d., 1966.
———. Letter to Josephine Schuyler. February 21, 1966. PDSP, SCRBC.
———. Notebook. 1964. PDSP, SCRBC.
———. Notebook. 1965. PDSP, SCRBC.
———. "Une Métisse a la Reserche de son ame." 1950. PSDSP, SCRBC.
———. *The Virgin and the Cross*. 1960. PDSP, SCRBC.
———. *The White Leopard of Katanga*. 1964. PDSP, SCRBC.
———. *Who Killed the Congo?* 1962. PDSP, SCRBC.
———. "Why I Don't Marry: Former Piano Prodigy Meets Many Men on World Concert Tours, but None Her Ideal." *Ebony* (July 1958) 78–80.
Second Vatican Council. *Orientalium Ecclesiarum* [Decree on the Catholic Churches of the Eastern Rite]. Washington, DC: National Catholic Welfare Conference, 1964. http://www.vatican.va/archive/hist_councils/ii_vatican_council/documents/vat-ii_decree_19641121_orientalium-ecclesiarum_en.html.
Segovia, Fernando. "Toward a Hermeneutics of the Diaspora: A Hermeneutics of Otherness and Engagement." In *Reading from this Place*. Vol. 1, *Social Location and Biblical Interpretation in the United States*, edited by Fernando Segovia and Mary Ann Tolbert, 57–74. Minneapolis: Fortress, 1995.
Sekyi-Otu, Ato. *Fanon's Dialectic of Experience*. Cambridge: Harvard University Press, 1996.
Sengstock, Mary C. "Traditional and Nationalist Identity in a Christian Arab Community." *Sociological Analysis* 35 (Autumn 1974) 201–10.
Shadid, Anthony. *House of Stone: A Memoir of Home, Family, and a Lost Middle East*. Reprint, Boston: Mariner, 2013.
Sheffer, Gabriel. *Diaspora Politics: At Home Abroad*. New York: Cambridge University Press, 2003.
Shenar, Gabriele. "Bollywood in Israel: Multi-Sensual Milieus, Cultural Appropriation, and the Aesthetics of Diaspora in Transnational Audiences." *Ethnos* 78 (2013) 226–54.
Smidt, Andrea J. "*Luces por la Fe:* The Cause of Catholic Enlightenment in Eighteenth-Century Spain." In *A Companion to the Catholic Enlightenment in Europe*, edited by Ulrich L. Lehner and Michael Printy, 403–52. Boston: Brill, 2010.
Snyder, Susanna. *Asylum-Seeking, Migration and Church*. Surrey: Ashgate, 2012.
Sobrino, Jon. *El Principio-Misericordia: Bajar de la Cruz a los Pueblos Crucificados*. Santander: Sal Terrae, 1992.
Sono, Ayako. "Shūkyō o tokutei shinai aratana kinenbyō no setsuritsu o" [Toward the Establishment of a Religiously Neutral Memorial Site]. *Jurist* 848 (1985) 32–34.
———. "Yasukuni ni mairimasu" [I Will Visit Yasukuni Shrine]. *Shokun* (September 2005) 36–41.
Spadaro, Antonio. "Interview with Pope Francis," August 19, 2013. http://w2.vatican.va/content/francesco/en/speeches/2013/september/documents/papa-francesco_20130921_intervista-spadaro.html.

———. "Wake Up the World! Conversation with Pope Francis about the Religious Life." Translated by Donald Maldari. *La Civiltà Cattolica* 1 (January 2014). http://jpicformation.wikispaces.com/file/view/Wake_up_the_world-2.pdf/495026180/Wake_up_the_world-2.pdf.

Stepick, Alex. *This Land is Our Land, Immigrants and Power in Miami*. Berkeley: University of California Press, 2003.

Stepick, Alex, et al. *Churches and Charity in the Immigrant City: Religion, Immigration, and Civic Engagement in Miami*. New Brunswick, NJ: Rutgers University Press, 2009.

Stevens-Arroyo, Anthony M. "A Marriage Made in America: Trent and the Baroque." In *From Trent to Vatican II: Historical and Theological Investigations*, edited by Raymond F. Bulman and Frederick J. Parrella, 39–60. New York: Oxford University Press, 2006.

Synott, Anthony. "The Beauty Mystique: Ethics and Aesthetics in the Bond Genre." *International Journal of Politics, Culture, and Society* 3 (1990) 407–26.

Talalay, Kathryn M. *Composition in Black and White: The Life of Philippa Schuyler*. New York: Oxford University Press, 1995.

Tan, Jonathan Y. *Introducing Asian American Theologies*. Maryknoll, NY: Orbis, 2008.

Tangney, June Price. "Shame and Guilt in Interpersonal Relationships." In *Self-Conscious Emotions: The Psychology of Shame, Guilt, Embarrassment, and Pride*, edited by June Price Tangney and Kurt W. Fischer, 114–42. New York: Guilford, 1995.

Tangney, June Price, and Ronda L. Dearing. *Shame and Guilt*. New York: Guilford, 2004.

Tani, Daiji. *Ijūsha to tomo ni ikiru Kyōkai* [A Church that Lives Together with Migrants]. Tokyo: Shinsho Henkei, 2008.

———. "Jimintō shinkenpō sōan o kenshō suru" [An Examination of the LDP Draft Constitution]. In *Shinkyō no jiyū to seikyō bunri* [Freedom of Belief and the Separation of Church and State], edited by the Catholic Bishops' Conference of Japan, 17–44. Tokyo: Catholic Bishops' Conference of Japan, 2007.

Tanner, Norman P., ed. *Decrees of the Ecumenical Councils*. Vol. 2. Washington, DC: Georgetown University Press, 1990.

Taylor, Charles. "The Politics of Recognition." In *Multiculturalism: Examining the Politics of Recognition*, edited by Amy Gutmann, 25–74. Princeton: Princeton University Press, 1994.

———. *A Secular Age*. Cambridge: Harvard University Press, 2007.

Taylor, Philip. *Goddess on the Rise: Pilgrimage and Popular Religion in Vietnam*. Honolulu: University of Hawaii Press, 2004.

Taylor, William B. *Shrines and Miraculous Images: Religious Life in Mexico Before the Reforma*. Albuquerque: University of New Mexico Press, 2010.

Tejirian, Eleanor H., and Reeva Spector Simon. *Conflict, Conquest, and Conversion: Two Thousand Years of Christian Missions in the Middle East*. New York: Columbia University Press, 2012.

Terada, Takefumi. "Editor's Note: Migrants and the Catholic Church in Japan." *Jōchi Aji Gaku* [The Journal of Sophia Asian Studies] 26 (2008).

Ter Haar, Gerrie. "African Christians in Europe: A Mission in Reverse." In *Changing Relations between Churches in Europe and Africa: The Internationalization of Christianity and Politics in the Twentieth Century*, edited by Katharina Kunter and Jens Holger Schjorring, 241–49. Wiesbaden, Germany: Harrassowitz Verlag, 2008.

Torresin, Antonio. "La Parrocchia Ospitale: L'Annuncio del Vangelo oltre la Retorica." *Regno Attualità* 2 (2014) 8–13.
Tracy, David. *The Analogical Imagination: Christian Theology and the Culture of Pluralism*. New York: Crossroad, 1981.
Tran, Peter. "Toward Multicultural Church Communities: A Pastoral Letter by Cardinal Peter Seiichi Shirayanagi of Tokyo." *Migration World Magazine* 26 (1998) 29–31.
Trevor-Roper, Hugh. "The Rise of Christian Europe." *The Listener*, November 28, 1963.
Trzebiatowska, Marta. "The Advent of the 'EasyJet Priest': Dilemmas of Polish Catholic Integration in the U.K." *Sociology* 44 (2010) 1055–72.
Tuan, Yi-Fu. *Space and Place: The Perspective of Experience*. Minneapolis: University of Minnesota Press, 1977.
Turner, Victor W. *From Ritual to Theater: The Seriousness of Human Play*. New York: Performance Art Journal, 1982.
———. *Ritual Process: Structure and Anti-Structure*. Ithaca: Cornell University Press, 1969.
Tweed, Thomas. *Our Lady of Exile: Diasporic Religion at a Cuban Catholic Shrine in Miami*. New York: Oxford University Press, 1997.
UN Department of Economic and Social Affairs Population Division. *International Migration Report 2013*. New York: United Nations, 2013. https://www.un.org/en/development/desa/population/publications/migration/migration-report-2013.shtml.
UN High Commissioner for Refugees (UNHCR). "UNHCR Statistical Yearbook 2012: 12th ed." December 10, 2013. http://www.unhcr.org/uk/statistics/country/52a7213b9/unhcr-statistical-yearbook-2012-12th-edition.html.
US Conference of Catholic Bishops. *Asian and Pacific Presence: Harmony in Faith*. Washington, DC: US Conference of Catholic Bishops, 2001.
———. *Economic Justice for All*. Washington, DC: US Conference of Catholic Bishops, 1986. http://www.usccb.org/upload/economic_justice_for_all.pdf.
———. "Strangers No Longer: Together on the Journey of Hope—A Pastoral Letter Concerning Migration." US Conference of Catholic Bishops, January 22, 2003. http://www.usccb.org/issues-and-action/human-life-and-dignity/immigration/strangers-no-longer-together-on-the-journey-of-hope.cfm.
US Conference of Catholic Bishops and Conferencia de Episcopado Mexicano. *Strangers No Longer: Together on the Journey of Hope*. Washington, DC: US Conference of Catholic Bishops, 2003. http://www.usccb.org/issues-and-action/human-life-and-dignity/immigration/strangers-no-longer-together-on-the-journey-of-hope.cfm.
US Conference of Catholic Bishops' Secretariat of Cultural Diversity in the Church. Subcommittee for Asian and Pacific Islander Affairs. "Asian and Pacific Catholics in the US: 2011." Unpublished survey.
van der Ven, J. A. *Ecclesiology in Context*. Grand Rapids: Eerdmans, 1993.
Vertovec, Steven. "Conceiving and Researching Transnationalism." *Ethnic and Racial Studies* 22 (1999) 447–62.
Vertovec, Steven, and Susanne Wessendorf. *Multiculturalism Backlash: European Discourses, Policies, and Practices*. London: Routledge, 2010.
Walls, Andrew F. "World Christianity, Theological Education, and Scholarship." *Transformation* 28 (2011) 235–40.
Walnut Ridge Consulting. "American Indian Proverbs," n.d. http://www.walnutridgeconsulting.com/?page_id=376.

Wan, Enoch. "Diaspora Mission Strategy in the Context of the United Kingdom in the Twenty-First Century." *Transformation: An International Journal of Holistic Mission Studies* 28 (2011) 3–13.
Ward, Graham. *Cities of God*. London: Routledge, 2000.
Warner, R. Stephen. "Religion and New (Post-1965) Immigrants: Some Principles Drawn from Field Research." In *A Church of Their Own: Disestablishment and Diversity in American Religion*, 232–52. Piscataway, NJ: Rutgers University Press, 2005.
Warner, R. Stephen, and Judith Wittner. *Gatherings in Diaspora: Religious Communities and the New Immigration*. Philadelphia: Temple University Press, 1998.
Washington, Mary Helen, ed. *Invented Lives: Narratives of Black Women, 1860–1960*. New York: Anchor, 1987.
Wayde Gayles, Gloria Jean. *Rooted Against the Wind*. Boston: Beacon, 1996.
Weaver, Alain Epp. *Mapping Exile and Return: Palestinian Dispossession and a Political Theology for a Shared Future*. Minneapolis: Fortress, 2014.
Webber, Jonathan. Forum for European Philosophy Panel Discussion, London School of Economics, London, February 21, 2013.
Werbner, Pnina. "Global Pathways: Working Class Cosmopolitans and the Creation of Transnational Ethnic Worlds." *Social Anthropology* 7 (1999) 17–35.
———. "Migration and Transnational Studies between Simultaneity and Rupture." In *A Companion to Diaspora and Transnationalism*, edited by Ato Quayson and Girish Daswani, 106–24. Malden, MA: Wiley Blackwell, 2013.
Wheatley, Catherine. *Michael Haneke's Cinema: The Ethic of the Image*. New York: Berghahn, 2009.
Wilbanks, Dana W. *Re-creating America: The Ethics of U.S. Immigration and Refugee Policy in a Christian Perspective*. Nashville: Abingdon, 1996.
Wright, Wendy. *The Lady of the Angels and Her City: A Marian Pilgrimage*. Collegeville, MN: Liturgical, 2013.
Yoon, David, and Ruth Chung. *Religion and Spirituality in Korean America*. Champaign: University of Illinois Press, 2008.
Yoon, Inshil Choe. "Martyrdom and Social Activism: The Korean Practice of Catholicism." In *Religions of Korea in Practice*, edited by Robert Buswell, 355–75. Princeton: Princeton University Press, 2007.
Younes, Robert. "Yvonne Haddad on Issues Concerning Arab-American Christians, Muslims." *Washington Report on Middle East Affairs* 24 (April 2005) 61.
Yousef, Odette. "Local Indian Catholics Allege Discrimination Within Their Own Church," *WBEZ News*, September 11, 2013. http://www.wbez.org/local-indian-catholics-allege-discrimination-within-their-own-church-108652.
Zarate, Robert. "The Filipinos in the Catholic Church in Japan." *Jōchi Aji Gaku* [The Journal of Sophia Asian Studies] 26 (2008) 25–39.

Scripture Index

Genesis
1:26–27	64
5:1–3	64
9:6	64
12	174n27
18	94

Exodus
1–14	70
20:2	69

Psalms
58	107

Jeremiah
29:5	1
29:7	1

Matthew
2:1–13	70n21
2:13–17	70
2:13–14	71
4:1–11	77
4:4	76, 77, 94
5:17–18	68
7:1–5	69
8:5–13	68
8:11	68
11:16–19	68
13:10–17	69
13:54–57	70n21
15:21–28	68
19:16–22	70n21
19:30	73
20:16	73
22:37–38	67
22:39	67
25:31–46	73
26:3–4	70n21
26:14–16	70n21
26:47–50	70n21
26:69–75	70n21
27:15–18	70n21
27:20–23	70n21
28:19	136n22

Mark
3:20–21	70n21
6:1–4	70n21
7:24–30	68
10:17–22	70n21
10:31	73
12:28–34	68
14:66–72	70n21
15:6–14	70n21

Luke
1:39	71
2:1–5	70
4:13–30	70n21
6:27–38	69
7:1–10	68
7:11–17	68
7:24–35	68
7:33–50	92
7:36–50	68
13:10–17	68
13:29–30	73
14:1–24	92
15:1–2	92
16:19–31	74
18:18–23	70n21
19:1–10	92, 94
22:4–6	70n21

Luke (continued)
22:30	68
22:54–62	70n21
23:13–23	70n21

John
7:41–43	70
7:52	70
11:47–53	70n21
18:2–5	70n21
18:15–18	70n21
18:25–27	70n21
19:5–7	70n21
19:14–15	70n21
19:36	109n39

Acts
1:8	1

Romans
1:18–20	71
3:21–24	71
10:14	44
13:9–10	71

1 Corinthians
11:7	64

2 Corinthians
5:6	106n30

Ephesians
2:11–22	91

Philippians
3:20	73, 153

Hebrews
11:13–16	73
13:14	73

James
3:9	64

Revelation
3:20	94

Subject Index

African Catholicism, 209, 212, 217
African Catholic diaspora, 9–10
  and migration, 214
  and transnationalism, 218–19
Asian Americans,
  and catholicity, 177
  and community, 8
  and epistemology, 168–70
  and ethnicity, 8
  as first generation immigrants, 168
  and identity, 57, 168–70
  liminality, Turner's concept of,
    169–70, 171, 178
  population in North America,
    53–54, 168
  and race, 8
  and religion, 57, 177
  See also specific groups
Asian American Catholics, 57–59
  "Asian in spirit," 4, 56–57
  and tradition, 56–61
Asian American Catholic studies, 180
Asian American studies, 8
  and diaspora, 179
  and Vietnamese diaspora, 179
Asian Catholic diaspora, 8
Asian and Pacific Islander (APA)
    Catholics, 56–59
  and celebrations, 54, 56, 59, 60, 61
  and dioceses, 48, 54–55, 58–59, 61,
    114, 116, 118, 128, 172–73, 175,
    186, 187
  and language use, 47, 48, 54, 58, 59,
    117–18, 119, 120, 169
  and martyrdom, 43, 44–45, 46, 48,
    60, 113, 187
  and Mary, 8–9, 60, 179–89
  (*see also* Marian apparitions)

  and pastoral care ministries, 54, 58,
    119, 120
  and population, 45, 53–55, 115,
    116–17, 164, 168
  and religiosity, 56, 60
Atlantic slave trade, 13
Augustine, Saint, 6, 96, 104–7, 181

Bonaventure, Saint, 6, 97, 106–7,
    109–10
borders, 3, 11, 63, 65, 67, 68, 69, 72,
    73, 74, 78, 79, 89, 102, 136

Catholic Church,
  as a church of migrants, 18, 20, 22,
    57–58, 97, 177
  and ethnicity, 53–54, 177, 218
  as global, 117, 202, 204, 205, 211,
    217, 218
  and immigration, 63–75
  and the state, 12, 65, 66, 68, 121,
    126, 128
  as transnational, 10, 18, 22, 202–3,
    205, 211, 218
  universality of, 2, 150, 216
Catholic faith,
  early church developments, 40–43
  and disciples, 40, 41, 68, 109, 136
  and displacement, 2, 3, 18–20, 22,
    141, 202, 207, 215, 218–19
  and immigration, 63–75
  and martyrdom, 42, 43, 44–45, 46,
    48, 51, 60, 113, 187
  and missionary activity, 4, 7, 22, 33,
    40, 44, 45, 46, 47, 48, 49, 55, 58,
    90, 92, 93, 113–14, 118, 136–37,
    144–45, 149, 150, 171, 173, 174n,
    175, 179, 213

243

SUBJECT INDEX

Catholic faith, *(continued)*
  and Protestantism, 49, 50, 86, 113, 130
  and transnationalism, 10, 22, 202–3, 218
Catholic identity, 4, 31, 58, 60, 180, 202, 205, 211, 218
Catholic schools, 114, 124n27, 126, 132, 135
catholicity, 2, 18, 22, 88, 171, 172–74, 91, 177
  Chilean Catholicism, 146, 147, 157
  See also Jesús Nazareno cult
Chilean Catholics, 7, 142–166
  See also Jesús Nazareno cult
Chiloé, 7, 142–166
Christianity,
  and Buddhism, 21, 56 127, 127n, 184
  and Confucianism, 44, 47, 56, 184, 184n8
  European model, 49, 114, 144, 147, 148, 157n34, 175
  and Islam, 3, 24, 26, 27, 33–34, 56
Christian identity, 22, 27,
Christian theology, 5, 67, 76, 84–85, 87, 103
  Augustinian, 6, 97, 104–8
  classical, 6, 152, 156
  feminist, 84
  and justice, 67
  liberation, 76n1, 84, 163n49, 165, 167
  liturgical, 156, 167
  migration, 76n2, 77, 85, 164
  postcolonial, 84
  Trinitarian, 91, 94, 107, 142n1, 151
  Western, 88
Cuban Catholics, 7, 131–141
  and Afro-Cuban religions, 133, 140
  and assimilation, 134
  Ermita, the, 140–41
  exodus, 134
  in Miami, 132, 133, 134, 135, 136, 137, 140, 141, 154
  in New York, 131

  and Our Lady of Charity, 7, 132, 137, 138–41
  and Second Vatican Council, 135
  in South Florida, 132, 134
  as "victim diaspora," 133
Cuban diaspora, 7, 131–141
  and *balseros*, 133, 134
  Cuban Revolution, 7, 131, 132
  Cuban War of Independence, 139
  and economic crisis, 133
  Fidel Castro, 131
  in Key West, 131
  in Miami, 12, 131–32
  in New York, 131
  in Tampa, 131

diaspora,
  and cosmopolitanism, 98–100, 101, 102, 103, 104, 106, 205, 215
  definitions of, 24, 25, 25n5, 133n12
  de-territorialized, 133n12, 204
  and loyalty to country of origin, 99, 100, 102
  and transnationalism, 3, 10, 16, 18, 134, 203–5
  See also diaspora communities; diaspora religion; diaspora studies
diaspora communities, 2, 11–22, 117, 122, 130, 180, 214
  and food, 19, 59, 91, 164
  and language, 18, 19, 23, 47, 48, 54, 58, 59, 97, 117, 118, 120
diaspora religion, 16–22
diaspora studies, 3, 8, 11–13, 13–16, 17, 18, 22, 133n12
  and Jewish communities, 13, 133n12, 203
  and physical space, 3, 15–16
  and race, 8, 9, 180
  and social space, 15, 16n5
  and transnational studies, 3, 11–13, 17, 202
displacement, 3, 18–20, 35, 46, 62, 63, 63n, 76n1, 168, 202, 203, 207, 215, 218
  and religion, 18–20, 22
  negative outcome, 20
  positive outcome, 20

SUBJECT INDEX 245

endogamy, 171, 172–74, 177
ethno-religious ideology, 37
Eucharistic liturgy, 6, 43, 45, 48, 85, 108, 108n37, 109, 110, 111

Fanon, Frantz, 9, 199–201
Filipino American Catholics, 6, 54, 58, 60, 61, 119, 119n17, 142n1
    Simbang Gabi, 60–61
Francis, Pope, 5, 77, 78, 79, 83, 84, 88, 92, 93
    and Lampedusa, 5, 78, 83
    on migration, 77, 79, 84

globalization, 8, 11, 117, 188, 203
    trend of contemporary migration, 203

homeland, 11, 12, 13, 14, 16, 17, 18, 19, 21, 137, 139, 140, 141, 149, 150, 153, 155, 188, 204, 218
    idealized, 15, 19, 24, 133n12, 203
    and identity, 4, 40, 72, 133–34, 159, 170
homogeneity, 6, 120
human dignity, 5, 63–66, 90
human populations,
    Asian Pacific Islander Catholic, 55
    Catholic, 52, 53–55
    Cuban Catholics, 7
    Korean, 44
    Korean American, 45
    as migrants, 203
    in Zimbabwe, 10
    See also movement of peoples

identity,
    Catholic, 4, 27, 31, 57–58, 60, 180, 202, 205, 211, 218
    cultural, 12, 30, 33, 74, 155, 159, 163, 164, 165, 166, 185
    and homeland, 4, 40, 72, 133–34, 159, 170
    hybrid, 204
    hyphenated, 168
    and liminality, 169
    migrant, 6, 96–111
    and multiplicity, 6, 96–111

immigrants,
    and belonging, 3, 32, 58, 97, 169, 205, 208, 213, 215, 217, 218
    to more than one place, 23, 101, 102, 204
    Catholic, 6, 18, 19, 23, 31, 38, 46, 55, 57–58, 86, 117, 117n10, 130, 132, 170, 202, 135, 150, 215, 218–19
    as children, 18, 79, 81, 85, 132, 134, 135
    first-generation, 15, 18, 29, 87, 168
    immigrant communities, 23, 31, 164, 176, 215
    as "other," 208
    See also migrants
immigration,
    and divine law, 67
    and justice, 5, 63, 64, 66–69, 71, 74
    undocumented, 67
    See also migration
Indian Catholics, 53, 54, 167–78
    and *kairos*, 167, 178
    See also SyroMalabar Catholics
International Organization for Migration (IOM), 203

Japanese Catholics, 112–130
    in Brazil, 117, 118, 119
    Catholic Toyko International Center (CTIC), 118, 119n17
    and the Constitution of Japan, 121, 122, 123, 124, 125n28, 126, 127–28, 129
    and the Fundamental Education Law, 121, 122, 125, 126
    and the Liberal Democratic Party, 121, 122, 124, 127, 129
    and nationalism, 120–21
    and neo-nationalism, 6, 120
    and the Occupation period, 113, 114, 121
    and patriotism, 121, 124, 125, 129
    and pluralization, 119, 120
    and religious freedom, 127–28
    and Shinto values, 121

SUBJECT INDEX

Jesús Nazareno cult, 142–166
   Caguach, 143–48; 149, 150, 152, 153, 157, 158, 159, 160, 163, 164, 165
   Chilote diaspora, 8, 145, 156, 160, 161
   Chilote emigration, 143, 149–50, 153, 159, 160
   Chilote tradition, 155, 159
   devotionalism, 163, 149, 157n34, 161
   image of Nuestro Padre Jesús Nazareno, 142, 143, 145, 151, 152, 153, 155, 156,157, 158
   Jesús Nazareno procession, 142, 155, 156, 157, 158, 159, 160, 165
   Punta Arenas, 142, 143, 150, 153, 155, 156, 157, 158, 159, 160, 161, 163, 165,166
   See also Chilean Catholicism; Chilean Catholics
Jewish experience, 13, 25, 133n12
   Babylonian Exile, 13, 137
John Paul II, Pope, 66, 160, 176, 181, 183, 187, 188
justice, 5, 63, 64, 66–69, 72, 74
   restorative, 71
   social, 90, 163, 163n49

Korean Catholics, 4, 43–51, 54, 58, 60, 118
   and China, 4, 44, 46
   and Confucianism, 44, 47
   faith communities in the US, 45–48, 168
   and the laity, 4, 43–44, 45–46
   and language use, 48, 118
   and martyrdom, 44–45, 46, 48, 60
   and persecution, 44
Korean diaspora, 4

Lampedusa, 5, 78, 81, 83, 85
   and Pope Francis, 83
Latin American Catholic Diaspora, 7–8
Levantine Catholics, 3, 23–39
   and cultural association with the West, 26, 27, 28, 30, 33–34

   and Islam, 26, 27, 32, 33, 38–39
   See also Levantine Christians
Levantine Christians, 3, 23–39
   Armenian, 25
   Chaldean, 25, 32
   and clericalism, 38
   and the Coptic community, 25, 26
   cultural identity, 33–36
   and European Colonialism, 28
   and the Evangelical community, 26
   immigration to the US, 23, 29
   and interreligious communication, 38
   and Islam, 3, 24, 26, 32, 33, 34, 38–39
   Maronite, 24, 25, 26, 31
   Melkite, 24, 25, 29, 31
   and Middle Eastern politics, 23, 29, 35–36, 38
   in North America, 25, 28–29, 29n15, 30–36
   and the Orthodox community, 26, 36
   and the Ottoman Empire, 3, 25, 26, 27, 28, 33, 34
   Palestinian immigration, 25, 29, 35
   racialization, 32, 34
   and the Roman Catholic Church, 25, 26, 26n7, 31, 33
   and sectarianism, 28
liberation theology, 76n1, 84, 163n49, 165, 167

Marian apparitions, 9, 181–86
   Fatima, 9, 183
   La Vang, 9, 181–84
   Lourdes, 9, 183
   Tra Kieu, 181
Marian devotion, 9, 60, 138, 179–89
migrant communities, 13, 17, 18, 101, 210
   study of, 17
migrants,
   and allegiance, 12, 97
   as asylum seekers, 10, 63, 76n1, 79, 80, 82, 206, 207, 208
   categorization of, 63

and Christ, 6, 73, 91, 108, 108n37, 109, 110, 111, 164
in the country of residence, 97, 99, 100, 104
and cross-cultural communities, 5, 92
and dehumanization, 5, 63, 64, 74
and discrimination, 79, 208
first generation, 15, 18, 29, 87, 168
and human dignity, 5, 63–66, 90
and human rights, 62, 65, 125, 139
and identity, 6, 96–111
as marginalized, 5, 15, 32, 66, 68, 73, 79, 92, 169, 177, 186, 205, 208
as "other," 69, 71–72
as refugees, 10, 12, 14, 15, 56, 62, 63, 63n7, 70, 73, 76n1, 77, 79, 80, 82, 83, 84, 89, 90, 93, 94, 95, 116, 118, 126, 134, 168, 180, 202, 206, 208, 219
second generation, 16, 23
sexual exploitation of, 79
and stereotypes, 64, 91
undocumented, 79, 85, 208
See also immigrants
migration,
and acceleration, 203
and borders, 3, 11, 63, 65, 67, 68, 69, 72, 73, 74, 78, 79, 89, 102, 136
and Catholic social teaching, 64–66
and "charity," 86
contemporary trends, 203
and differentiation, 203, 218
and displacement, 3, 18–20, 35, 46, 62, 63, 63n, 76n1, 168, 202, 203, 207, 215, 218
and economic factors, 8, 11, 29, 45, 46, 62, 63, 76n1, 80, 120, 131, 133, 191, 206
and environmental factors, 11
and ethnic theology, 87, 88, 88n36, 165
and feminist theology, 84
feminization, 203
and globalization, 8, 11, 117, 188, 203

and human relationships, 15, 77, 90, 91, 93, 94, 95
internal, 29, 149
laws, 66, 67, 68, 81, 101, 208
and multiculturalism, 6, 12, 58, 59, 84, 86, 92, 99, 112–30, 141, 187, 201, 208
and multiplicity, 6, 96–111
and Passover narratives, 5, 62–75
and politicization, 203
and Pope Francis, 5, 77, 78, 79, 83, 84, 88, 92, 93
and postcolonial theology, 84, 171, 204
as a social phenomenon, 168
and solutions, 82
cosmopolitan, 98–100
postmodern, 100–103
See also immigration
migration corridors, 203
missionary movement, 22, 33, 114
movement of peoples, 1, 2, 3, 5, 10, 13, 24, 73, 206, 214
multiculturalism, 6, 12, 58, 59, 84, 86, 92, 99, 112–30, 141, 187, 201, 208
multiplicity, 6, 96–111

nationalism, 5, 19, 63, 69, 72–74, 139, 140, 147n14
romantic, 159
nation-state, 12, 18, 203
neo-nationalism, 6, 112–30
Nogales, 5, 78

particularity, 2
Passover narratives, 5, 62–75
Philippine Catholics, 115, 116, 117, 118–20, 162
in Japan, 118–20
Philippine Migrant Workers Center, 118
See also Filipino American Catholics
pilgrimage metaphor, 177, 178
Protestant Reformation, the, 49, 50

Protestantism, 26, 49, 50, 86, 113, 115, 117n, 124, 124n26, 124n27, 130, 218
Punta Arenas, 7, 142–66

refugees, 10, 12, 14, 15, 56, 62, 63, 63n7, 70, 73, 76n1, 77, 79, 80, 82, 83, 84, 89, 90, 93, 94, 95, 116, 118, 126, 134, 168, 180, 202, 206, 208, 219
religiosity, popular, 4, 7, 56, 60–61, 147, 149, 157n34, 163n49, 165, 166
rights,
  human, 62, 65, 125, 139
  sovereign, 65, 66

Schuyler, Philippa, 190–201
  as a child prodigy, 9, 190, 191, 198
  Cold War context, 192, 201
  death, 199
  and Frantz Fanon, 9, 199–201
  as multiracial, 191, 192
  and plays, 191, 196
  and prospective husband, 197, 198
  and race, 192, 194, 199, 201
  and racism, 192, 194, 199, 200, 201
  and sexism, 192
  and stereotypes, 191, 192
  as war correspondent, 199
  as writer, 191, 192, 194, 195, 196, 199
Second Vatican Council, 72, 87, 106, 114, 135, 161, 162, 167, 175, 176, 206
social ethics, 5
social justice, 90, 163, 163n49
Syrian Christians, 170–78
  Eastern Catholic Community, 171
  Hindu social structures, 171, 172, 173, 175n30
  See also Indian Catholics; SyroMalabar Catholics
SyroMalabar Catholics, 170–78
  and catholicity, 171, 172–74, 177
  in diaspora, 167–78
  and endogamy, 171, 172–74

  the irruption of migrants, 167, 168, 177, 178
  and John Paul II, 176
  and *kairos*, 167, 178
  Knanaya Catholics, 171–74
  Mar Thoma Silva, 174, 174n27
  migration of, 167, 168, 170, 171, 172, 173, 176, 177
  and North American Catholic practices, 171, 172
  and Second Vatican Council, 167, 175
  and Thomas Christians, 171–76
  See also Indian Catholics; Syrian Christians

Thomas Christians, 171–76
  and latinization, 175, 175n30
  Orientalium Ecclesiarum, 174, 175
  Synod of Diamper, 175
transnational studies, 3, 11–13, 17, 202
transnationalism, 3, 10, 16, 18, 22, 134, 202–5, 218–19
  and diaspora, 3, 10, 16, 18, 134, 203–5

Vietnamese American Catholics, 80, 187
Vietnamese Bishops' Conference, 185
Vietnamese Catholic diaspora, 9, 179, 187
  Center of Pastoral Apostolate for Overseas Vietnamese, 187
  and race, 179, 180
Vietnamese Catholics, 8, 9, 58, 179–89
  and Buddhism, 184
  and French colonization, 182, 185
  and Mary, 9, 179–89
    and goddess worship, 184, 185, 188
    La Vang apparition, 9, 181–84
    Our Lady of La Vang in Orange County, 21, 180, 187
    Tra Kieu apparition, 181
  postcolonial period, 180, 187
Vietnamese refugees, 180

Zimbabwe Catholic Bishops Conference, 206
Zimbabwean Catholics in Britain, 206–19
   and community, 206–207, 209, 210, 211, 216, 217, 218
   and discrimination, 208
   Economic and Social Research Council study, 202
   and ethnicity, 218
   and hymns, 210–11, 215
   and identity, 205, 211
   as immigrants, 209, 212, 214, 215, 218, 219
   language use, 218
   Men's Forum, 213, 217
   and public spaces, 213
   and racism, 207, 208
   as refugees, 219
   reverse evangelization, 214
   and reverse mission, 213–15
   transnationalism, 202, 203, 204, 205, 208, 210, 211, 213, 218
   and women's guilds, 210, 211–13; 215, 217, 218
Zimbabwean diaspora in Britain, 202–19
   as refugees, 202, 206, 208, 219

www.ingramcontent.com/pod-product-compliance
Lightning Source LLC
Chambersburg PA
CBHW021938240426
43669CB00047B/270